RUSSIAN INHERITANCE LAW

STUDIES IN RUSSIAN, EAST EUROPEAN, AND EURASIAN LAW

WILLIAM E. BUTLER (SERIES EDITOR)

1. Butler, W. E., Russian Law and Legal Institutions. 3d ed.; 2021. ISBN 978-854901449

2. Il'in, I. A., On the Essence of Legal Consciousness, ed., introduced, & transl. W. E. Butler, P. T. Grier, and Paul Robinson. 2d rev. ed.; 2023. ISBN-13 978-1-61619-679-03.

3. Butler, W. E., Russian-English Legal Dictionary. 2d rev. ed.; Clark, New Jersey, Talbot Publishing, 2023. ISBN 978-1-61619-682-0

4. Butler, W. E., Russian Inheritance Law. 2d rev. ed.; Clark, New Jersey, Talbot Publishing, 2025. ISBN 978-1-61619-692-9

Studies in Russian, East European, and Eurasian Law

RUSSIAN INHERITANCE LAW

SECOND REVISED EDITION

William E. Butler

John Edward Fowler Distinguished Professor of Law,
Penn State Dickinson Law
Emeritus Professor of Comparative Law,
University College London
Foreign Member, Russian Academy of Natural Sciences,
National Academy of Sciences of Ukraine, and
National Academy of Legal Sciences of Ukraine

TALBOT
PUBLISHING
Clark, New Jersey
2025

Russian Inheritance Law
ISBN: 978-1-61619-692-9

TALBOT PUBLISHING AN IMPRINT OF
The Lawbook Exchange, Ltd.
33 Terminal Avenue
Clark, New Jersey 07066-1321

Please see our website for a selection of our other publications and fine facsimile reprints of classic works of legal history www.lawbookexchange.com

Library of Congress Cataloging-in-Publication Data

Names: Butler, William Elliott, 1939- author.
Title: Russian inheritance law / William E. Butler, John Edward Fowler Distinguished Professor of Law, Penn State Dickinson Law, Emeritus Professor of Comparative Law, University College London, Foreign Member, Russian Academy of Natural Sciences, National Academy of Sciences of Ukraine, and National Academy of Legal Sciences of Ukraine.
Description: Second revised edition. | Clark : Talbot Publishing, an Imprint of The Lawbook Exchange, Ltd., 2025. | Series: Studies in Russian, East European, and Eurasian law | Includes bibliographical references and index. | Summary: "A treatise on the origins, sources, history and current state of Russian inheritance law"-- Provided by publisher.
Identifiers: LCCN 2024043981 | ISBN 9781616196929 (hardcover)
Subjects: LCSH: Inheritance and succession--Russia (Federation)
Classification: LCC KLB770 .B88 2025 | DDC 346.4705/2--dc23/eng/20240918
LC record available at https://lccn.loc.gov/2024043981

Printed in the United States of America on acid-free paper

Contents

ANNEXES

PREFACE TO SECOND EDITION

In the decade that has elapsed since the first edition of this work, major changes have been introduced into the inheritance law of the Russian Federation that collectively seek to strengthen the unobstructed passage of commercial assets from generation to generation while minimizing the likelihood of fractionating family businesses by inadvertently requiring their dispersion among heirs uninterested in such an enterprise or untalented in matters entrepreneurial. These aspirations are collectively addressed through the introduction of the joint will, inheritance contract, and inheritance foundation. No less significant, but not as well known, has been the extension of obligatory shares of an inheritance to all females aged 55 or over and all males aged 60 or over.

In all other respects the structure and range of the previous edition remain as before.

PREFACE TO FIRST EDITION

Inheritance is perhaps taken for granted in western Europe and the United States. Whatever limitations may have been imposed on the right to inherit over the generations, the right to inherit has never been repealed or abolished, nor has there been serious discussion of taking such a step. Russian experience is otherwise, as this volume will amply demonstrate.

Inheritance was not merely abolished on 18 April 1918 by the Government of the Russian Soviet Federative Socialist Republic (RSFSR). It was reconceptualized so that the passing of any property to a decedent's immediate family was conceived of as a form of social security. From 1918 until the mid-1920s the property of a decedent was effectively divided between the State and designated categories of individuals close to the decedent. Even though that system was relaxed thereafter, the pressures imposed by the early tenets of Soviet Marxist-Leninist practices endured throughout the existence of the Soviet Union.

Not until early in the twenty-first century was the entire system of Russian inheritance rethought. Many procedures were retained intact or with minor modifications. The Russian legislator has, however, been mindful of the need to elaborate a new approach. The right to inherit is ensconced in the 1993 Russian Constitution as part of the section of human rights provisions that operate directly and deliberately are almost impossible to amend. Inheritance is conceived of as being derivative from the civil legal capacity of a natural person.[1] This comes close, some would say is tantamount, to treating inheritance as a natural right of man and citizen.

The post-Soviet approach contrasts starkly with the original position adopted in the 1918 Dekret: "inheritance ... shall be abolished" (Article 1) – a proposition that suggests the legislator has the right to do precisely that, with nothing in Russian constitutional history to suggest such a measure might be challenged. The draftsmen of the 1922 RSFSR Civil Code worked from the same premise of free discretion on the part of the State to treat with inheritance as the State wished: inheritance "shall be permitted" (Article 416), which meant within the confines of the strictures laid down by the State and insofar as the State may wish to "permit". The 1964 RSFSR Civil Code and the 1991 Fundamental Principles of Civil Legislation of the USSR and Union Republics (FPCivL), in force until 2002 in the Russian Federation with respect to inheritance, merely provided laconically that "inheritance shall be effectuated", without grounding the right to inherit in something more fundamental by way of legal principle.

How far post-Soviet Russia has moved in the direction of implementing an approach to inheritance consistent with what Russian jurists view as "world civilization" may be judged to a significant extent by the present study, which is to date the most

[1] Russian jurists have in mind the 1966 International Covenant on Civil and Political Rights, which provides in Article 16: "Everyone shall have the right to recognition everywhere as a person before the law". 999 UNTS 171. The Russian legal mentality understands this to mean, as expressed in the Russian translation of the Covenant: "Everyone wherever situated shall have the right to recognition of his legal capacity".

comprehensive account of Russian inheritance law undertaken in the English language. It is based on an extensive reading of Russian doctrinal writings, legislation, and judicial practice. The major relevant provisions of the Civil Code of the Russian Federation and the Family Code of the Russian Federation addressing inheritance are reproduced in the Annex, in the author's translation.

To the extent that transliteration appears, the Library of Congress system is used in its short form, without diacritical markings. Unless indicated otherwise, books printed in the Russian language were published at Moscow. I am greatly indebted to Consultant+ for the use of a data base giving full access to Russian legislation, in fully amended and integrated form, and international treaties. Certain documents consulted when preparing the present volume were available only on Consultant+ and otherwise unpublished. All decrees, rulings, opinions, orders, and judgments of Russian courts mentioned herein are available on Consultant+.

W. E. Butler

Newville, Pennsylvania

Status juris: 15 October 2024

Abbreviations

FPCivL	Fundamental Principles of Civil Legislation (1961 or 1991)
RSFSR	Russian Soviet Federative Socialist Republic
CIS	Commonwealth of Independent States
СЗ РФ	Собрание законодательства Российской Федерации
USSR	Union of Soviet Socialist Republics

Chapter 1

Historical Introduction to Russian Inheritance Law

Inheritance is regarded by Russian legal historians as a part of the civil law deeply embedded in the ownership relations of society. The transition of the Russian Federation from a socialist planned economy which followed the Revolutions of 1917 to a market economy of a type undetermined cannot fail, in their view, to affect the law of inheritance; but neither is this transition the first such in Russian historical experience. Changes in the law of ownership will, as a rule, one way or another affect the right to inherit or what may be inherited, or who may inherit. Modern Russian jurists are inclined to see the right to inherit property as a "stimulator of the development of productive forces in society", a "powerful incentive to more effective labor".[1] Inheritance promotes entrepreneurship and stability in society, the preservation of family foundations and values, generates a material base for the rising generations, and protects the interests of the creditors and debtors of the decedent – acknowledging at the same time that inheritance may contain negative elements in the form of greater social inequality or even the creation of a parasitic stratum of society.

These are themes that transcend the present Russian law of inheritance and reach far back into the past. For all of the need to break with the Soviet past insofar as ownership relations are concerned, the law of inheritance in Russia is rather conservative and inclined to change in measured fashion rather than by way of counter-revolution. This makes knowledge of Russian historical experience in respect of inheritance all the more germane to understanding the present.

[1] See S. P. Grishaev, Наследственное право [Inheritance Law] (2014), p. 5.

INHERITANCE IN KIEVAN RUS

The right of inheritance is widely regarded in Russian and Ukrainian legal doctrine as having been a long-established element of Slavonic customary law whose existence was formally acknowledged, *inter alia*, in the Peace Treaty concluded between Rus and Byzantium in the year 911 (Article 13): "If someone of them dies without bequeathing his property and his relatives are not with him in Greece, let all the property return to close relatives in Rus. If he draws up a will, let he to whom an instruction was written inherit the property take the property and inherit it".[2] The word "written" has attracted the attention of Russian and Ukrainian prerevolutionary and Soviet historians because the formulation suggests a level of literacy and recognition of the written form of a testamentary disposition.[3] Others have contended that Article 13 reflected Byzantine law, rather than that of Kievan Rus, and was intended to operate only on Byzantine possessions in Greece.[4] The aim of the provision, it has been suggested, was to address conflicts of law issues and discourage local authorities from appropriating the property of the deceased individual.[5]

[2] See K. A. Nevolin, История российских гражданских законов [History of Russian Civil Laws] (Spb., 1857; reprint ed., 2006), III, pp. 266-267. Also see P. P. Tsitovich, Значение договоров русских с греками в истории русского наследственного права [Significance of Treaties of the Russians with the Greeks in the History of Russian Inheritance Law] (Kharkov, 1870).

[3] See L. I. Rudnev, О духовных завещаниях по русскому праву [On Spiritual Testaments under Russian Law] (Kyiv, 1894), p. 41; A. A. Zimin (ed.), Памятники русского права Киевского государства X-XII вв. [Monuments of Russian Law of the Kievan State X-XII Centuries], (1952), I, p. 23. For a contrary skeptical view which questioned the existence of literacy in Kievan Rus in the early tenth century, see A. Stanislavskii, Исследования начал имущественных отношений в древнейших памятниках русского законодательства [Studies on the Principles of Property Relations in Ancient Monuments of Russian Legislation] (Kazan, 1855), p. 13.

[4] V. Sergeevich, Лекции и исследования по древней истории русского права [Lectures and Studies on the Ancient History of Russian Law] (Spb., 1903), p. 541. Shershenevich said of the treaty: "Reflecting foreign views, they cannot serve as an expressor of a purely Russian procedure for inheriting". Quoted in E. A. Kirillova, Основания наследования в гражданском праве Российской Федерации [Grounds of Inheriting in the Civil Law of the Russian Federation] (2012), p. 6.

[5] L. V. Sannikova, Институты частного права в Русской Правды [Institutes of

Detailed provisions on inheritance are found in the Expanded Version of the *Russkaia Pravda*, composed not earlier, it is believed, than 1113. Moveable property passed by way of inheritance: house, goods, slaves, livestock, the courtyard; land was not among the objects of inheritance. If a peasant died, his property passed to the prince; if the deceased had unmarried daughters, a portion of the estate went to them (Article 90). In the case of a boyar or retainer of the prince, the estate passed to the sons; should there be no sons, the daughters inherit. Property might be distributed to heirs on two grounds: by will, in which event the division stipulated stands; if intestate, the property is divided evenly among all his children with one portion to the church in memory of his soul (Article 92). A widow who remains unmarried was entitled to a share of her husband's estate, but if she was given property by the husband while still alive, she has no need of her husband's estate (Article 93). Should there be children from more than one marriage, the children of the first wife take the property of their mother even if their father's wife left the property to the second wife (Article 94). If there be a sister in the house, she received nothing from the estate, but her brothers give her in marriage as best they can (Article 95).[6]

A husband did not inherit after a wife; those children with whom the mother lived inherited after her. It has been suggested that under this approach to inheritance the family was viewed as something continuous along the male line and women were not regarded as being firmly attached to their lineage but rather passed from the moment of marriage into the family of their spouse. On this view, the will, which might be oral, did not change the sequence of inheritance. Rather a will distributed property among the heirs by operation of law and instructed on how the property should be managed. Collateral lines were not among heirs in the *Russkaia Pravda*. Or so it would seem.

Private Law in the Russkaia Pravda] (2014), p. 42.

6 For the English translation of all three texts of the *Russkaia Pravda*, see D. H. Kaiser (transl. & ed.), *The Laws of Rus' – Tenth to Fifteenth Centuries* (1992), pp. 30-31.

Russian doctrinal writings of early and recent origin contain a considerable diversity of views as to how the *Russkaia Pravda* should be understood. Sannikova has observed: "... the norms contained in the said Articles of the *Russkaia Pravda* regulated with insufficient completeness the relations of inheritance by will and do not give a general impression of inheritance by will in Medieval Rus".[7] By way of example of the conflicting interpretations, the question arises of what the word "children" means in Article 92 of the Expanded Version. The first clause of Article 92 refers to "children" in the context of inheritance by will, and in the second clause, in the context of inheritance by operation of law. Many rely on a literal interpretation of the word "children" – that is, assuming the word itself contains no indication of gender. If that understanding of the word is accepted, Article 92 is clearly in contradiction with Articles 90 and 91. Should the word "children" be understood to mean sons and daughters, or only sons?[8]

However the word "children" is understood, the question arises as to the extent to which a Russian testator might expand the group of heirs by will. A trend in that direction by the thirteenth and fourteenth centuries has been noted by commentators,[9] although examples of birchbark wills are known in this connection as early as 1160 to 1180; it is plausible to conclude that the *Russkaia Pravda* did not prohibit bequeathing property to other relatives.[10] As for collateral relatives, it has been persuasively suggested that, given the absence of evidence to the contrary, "the silence of the *Russkaia Pravda* concerning inheritance by collateral relatives in and of itself cannot serve as

[7] Sannikova, note 5 above, p. 43.

[8] Compare Sergeevich, note 4 above, with M. F. Vladimirskii-Budanov, Обзор истории русского права [Survey of the History of Russian Law] (reprint ed.; 1995), p. 461.

[9] See V. V. Momotov, Берестяные грамоты – источник познания русского права XI-XV вв. [Birchbark Instruments – Source of Cognition of Russian Law XI-XV Centuries] (1997) (abstract of kandidat dissertation), p 19.

[10] Sannikova, note 5 above, p. 44.

evidence of their exclusion from inheritance; because the *Pravda* had no need to set out a detailed sequence of inheritance".[11]

The right of a mother to bequeath her property was addressed with greater definitude in the *Russkaia Pravda*. The children were to have no part of their mother's (widow's) portion, but the mother might designate an heir(s) from among her own children or share the property between them. If she died without making a disposition of her property, whomsoever she lived with and received support from would take her property (Article 103). Article 106 enlarged upon this situation: a mother who had a good son, irrespective of whether of the first or second husband, might leave her property to that son; if all the sons were bad, that is, did not support the mother, she might leave her property to the daughter who feeds her. This has been construed as the creation by the *Russkaia Pravda* of a certain "gradation" in the choice of children: the mother must first try living with her sons, and only when they all proved to be "bad", might she move on to the daughters.[12] Modern writers have rejected this interpretation of the clauses. The reference in Article 106 to "sons", in this view, is better explained not as the duty of the mother to "try" to live with her sons, but rather by a custom long established under which the duty of sons to support their mother flows from the son as the head of the household. A daughter of the mother who has married was regarded as having joined another family and no longer is able to express her own independent will.

The right of a mother to make a "disposition" during the times of the *Russkaia Pravda* has been challenged on linguistic grounds: the controversy turns on the use of the term "ряд", when translated as "disposition". The Russkaia Pravda does not use this term in connection with a mother's property, which has led some commentators to suggest that a mother did not

[11] V. Nikol'skii, О началах наследования по древнему русскому праву [On the Principles of Inheritance under Medieval Russian Law] (1859), p. 371.

[12] Tsitovich, Исходные моменты в истории русского права наследования [Basic Moments in the History of the Russian Law of Inheritance] (Kharkov, 1870), p. 166.

"dispose" of her property, but made a gift of this property; different terms, it was believed, were used to distinguish inheritance after a father or mother.[13] Empirical evidence is directly to the contrary. Birchbark wills use the term "will" [завещание] of women and invoke the usual prefatory language of a last will and testament. The issue is whether the surviving birchbark wills represent a change from the terminology of the *Russkaia Pravda* or whether the absence of the terminology of "disposition" had no material significance in this connection.

As noted above, the Rus-Byzantium Treaty of 911 made reference to the written form of a will. The *Russkaia Pravda* is silent with respect to the form of a will. The legal historians are divided as to how such silence should be construed. Some consider the "oral conclusion of a will to have been the customary form";[14] Nikol'skii did not consider the term "disposition" in Article 92 of the Russkaia Pravda as referring to a legal document or act and believed that a will might be in written or oral form.[15] A significant number of birchbark documents discovered in recent times are, in fact, wills, which suggests that the written form, whether essential or not, was extensively used.[16] Although instruments dating from 1120 to 1140 mention the participation of a clergyman or scribe as having to be present when drawing up a will,[17] it seems unlikely that this was regarded as an imperative requirement for the validity of the testament. Whether, on the other hand, one can go so far as to say that the absence in the *Russkaia Pravda* of any provisions relating to the form of a will meant the complete absence of any formal requirements for the form of a will is unlikely, even though the practice of oral wills would seem contrary to this proposition. Surviving evidence of wills would suggest that they sometimes were oral in form, sometimes were

[13] L. I. Rudnev, note 3 above, p. 16.

[14] Vladimirskii-Budanov, note 8 above, p. 463.

[15] Nikol'skii, note 11 above, p. 341.

[16] Sannikkova, note 5 above, p. 47.

[17] Mamotov, note 9 above, p. 19.

written out by the testator himself, and sometimes were drawn up or written down by a clergyman or other individual from the words of the testator.

The surviving texts suggest that a written will was drawn up according to certain rules: an appeal to the Almighty, the basis of the testator's rights to the property which he is bequeathing, an enumeration of debtors who owed him money, or the imposition of a testamentary legacy or the designation of an executor. Although structured wills date from the fourteenth and fifteenth centuries, some believe that earlier enumerations of debtors were a form of will.[18]

Inheritance by operation of law is among the most controversial of subjects in the subsequent historiography of the *Russkaia Pravda*. Article 90 of the Expanded Version of the *Russkaia Pravda* begins as follows: "If a peasant dies, then his estate [escheats] to the prince". Read literally, the formulation would mean, in effect, no inheritance. Some manuscript versions, however, add the words "without children" to the formulation, and the majority of commentators have understood Article 90 in this sense and, moreover, also to mean only sons.[19] On this view, a daughter might inherit only if she were unmarried, but in that event only a respective portion.

Part of the debate turns upon the definition of what was meant by the term "peasant". What Grekov suggested six decades ago remains the case: "one may boldly say that there is no historian in Russia who has not attempted to determine the legal nature of the peasant, and nonetheless the question remains open".[20] From the standpoint of inheritance, the question is whether the term "peasant" encompassed both dependent and free peasants. Ultimately, this discussion

[18] See V. F. Andreev, Новгородский частный акт XII-XV вв. [Novgorod Private Act of the Twelfth to Fifteenth Centuries] (1986). Sannikova persuasively points out that "there are no grounds to qualify such as wills". Sannikova, note 5 above, p, 48.

[19] See Sergeevich, note 4 above, p. 544; also see A. E. Presniakov, Княжее право в Древней Руси [Princely Law in Medieval Rus] (St. Petersburg, 1909), p. 281.

[20] B. D. Grekov, Киевская Русь [Kievan Rus] (Leningrad, 1953), p. 242.

reduced to whether there was any different of consequence between the rights of peasants, on one hand, and boyars and retainers, on the other, to inherit, especially with regard to unmarried daughters. Probably the better view in doctrinal writings is that after the death of a boyar or retainer, only sons are heirs, who in turn must be concerned about the marriage of a sister with a share of property going to her in the form of dowry. This rule is regarded as universal in character rather than directed to a particular estate.

Article 98 of the Expanded *Russkaia Pravda* addresses the situation when a man has children by his slavewoman. They are to receive nothing; however, when the man dies, the slavewoman and the child are to receive their freedom. Many Russian historians consider this provision to have been introduced into Russian Law under the influence of the Church in order to distinguish between legitimate and illegitimate children. The position there was that legitimate sons inherited after their father, and in the absence thereof, daughters, except for the daughters of peasants.

Under the Expanded *Russkaia Pravda* (Article 100) the residence passed to the youngest son without any division – a principle regarded as codifying a custom of the Slavonic peoples.[21] The question is whether this rule applied only to inheritance by operation of law or also limited the freedom of disposition by will.[22] The commentators are divided.

If a widow remarried, the second husband administered her property. Having grown up, the sons of the first marriage might demand that their stepfather transfer the property of the first marriage to them, pursuant to Article 105 of the *Russkaia Pravda*. If the stepfather died, having squandered the property of his stepchildren, the half-brother was liable to pay compensation for the losses caused by his father to the inheritance property.

[21] Sannikova, note 5 above, p. 54.

[22] Contrast Vladimirskii-Budanov, note 8 above, p. 467, with N. A. Maksimeiko, in B. D. Grekov (ed.), Правда Русская: Комментарий [Pravda Russkaia: Commentary] (1947), II, p. 667.

Witnesses assisted in establishing the extent of the losses. The principle has led some observers to postulate the existence of a principle of universal succession in medieval Russian law[23] to the debts of the decedent. On the contrary, the special instances in which succession to debts is indicated suggests that universal succession was not a principle of medieval Russian law.

INHERITANCE IN MUSCOVY

Inheritance by will and inheritance by operation of law were distinguished in the Pskov Judicial Charter of 1467 (Article 55).24 Both moveable and immoveable property could be inherited. A will might be drawn up to the benefit of heirs by operation of law and/or to those outside the category. The written form was required if the heirs fell outside the category of heirs by operation of law, as was a special procedure for confirmation of the will. Oral, or parol, wills were permitted for heirs by operation of law (Article 100).

Heirs by operation of law included: father, mother, son, brother, sister, or others of close kinship. Sons were called to inherit together with the mother. If a son does not maintain his father or mother until their death, but deserts their home, he may not receive property after their death (Article 53). Inheritance by a surviving spouse consisted not only of receiving part of the property in ownership, but for life or until a second marriage of all the other property of the deceased (Articles 88-89).

Accordingly, the Pskov Judicial Charter expanded the group of individuals who could inherit by operation of law by including within that group the parents of the deceased and certain collateral relatives and by allowing inheritance by will in favor of individuals who were not kin of the decedent.

The *Sudebniks* of 1497 and 1550 contained provisions on inheritance that were virtually identical: if the decedent left no will, all his moveable and immoveable property passed to

[23] See Rudnev, note 3 above, p. 15.

[24] For a translation of the Charter, see note 6 above, pp. 87-105.

the sons, and in the absence thereof, to the daughters. If the decedent had no children, the estate passed to the closest relative (Article 60, 1497 *Sudebnik*; Article 92, 1550 *Sudebnik*). Both *Sudebniks* permitted inheritance by collateral heirs, depriving the surviving spouse and parents of the right to inherit.[25] In 1562 women were eliminated entirely from the right to inherit patrimonial landed estates, a provision confirmed in 1572.

INHERITANCE UNDER THE 1649 SOBORNOE ULOZHENIE

The 1649 *Sobornoe ulozhenie,* the bedrock on which the legislation of the Russian Empire was constructed, contained the accumulated collective wisdom from earlier Muscovite legal experience.[26] It legalized the enserfment of the peasantry and consolidated legislatively the possibility to transfer peasants by inheritance together with other property.

In matters of inheritance the sequence of being called to inherit depended upon the types of property which comprised the estate. Special rules were established for patrimonial estates (inherited, purchased, or received as a reward for service) and granted estates. In general there was a gradual expansion of the group of heirs by operation of law at the expense of collateral relatives up to the fifth degree of kinship and a limitation of the powers of the decedent by creating exceptions from the free disposition of individual types of immoveable property that, as a rule, constituted the most valuable core of the estate.[27]

[25] K. A. Nevolin suggested that this sequence of inheritance may have been drawn from the Old Testament as recorded in the Kormchaia kniga of the Russian Orthodox Church: "... If a man die and have no son, then ye shall cause his inheritance to pass unto his daughter. And if he have no daughter, then ye shall give his inheritance unto his brethren. And if he have no brethren, then ye shall give his inheritance unto his father's brethren. And if his father have no brethren, then ye shall give his inheritance unto his kinsman that is next to him of his family ...". Numbers, 27, 8-11 (King James version). See Nevolin, note 2 above, III, p. 325.

[26] See W. E. Butler, *Russian Law and Legal Institutions* (3d ed.; 2021), pp. 57-59.

[27] See M. S. Abramenkov and P. V. Chugunov, Наследственное право [Law of Inheritance], ed. V. A. Belov (2013), p. 50.

A will in addition to specifying the principal heir might contain instructions for testamentary legatees. As a rule, the legal heirs or relatives up to the fifth degree of kinship or the church would be designated as heirs, and outsiders as testamentary legatees. Property could be bequeathed to one of the heirs while excluding a wife and close relatives, subject to certain exceptions (for example, in 1580 it was prohibited to bequeath all property to the church to the exclusion of the wife and close relatives). The freedom of testamentary dispositions was limited in 1689 by a prohibition against bequeathing inherited patrimonial estates or those received as a reward for service. A will in written form had to be signed by the testator or only by witnesses and confirmed by church authorities. Oral wills were permitted until the late seventeenth century.

Children, spouse, and collateral relatives were called to inherit by operation of law. The rights of each heir depended upon what property was left by the decedent. According to the *Sobornoe ulozhenie* (Article 2, Chapter 17), patrimonial estates and those received as a reward for service passed to the son of the decedent; in the absence of a son, to the daughters, and if there were no daughters, to the closest kin. The surviving spouse of a childless decedent had a right to one-fourth of the moveable property and her dowry. The same Article provided that childless mothers and wives of owners of a patrimonial estate might receive maintenance for life from patrimonial estates that were a reward for service until they remarried or took the veil; however, they could not sell, pledge, or take such an estate as dowry. As regards patrimonial estates purchased from private individuals, the widow had the right of ownership to such and could freely dispose of it. Patrimonial estates purchased from treasury lands passed to the wife and children of the decedent, and if there were no wife and children, to the relatives of the decedent. If a childless widow remained after the decedent, she received a purchased patrimonial estate in possession and use for life until she remarried or took the veil – in which event the property passed to the relatives of the decedent. Escheated estates passed to the sovereign.

The portion of a granted estate due to a widow was subject to determination in each individual instance and ranged from a one-third to a one-seventh part. After 1644 the percentage was affected by whether the husband perished in combat, died while on a march, or was simply in service. The widow was entitled to one-fourth of the moveable property of the decedent. Inheritance by collateral relatives was initially permitted only with respect to natural brothers and their descendants up to the fourth degree of kinship; in 1676 this was extended to first cousins once removed and brothers up to the fifth degree inclusive.

On the whole, the 1649 *Sobornoe ulozhenie* sought to keep immoveable property, especially patrimonial estates, in the possession of the male line. This was achieved partly by limiting the inheritance rights of women – wives, mothers, and sisters of the decedent – who were to be supported by the males (spouses, sons, or brothers).

Material changes in the Russian law of inheritance were introduced by Peter the Great (1672-1725) in the 1714 Edict on Primogeniture, expressly intended to reduce what was perceived as harm to the State caused by the splitting of patrimonial immoveables. Under the general rule, immoveable property passed to one of the sons of the decedent named in the will or to the eldest son if property passed by operation of law, or to the daughters if there were no sons. Moveable property passed to the other children in accordance with their participatory shares established by the will or, in the absence of a disposition, in equal shares.

If the testator had no children, the property was distributed as follows: by will he should have passed immoveables to one of the relatives, and moveable property to anyone; in the absence of a will, an immoveable should pass to the closest relative of the deceased, and the rest of the property to other relatives in equal shares. If the testator as the last male in the line transferred immoveable property to his female relative on condition that her husband take the surname of the testator, and this was not complied with, the immoveable passed to the treasury. For a childless widow the immoveable of her late husband remained with her until death, taking the veil, or remarriage, whereupon the immoveable returned to the eldest kin of her late husband. The Edict was not retroactive.

The 1714 Edict on Primogeniture was repealed in 1731 during the reign of Empress Anna Ioannovna (1693-1740). Both moveable and immoveable property passed under the 1731 Edict in equal shares to all sons of the decedent; grandchildren were called to inherit by right of representation and received the share of their father who died before the opening of the inheritance. Patrimonial immoveable property was subject to inheritance only by operation of law. When there were sons, daughters received 1/14 of immoveable and 1/8 of moveable property of the father. In the absence of descending relatives, the property passed to the brothers of the decedent. The surviving spouse was entitled to 1/7 of immoveable and 1/4 of moveable property. Parents after the death of their childless children received back in ownership everything they had passed to their children, together with the right to use for life of property acquired in good faith. The aspiration to keep property in the male line persisted.

INHERITANCE UNDER THE DIGEST OF LAWS (1832-1917)

Law reform undertakings initiated by Emperor Alexander I (1777-1825) during the first decade of the nineteenth century, initially influenced greatly by the ideas of Jeremy Bentham (1748-1832) on codification and later indebted to the writings of F. C. von Savigny (1779-1861), addressed inheritance in a Draft Civil Ulozhenie of 1814. For sundry reasons, including the Napoleonic invasion of Russia, the draft was never enacted, although in some modern Russian works on inheritance attention is given to the contemplated changes.[28] This was

[28] Ibid., pp. 53-58. The draft was published in Архив Государственного совета – Т. 4: Царствование императора Александра I (с 1810 по 19 ноября 1825 г.): журналы департамента законов [Archive of the State Council: Vol. 4: Reign of Emperor Alexander I (from 1810 to 19 November 1825): Journals of the Department

an aborted attempt at genuine codification, as distinct from systematization.

Under Emperor Nicholas I (1796-1855) inheritance legislation was significantly reworked in connection with the preparation of the Свод законов Российской империи [Digest of Laws of the Russian Empire], which incorporated the 1831 Statute on Wills. Inheritance was defined as the "aggregate of properties, rights, and obligations which remained after the deceased" (Article 1104). Inheritance was by will or by operation of law, with the legislator specially stipulating that foreigners, children conceived during the life of the father and born after his death, and the dumb, deaf, and insane were not prevented from inheriting (Article 1106). An estate opened from the moment of death or from the moment of deprivation of all rights of status, taking of monastic vows, or being missing.[29]

Inheritance by operation of law occurred when patrimony formed part of the estate and when the deceased left no will concerning other property or a court deemed the will to be invalid. The potential group of heirs by operation of law was unlimited, extending until the complete extinction of the male or female generations (Article 1111). Kinship was the link between persons born in a legal marriage based on their origin from a common ancestor even if they did not have the name or nickname thereof (Article 1112). Kinship was determined by degrees and lines. A degree represented the link of persons by birth, and a line, the link of degrees continuing without interruption. Lines were divided into ascending, descending, and collateral (Article 1114-1117).

The Digest of Laws provided that, generally speaking, inheritance by operation of law proceeded first to relatives of the deceased along the descending line and only in the event

of Laws] (St. Petersburg, 1874).

[29] G. F. Shershenevich, Учебник русского гражданского права [Textbook of Russian Civil Law] (reprint ed.; 2005), II, p. 337; Iu. M. Goncharov, Брачно-семейное право Российской империи XIX-начала XX вв. [Marriage-Family Law of the Russian Empire XIX-Beginning of XX Centuries] (2019), pp. 113-117.

of the "insufficiency thereof" might property pass to the collateral and ascending lines. The closest degree of relative of one line eliminated more remote relatives (Articles 1121-1122). Inheritance by right of representation was recognized (Article 1123). The heirs by representation received that portion which there deceased ancestor would have received.

Kinship by blood was thus the basic principle used to form the heirs by operation of law, and not family proximity. The closest heirs were the descending line of the deceased: his children and, by right of representation, their ancestors (Article 1127). The children divided property between themselves equally. Until a special law was adopted in 1912, daughters were eliminated from inheriting if there were sons or descendants thereof, receiving 1/14 on immoveable and 1/8 of moveable property of the father (the so-called "edict share"). Sisters who had brothers alive inherited nothing.[30] After 1912, women were equated with males an inheritance rights, except for land outside urban areas, of which they received a 1/7 share, subject to certain exceptions if there were no sons or descendants thereof or if there were a large number of daughters (Article 1128).[31] Adopted children were equated in their property rights and duties with legitimate children and could inherit property of the adoptive parent. Descendants of an adopted child inherited after the adoptive parent by right of representation.

In the absence of descending relatives the estate passed to the collateral line, in which event the closest collateral line excluded those more remote. If there were more than one equal collateral line, the inheritance was divided just as though there were descending lines, including with the right of representation

[30] The Journal of the Minister of Justice observed in 1864: "of all the legislation of civilized peoples there is not one in which a woman would be in regard to the right of inheritance by operation of law in a position as disadvantageous as in our fatherland". See Журнал Министерства юстиции [Journal of the Ministry of Justice], XX (1864), p. 412.

[31] A. G. Goikhbarg, Закон о расширении прав наследования по закону лиц женского пола и права завещания родовых имений [Law on Expansion of Rights of Inheritance by Operation of Law of Persons of Female Sex and Right to Bequeath Ancestral Estates] (1914), p. 120.

(Article 1136). The rights of parents to the property of deceased children were regulated specially (Article 1141-1146).

A surviving spouse had the right to receive a 1/7 "edict share"[32] of immoveable property and a 1/4 portion of moveable property, irrespective of whether the deceased had descending heirs. Author's right passed entirely to the surviving spouse (Articles 1148-1161).

In general, Shershenevich wrote: "if in general the right of inheritance of remote relatives with whom in a large number of instances the decedent was not linked by feelings of affection is from the modern point of view rather difficult to explain, this is undoubtedly unjust when this entails the elimination of other persons closer to the decedent – spouse, parents, illegitimate children, adopted persons. Such is Russian legislation in force".[33]

Not long before the Digest of Laws was published, the Statute on Wills (1831) was adopted. This Statute established two basic forms of will: the public will (крепостной), which is drawn up with the participation of public authorities, such as an uezd court, magistrate, civil chamber, or others and later came to be known as a "notarial will", which was drawn up with the participation of a notary and three witnesses; and the domestic will (домашний), which is drawn up by the testator at the place of his whereabouts.[34] The Digest of Laws defined a testament as the "legal declaration of the will of the possessor concerning his property in the event of his death" (Article 1010). "Legality" here meant that the testament or the testator had to satisfy certain criteria: to be of "sound mind and firm

[32] Russian jurists disagreed about the legal nature of the "edict share". Some argued that spouses who received an "edict share" were not heirs and the edict share was not an inheritance. Others believe that although the amounts of an edict share and an inheritance share were different in amount, the recipient of an edict share enjoyed inheritance rights to the property of a deceased spouse. The Ruling Senate put an end to the disagreement by decreeing there was no other legal means f or the spouse to acquire the rights to the property. See Goncharov, note 29 above, pp. 121-122.

[33] Shershenevich, note 29 above, II, p. 386.

[34] Nevolin, note 2 above, pp. 295-310.

memory" (Article 1016); have the right to dispose of property, which meant at least 21 years of age, not deprived of all rights of status when convicted of a crime, or taking of monastic vows; and to be in proper form, either notarial or domestic (Article 1012). Oral wills were expressly prohibited (Article 1023), as were those which combined the dispositions of two persons in a single document (Article 1032). Virtually the sole limitation on the freedom of dispose of property by will was a prohibition against bequeathing patrimony (Article 1068).

The notarial will was entered in the notarial book of documents and signed by the testator, who was thereupon issued with an extract from the notarial register; the extract had the force of a genuine will (Articles 1036-1040). Domestic wills written at the place where the testator was could be on paper of any format and dimensions provided that the document had to be written on a single sheet. The testator himself could write out the will or at his request and from his words, other persons could do so. For reasons of illiteracy or other considerations, the will might be signed not by the testator, but by an executor (Article 1053). The testator could keep a domestic will himself or lodge it with agencies or officials designated in legislation, such as a notary.

Russian law also recognized so-called "special" wills (of military servicemen abroad on campaign), wills drawn up on a naval vessel or on a merchant ship during a voyage, wills drawn by Russian subjects abroad, and wills of widows and maidens.

When an inheritance opened, a will had to be submitted to the relevant Russian court at the place of residence of the testator or location of property within a year (or for persons abroad, within two years); otherwise the will was considered to be null, subject to exceptions that would exclude this general period of limitation (Article 1066).

The executor designated in the will or the heirs themselves were responsible for executing the will. Heirs had the right to accept or to refuse the inheritance. Acceptance could take the form of a declaration before competent agencies or by the performance of actions, such as taking possession of property. Refusal, however, required a formal declaration before an appropriate official or agency. Provisions were made for preserving or managing property after an inheritance was opened, summoning heirs, and inventorying property.

Debts of the decedent followed the estate property and fell to the heirs accordingly. Children were specifically excluded from the duty to pay debts for parents unless they received property from the estate (Article 1262). Special provisions addressed escheat; when property went to the State by way of escheat, the treasury assumed the duty to pay debts of the deceased under the general rules.

The prerevolutionary approach to inheritance has been described by modern observers as being structured solely on the kinship principle: "in principle the purpose which the legislator pursued was sufficiently clear – to avoid the fractionalization of inheritance property. However, the answer to questions: why was the group of heirs to structured? By what models were the draftsmen of legislative act guided? – we did not find in the literature".[35]

During the second half of the nineteenth century the transfer of property by will rather than by operation of law is believed to have become the dominant practice – a practice that reflected the "growing individualization of property rights". Detailed rules for the distribution of an estate were minimal. Testamentary freedom meant the decedent might determine the future fate of his or her property, group of heirs, and share of each in the estate. Priority in practice was given to male heirs – sons and grandsons. Conditions were commonly encountered on a wife inheriting: "Do not change my surname, and if my wife remarries, all my property locate in suitable places".[36]

[35] Abramenkov and Chugunov, note 27 above, p. 65.

[36] Goncharov, note 29 above, p. 116, quoting State Archive of Altai Territory, fond 14, opis 1, file 330, folio 5.

Renewed attention to inheritance was given in the draft Civil *Ulozhenie* of 1906,[37] including a return to a concept considered in the 1814 draft – unworthy heirs. However, the First World War put an end to any prospects of adopting this advanced civil code, although the draft was impressive for its quality and used by Russian law reformers after 1991.

SOVIET INHERITANCE LAW (1917-1991)

In the eyes of the early Soviet leadership, inheritance was closely linked with the perpetuation of private wealth in the instruments and means of production. A Dekret of the All-Russian Central Executive Committee, "On Abolition of Inheriting", of 27 April 1918[38] abolished, or depending upon the interpretation of the Dekret, drastically limited, testamentary and intestate succession. The Dekret was retroactive. Except for the family of a deceased working male that otherwise might be left destitute, all property left by individuals upon death passed to the State. Estates not exceeding 10,000 rubles in value and comprising a dwelling house, furnishings thereof, and an individual worker's means of production would pass to those relatives who resided with and were dependents of the deceased. Peasant households were treated similarly, but without any ceiling value. Local soviets undertook to provide for a surviving spouse, children, and ascending or descending relatives, drawing upon the excess value of the estate. No distinctions were drawn between legitimate or illegitimate children, or adopted, adoptive, or blood relations insofar as their inheritance rights were concerned. Wills were abolished as a basis for inheritance.

The Dekret provided that the local soviets were to manage the property of a deceased. A notice of death would be published and persons who had the right to receive support were called.

[37] See I. M. Tiutrimov (ed.), Гражданское уложение. Проект [Civil Ulozhenie: Draft] (2008), IV, pp. 1-285.

[38] СУ РСФСР (1918), no. 34, item 456.

The question that engaged Soviet jurists at the time was whether the estates that could pass under the Dekret were "inheritance" in camouflaged form or a form of social security. Under the second approach, what passed as social security was "labor ownership". Serebrovskii was among those who supported the first approach: "Thus, without calling the transfer of property by way of Article 9 of the Dekret of 27 April 1918 inheritance, judicial practice in essence recognized that persons who received property in their time 'in management and disposition' possess all the rights of owner to this property".[39] Goikhbarg (1883-1962) wrote at the time:

> A lethal blow is inflicted by this Dekret on the institute of private ownership … Private ownership is transformed at a maximum into possession for life: property remains attached to an individual person at most for the period of his lifetime and not more. After the death of each individual possessor, it becomes the weal not of an individual, but of the collective – the proletarian State. It is essential to recall that after the publication of the law on the abolition of inheritance nothing remained of the institute of private inheriting, this institute was not preserved in any guide or in any part: all and every property of the deceased becomes the weal of the Russian Soviet Socialist Republic".[40]

The characterization of the property passing under the Dekret as "social security" was expressed by Brunkman as follows: "from the death of a natural person his legal personality dies away and this complex of property rights and duties passes as a whole to the State" and property lower than 10,000 rubles

[39] See V. I. Serebrovskii, «История развития советского наследственного права» [History of the Development of Soviet Inheritance Law], in Вопросы советского гражданского права [Questions of Soviet Civil Law] (1945), I, p. 160.

[40] See A. G. Goikhbarg, «Отмена наследования (Декрет ВЦИК от 27 апр. 1918 г. об отмене наследования)» [Abolition of Inheritance (Dekret of the VTsIK of 27 April 1918 on the Abolition of Inheriting[, Пролетариат и право: сборник статей [Proletariat and Law: Collected Articles] (1919), p. 112. On Goikhbarg, see O. Iu. Shilokhvost, Александп Гойхбарг: Горькая судьба Красного Трибониана [Aleksandr Goikhbarg: Bitter Fate of the Red Tribonian] (2020).

in value passes "to the persons enumerated in point 2 of the Dekret to persons in the form of and by way of social security ...".[41]

The Dekret was implemented pursuant to an Instruction of the People's Commissariat of Justice of 11 June 1918 "On the Procedure for the Introduction into Operation of the Dekret on the Abolition of Inheriting"[42] and the Joint Decree of the People's Commissariat of Justice and the People's Commissariat of Finances of 31 December 1918 "On the Exemption from Duties and Charges of Issuances Established by the Dekret on the Abolition of Inheriting".[43] The first of these Dekrets recommended that local courts not accept applications to call heirs and that newspapers not publish statements to call heirs. All cases before the courts concerning inheritance disputes were terminated and property exceeding 10,000 rubles in value was transferred to the jurisdiction of the soviets of working people's deputies. The second Dekret treated the transfer of property to relatives of the deceased solely as a type of social security. In practice doctrinal writings of the period indicated that there were virtually no instances of property passing to the State on the basis of these Dekrets (excluding, of course, the confiscation and nationalization of property under other legislation unrelated to inheritance).[44]

On 1 December 1918 the Council of People's Commissars of the RSFSR adopted a Dekret "On Deeming Scientific, Literary, Musical, and Artistic Works to be the Weal of the State".[45] Under this Dekret author's royalties became the weal of the State after the author's death, and relatives of the author received the

[41] A. Brunkman, «Некоторые юридические проблемы социалистического строя» [Certain Legal Problems of the Socialist System], Пролетарская революция и право [Proletarian Revolution and Law], no. 2-4 (1919), pp. 53, 55.

[42] СУ РСФСР (1918), no. 46, item 549.

[43] СУ РСФСР (1918), no. 100, item 1031.

[44] See A. G. Goikhbarg, Хозяйственное право РСФСР. Гражданский кодекс [Economic Law of the RSFSR. Civil Code] (1923), I, p. 176.

[45] СУ РСФСР (1918), no 86, item 900.

right to social security from this property by proceeding from the general rules of the Dekret on the Abolition of Inheriting. Analogous norms with regard to relatives of a deceased inventor were contained in the Dekret of the Council of People's Commissars of the RSFSR of 30 June 1919 "On Inventions".[46]

The abolition of inheriting inclined people to circumvent the situation by giving their property to relatives before death and avoiding the consequences of the Dekret abolishing the right to inherit. The authorities attempted to cut off the attractiveness of this option through the Dekret on Gifts of 20 May 1918;[47] this Dekret provided that a gift or other gratuitous transfer, assignment, and so on of property in an amount exceeding 10,000 rubles would be deemed to be invalid (Article 1), as would multiple gifts to relatives which in aggregate exceeded 10,000 rubles (Article 4). Any future gifts exceeding that amount also would be invalid. Steps were taken to curtail cash gifts exceeding 1,000 rubles without observing legal formalities (direct transfer, oral promises, etc.).

Dekret of 22 May 1922

The introduction of the New Economic Policy in 1921 signaled a change in civil-law relations, including inheritance. The situation was partially redressed by the adoption of the Dekret of 22 May 1922, "On Basic Private Property Rights Recognized by the RSFSR, Protected by its Laws, and Defended by Courts of the RSFSR", which recognized the "right of inheriting by will and by operation of law".[48] This Dekret also imposed a limit on the size of an estate that might pass by way of inheritance: 10,000 gold rubles, which in those days was a sizable amount and much larger than the 10,000 ordinary rubles authorized by the 1918 Dekret.

46 СУ РСФСР (1919), no. 34, item 341.

47 Декреты советской власти [Dekrets of Soviet Power] (1959), II, pp. 293-294.

48 СУ РСФСР (1922), no. 36, item 425.

The reintroduction of inheriting raised the question of whether this represented a return to or a revival of prerevolutionary Russian approaches to inheriting. The suggestion has been made that merely the "form" of inheriting was reintroduced, but that the content of Soviet inheritance differed cardinally from what had existed prior to 1918: the Soviet approach contained a strong public-law aspect, a priority of the interests of the State over individual interests, and a perception by the authorities that inheritance should be used as a means of ensuring the economic interests of the State.[49]

Soviet jurists at the time criticized the Dekret of 22 May 1922 on other grounds. Inheritance by will was in practice impossible, it was noted, because there were no notarial agencies empowered to enter wills in the notarial registers; moreover, any inheritance required the payment of inheritance duties, and these were introduced only from 1 January 1923. On this view, the Dekret did not in fact reinstate inheriting except on paper. The contrary position was set out by Vol'man: "If a law does not provide for the forms of a particular act but the act is permitted, this does not mean that the transaction itself cannot have force. The task of the court and appropriate agencies of power is to give a particular law the proper construction for the application thereof in practice. This is the duty of the appropriate agencies of power on which this lies according to the law ...".[50]

[49] See A. A. Demichev and A. B. Dukhan, Институт наследования в российском праве в XX – начале XXI в. в контексте соотношения интересов государства и личности [Institute of Inheritance in Russian Law in the XX and Early XXI Centuries in the Context of the Correlation of the Interests of the State and the Individual] (2014), p. 30.

[50] I. S. Vol'man, «Допускается ли наследование декретом от 22 мая 1922 г.» [Is Inheriting Permitted by the Dekret of 22 May 1922], Еженедельник советской юстиции [Weekly of Soviet Justice], no. 35 (1923), pp. 794-795. Vol'man gave short shrift to the inheritance duties argument, noting that Russian law "knows the transfer of property by inheritance without any duties". In his view, if duties were to be imposed from 1 January 1923, any transfers prior to that date occurred without the payment of duties. In fact, duties were introduced by the Dekret of the All-Russian Central Executive Committee of the RSFSR of 11 November 1922, "On Inheritance Duties". Duty was not recovered on an individual heir who received less than 1,000 gold rubles. A progressive rate applied to larger sums. СУ РСФСР (1922), no. 71, item 905.

1922 RSFSR Civil Code

The 1922 RSFSR Civil Code,[51] adopted 31 October 1922 and in force from 1 January 1923, accorded a separate section comprising twenty articles (Articles 416-435) to inheritance.[52] The Code broadened the ambit of heirs but initially retained a ceiling on the value of estates of 10,000 gold rubles, excluding rights arising from contracts concluded by State agencies with private persons (lease, concession, and so on),certain debts of the decedent, burial expenses, and designated taxes. The group of heirs by will and by operation of law completely coincided: direct descendants of the deceased (children, grandchildren, great-grandchildren, surviving spouse, and indigent or persons unable to work who were actually entirely dependent on the deceased for not less than a year preceding his death). Thus, property could pass by will only to beneficiaries within the statutory group of heirs, or to State or social organizations. Estates were distributed per capita with no right of representation. There were no priorities of calling to inherit.[53] This liberalization was tempered shortly after the 1922 Civil Code entered into force by the Dekret of 18 May 1923 confirming the Instruction on Inheritance Duties and Inheritance Property Passing to the State.[54] Under this Instruction only property whose value was less than 1,000 rubles was exempted from inheritance tax and a progressive inheritance tax up to 50 per cent was levied; when the ceiling on estates was abolished in 1926, the tax rate became up to 90 per cent, although State bonds and later cash

[51] СУ РСФСР (1922), no. 71, item 904.

[52] Bugaevskii wrote at the time: "no single part of the 1922 RSFSR Civil Code represented such a complete break with our past, prerevolutionary law as the part devoted to inheritance law". See A. A. Bugaevskii, Советское наследственное право [Soviet Inheritance Law] (Odessa, 1926), p. 3.

[53] These provisions, it was said at the time, facilitated the "squeezing and liquidation of capitalist elements". V. I. Serebrovskii, Избранные труды по наследственному и страховому праву [Selected Works on Inheritance and Insurance Law] (1923), p. 48.

[54] СУ РСФСР (1923), no. 59, item 565.

deposits held in banks were exempted from the normal rules on inheritance.

The 1922 Civil Code permitted wills drawn by individuals who had reached the age of 18. Although they could not change the ambit of heirs by operation of law, they might change the procedure for dividing the inheritance among them or they might deprive one, several, or all heirs by operation of law. Substitution was permitted in a designated heir in a will died before the inheritance was opened. Provision was made for a testamentary legacy, performance of which was enforceable through a court. Reviving prerevolutionary practice, a will had to be entered in the register of a notary and an extract issued from the register which had the legal force of a genuine will.

The registry for acts of civil status (ZAGS)[55] notified the competent people's court about the death of the decedent. The court was to take measures to protect the decedent's property until the heirs appeared for a period of up to six months. Heirs who were present had three months after the estate was opened to refuse or accept, but failure to refuse within that period constituted acceptance. The share due to an heir who refused the inheritance passed to the State. Absent heirs had up to six months to accept an inheritance.[56] Heirs might ask the people's court to issue a certificate confirming their right to inherit. Responsibility of an heir for debts of the decedent was limited to the actual value of the inherited property. If heirs failed to appear within six months or refused the inheritance, excluding instances of substitution, the property was escheat and passed to the State.

[55] On ZAGS, see W. E. Butler, *Russian Law* (3d ed.; 2009), paras. 6.156-6.159; Butler, note 26 above, pp. 259-260.

[56] No provision was made in the Code for seeking heirs through publications in the press or other means. This has been regarded as the preference of the legislator for persons close to the decedent inheriting and those who were not in regular contact, did not correspond with the decedent, lacked close family links would be less likely to inherit. See T. E. Novitskaia, Гражданский кодекс РСФСР 1922 г. История создания: общач характеристика. Текст. Приложения [1922 RFSR Civil Code. History of Creation: General Characteristics. Text. Annexes] (2d ed.; 2002), p. 106.

Between 1923 and 1945 a number of changes were introduced in the law of inheritance, although the 1922 Civil Code remained in force. In 1928 adopted persons and their descendants were added to the group of heirs by operation of law.[57] It also was expressly authorized to draw up wills to the benefit of the State, State agencies, Party, trade union, and cooperative organizations.[58] The "obligatory participatory share" was introduced: a testator could not deprive minor heirs of an inheritance of grant them property amounting to less than 3/4 of their participatory share by operation of law. A testator was given the right to place on heirs by will the duty to perform any actions which served to achieve a generally useful purpose (testamentary imposition).

In 1926 the procedure for entering wills in the register book was changed to allow notarial certification. Soviet consuls were given the right to certify wills in 1929 if a Soviet citizen drew up a will abroad; the same right was accorded to masters of seagoing ships in 1929, and, from 1930, to masters of vessels of internal navigation. The powers to protect inheritance property passed from 1930 to notarial agencies, but such measures thence need be taken only when this was considered to be advisable in the interests of the State or of the heirs. The 1936 Constitution of the USSR expressly consolidated the right of citizens to inherit articles of personal ownership (Article 10). Following the adoption of the new Constitution, Soviet jurists began to discuss in detail changes in inheritance legislation in

[57] See O. E. Blinkov, «Унификация советского наследственного права в Указе Президиума Верховного Совета СССР от 14 марта 1945 г. «О наследниках по закону и по завещанию» [Unification of Soviet Inheritance Law in the Edict of the Presidium of the USSR Supreme Soviet of 14 March 1945 'On Heirs by Operation of Law and by Will'], История государства и права [History of State and Law], no. 4 (2006), pp.

[58] At times there was a virtual campaign encouraging individuals to leave their estates to the State. One Soviet jurist, in making the case for allowing wills in favor of juridical persons, observed: "Is it advisable to constrain the freedom of dispositions upon death when they are directed towards … all-State purposes?". See B. Aleksandrov, «Допустимы ли по Гражданскому кодексу завещания в пользу юридических лиц?» [Are Wills Permissible under the Civil Code in Favor of Juridical Persons?], Еженедельник советской юстиции [Weekly of Soviet Justice], no. 2 (1925), p. 28.

the legal media. Most favored enlarging the group of heirs, the introduction of priorities for inheriting, and the removal of limitations on inheriting. However, significant changes only followed during the 1940s, after the Second World War had commenced.[59] A simplified procedure for certifying the wills of persons was introduced in a Decree of the Council of People's Commissars of the USSR of 15 September 1942 for individual military units of the Army and Navy.[60] By an Edict of 10 April 1942 the progressive inheritance tax was replaced by a scheme of notarial fees levied for issuing an inheritance certificate.[61] The Plenum of the USSR Supreme Court by Decree No. 15/M/16/y of 15 September 1942 had suspended the running of periods to accept an inheritance in Articles 430 and 433 of the 1922 RSFSR Civil Code and corresponding articles in the civil codes of other union republics.[62]

USSR Edict of 14 March 1945

Further reforms were introduced to liberalize succession by the Edict of the Presidium of the USSR Supreme Soviet "On Heirs by Operation of Law and by Will" of 14 March 1945.[63] Modern Russian jurists consider this Edict in retrospect to have had "exceptional significance and became the turning point in the history of Soviet inheritance law".[64] Comprising less than a single page and containing only four articles, the Edict "cardinally

[59] For a summary of the principal literature, see Demichev and Dukhan, note 49 above, p. 65.

[60] СП СССР (1942), no. 8, item 133; cited in Demichev and Dukhan, note 49 above, p. 70.

[61] Ведомости Верховного Совета СССР (1942), no. 13. Further exemptions from the payment of duties for certificates of the right to inherit were introduced by an Edict of 9 January 1943 and again on 28 December 1943 for heirs of persons who died in action.

[62] Судебная практика Верховного Суда СССР [Judicial Practice of the Supreme Court of the USSR] (1942), I, p. 5.

[63] Ведомости Верховного Совета СССР (1945), no. 15.

[64] E. Berezovskaia, «Этапы и закономерности развития наследственного права России» [States and Laws of Development of Inheritance Law of Russia], Юрист [Jurist], no. 12 (2006), p. 33.

altered the institute of inheritance in Soviet law and became the basis for changing the norms of inheritance law in the union republics, including the RSFSR".[65] Of considerable significance was the fact that the changes were introduced by all-union legislation, for in pursuance of the 1936 USSR Constitution it was contemplated at the time that civil law would become a matter for the Union as a whole rather than its constituent republics. A Draft Civil Code of the USSR was underway; no doubt the Edict of 14 March 1945 was a preliminary step in that direction.

The major innovation of the Edict was to enlarge the range of heirs and for the first time in Soviet inheritance law to establish priorities for being called to inherit. Three priorities were created: (1) children of the decedent, including adopted children, spouse, and parents not capable of working, and other persons not capable of working who were dependent of the deceased for not less than a year before his death; (2) parents of the deceased capable of working; (3) the brothers and sisters of the deceased. The freedom to bequeath was broadened: in the absence of heirs by operation of law, property might be bequeathed to any person.

Inheritance by children had not created any special difficulties in the Soviet Union until the enactment of the Edict of the Presidium of the USSR Supreme Soviet of 8 July 1944 on increasing State assistance to pregnant women, mothers with many children, and single mothers,[66] which provided that persons in *de facto* marital relations before 8 July 1944 might formalize those relations by registering their marriage and indicating in so doing how long they had been in a *de facto* relationship. State registration was therefore required for a *de facto* marriage to have legal significance. As a result, not all children received the right to inherit after both parents, but each child might inherit after its mother.

[65] Demichev and Dukhan, note 49 above, p. 73.

[66] Ведомости Верховного Совета СССР (1944), no. 37.

An analysis undertaken at the time of children who might inherit after both parents identified these categories: (1) children born of parents in a registered marriage; (2) children born before the Edict of 4 July 1944 of parents in *de facto* marital relations who officially formalized these relations after the date of the Edict by registering the marriage if the father recognized them as his children; (3) children born before 8 July 1944 of parents whose marriage was not registered if the deceased had been registered as the father of the children at a ZAGS office; (4) children born after 8 July 1944 to a single mother if she later entered into a registered marriage with the father of those children who recognized his paternity.[67]

Adopted children being included in the first priority was no surprise given that such children under the 1926 RSFSR Code of Laws on Marriage, Family, and Trusteeship were equated in personal and property rights to the natural children of the adoptive parents. Inheritance rights did not extend, however, to foster children. A spouse was eligible to inherit in the first priority if (1) the marriage between the spouses was official registered; (2) the spouses were in *de facto* marital relations before 8 July 1944 but the marriage was officially registered before the death of one of the spouses; (3) the spouses were in *de facto* marital relations and the marriage was determined in a special procedure set out in an Edict of the Presidium of the USSR Supreme Soviet of 10 November 1944 "On the Procedure for Recognizing *De Facto* Marital Relations in the Event of the Death or Missing on the Front of One Spouse".[68]

Parents of the deceased not capable of working were included in the first priority in the interests of social justice. Situations were encountered when during the Second World War parents remained alive after the death of their children but formally could not become heirs even if the deceased had no heirs by operation of law. It was decided that parents were

[67] G. N. Amfiteatrov and A. P. Solodilov, Право наследования в СССР [Law of Inheritance in the USSR] (1946), p. 11.

[68] Ведомости Верховного Совета СССР (1944), no. 60.

more deserving heirs of homes belonging to children who died in action than the State.[69] Prior to 8 July 1944, parents had not inherited after their deceased children unless they were indigent dependents not capable of working. Although the Edict of 14 March 1945 liberalized the position, not all parents were first priority heirs, only those not capable of working. This category included men aged 60 or above, women aged 55 or above, and persons have I or II group disability. Whether such parents were living with their children was immaterial. Parents who were capable of work fell into the second priority of the right to inherit.

In practice the Edict of 8 July 1944 operated retroactively to some extent. It applied to inheritances opened before it was issued that had not been accepted by heirs and not passed to the State as escheat. This gave rise to problems of interpretation which ultimately were addressed in decrees of the Plenum of the USSR Supreme Court of 10 January 1946[70] and 20 June 1947.[71] Pursuant to the Edict of 14 March 1945, the Presidium of the RSFSR Supreme Soviet made changes in Articles 418, 420, 421, 422, and 423 of the 1922 RSFSR Civil Code to record the changes instructed at the all-union level on 12 June 1945.

Additional changes were made in the 1922 Civil Code during 1945 that repealed the rule on the passing the State of property whose inheritance was refused by the heir; now such property passed to the other heirs by operation of law, which in effect meant that inheritance participatory shares could increase.

[69] Z. I. Mozzhukhina, Наследование по завещанию в СССР [Inheritance by Will in the USSR] (1955), pp. 14-15.

[70] Decree of the Plenum of the USSR Supreme Court No. 1/2y, 10 January 1946, "On the Application of Article 3 of the Edict of the Presidium of the USSR Supreme Soviet of 14 March 1945 'On Heirs by Operation of Law and by Will'", Судебная практика [Judicial Practice], no. 2 (1946), pp. 4-5.

[71] Decree of the Plenum of the USSR Supreme Court No. 9/4y, 20 June 1947, "On the Application of the Edict of the Presidium of the USSR Supreme Soviet of 14 March 1945 'On Heirs by Operation of Law and by Will' and Other Questions of Inheritance", Судебная практика [Judicial Practice], no. 4 (1947), pp. 5-7.

1961 FPCivL

In the four decades during which the 1922 Civil Code operated, a large number of gaps and inconsistencies were identified that could only be partly addressed by additions and changes, or by judicial and notarial practice. These were addressed in appreciable measure by the Fundamental Principles of Civil Legislation of the USSR and Union Republics (1961 FPCivL), adopted 8 December 1961 and in force as from 1 May 1962.[72] Section VII, containing five Articles 117-121, was devoted to inheritance. The 1961 FPCivL removed the restrictions on individuals to whom property may be left. Inheritance by operation of law occurred only when and insofar as not established otherwise by a will. If there were no heirs by operation of law or by will, or the heirs refused the estate, or all heirs had been deprived by the testator, the property escheated to the State.

Only the first priority of heirs was established by the 1961 FPCivL: children, including those adopted; spouse, and parents, including adoptive, and a child of the decedent born after his death. Grandchildren and great-grandchildren were called to inherit by right of representation. Additional priorities of heirs were left to union republic legislation. Although any person might inherit under a will, an obligatory share was reserved for minor children or those incapable of working, including adopted children; a spouse not capable of working, parents, including adoptive, and dependents of the deceased; the obligatory share was to be not less than 2/3 of the participatory share due to each of them under inheritance by operation of law. If obligatory heirs had a right to ordinary household articles and the like, this was counted towards their participatory share. Deposits in savings accounts were disposed of outside these provisions pursuant to the charters of the banks concerned or other special rules.

[72] Ведомости Верховного Совета СССР (1961), no. 50, item 525; transl. in W. E. Butler (ed. & transl.), *The Soviet Legal System: Legislation and Documentation* (1978), pp. 393-430.

The 1961 FPCivL operated as an all-union act binding throughout the entire Soviet Union and accordingly addressed what were regarded as "basic principles" of civil legislation. Each union republic was to adopt its own civil code incorporating the FPCivL and elaborating those provisions in accordance with their special circumstances and conditions. The Civil Code of the RSFSR, adopted in 1964 to this end, devoted 35 Articles to inheritance (Articles 527-561).

1964 RSFSR Civil Code

A major innovation of the 1964 Civil Code was a revival of a matter discussed but never enacted in the 1814 and 1906 draft civil codes: deprivation of unworthy heirs of the right to inherit. Citizens who by their unlawful actions directed against the decedent, or any of his heirs, or against the effectuation of the last will of the decedent expressed in a testament which furthered their being called to inherit, provided that such circumstances were confirmed in a judicial proceeding, were deprived of the right to inherit. Moreover, parents who were deprived of parental rights and had not been restored in them at the time the inheritance was opened could not inherit, nor could parents and children who had reached majority who maliciously avoided performing the duties to maintain the decedent placed on them by law, provided that this circumstance was confirmed in a judicial proceeding (Article 531).

The freedom of testamentary disposition was formulated more expansively in the 1964 Civil Code (Article 534): the testator might bequeath his property or part thereof to any person at his discretion. Provision was made for the right to subdesignate an hair if the principal heir specified in a will died before the opening of the inheritance or refuses the inheritance (Article 536). Both a testamentary legacy and a testamentary imposition were provided for (Articles 538, 539), as was the possibility of revoking or changing a will (Article 543). A will had to be in writing, with specification of the date and place of drawing it and be notarially certified. Certain specified wills were equated to notarially certified (for example, wills of military servicemen certified by the command of a military unit). As a rule, the heirs were responsible for executing a will, but an executor who was not an heir might be indicated. Consent to serve an executor was indicated on the will itself or a document appended to the will.

If an heir refused to accept an inheritance, this was performed before a notary. A refusal might be "simple, in which event the heir did not indicate to whose benefit he was refusing his portion of the inheritance property, or might be "directed", when the refusing heir transferred the property to other heirs by operation of law or will or to the State or a collective formation (Article 550).

The 1964 Civil Code further consolidated the principle of increments to participatory shares of an inheritance. If an heir by operation of law did not accept an inheritance or his refusal of the inheritance was simple, or he was deprived by the testator of the right to inherit, his participatory share went to the other heirs by operation of law and was distributed equally to them. Analogous rules operated for situations when an heir did not take and a substitute heir was not designated by the testator (Article 551).

The State might receive inheritance property in full or in part under the 1964 Civil Code: (1) if the property was bequeathed to the State; (2) if the decedent had no heirs by operation of law or by will; (3) if all the heirs were deprived by the testator of the right to inherit; (4) if none of the heirs accepted the inheritance; (5) if one of the heirs refused the inheritance in favor of the State; (6) if in the absence of heirs by operation of law only part of the decedent's property was bequeathed (Article 552).

An inheritance could not be accepted or refused with conditions or reservations and was irrevocable (Articles. 546, 550). An heir, including the State, who accepted an inheritance was liable for the debts of the decedent within the actual value of the inheritance property which passed thereto (Article 553). Creditors of the decedent had six months from the day of opening the inheritance to present their claims to the heirs who accepted the inheritance or to the executor, or to the notarial office at the place of opening the inheritance, or to file suit in court.

The inheritance property was divided by agreement of the heirs who accepted the inheritance in accordance with the participatory share due to each of them; if they could not agree, the division was by a court.

Special rules operated for certain types of property. Household articles passed to heirs by operation of law who lived together with the decedent before his death for not less than one year. Members of a collective farm household or one-man peasant farm did not divide inheritance property (Article 560). Citizens who had deposits in a State Labor Savings Bank or the USSR State Bank could dispose of their account to any person, in which case the deposit was not part of the inheritance property. If there was no special disposition of the account, inheritance proceeded on the general grounds.

The 1964 RSFSR Civil Code was the subject of explication and clarification on three major occasions during the Soviet era with respect to inheritance by the supreme courts of the USSR and RSFSR: Decree of the Plenum of the USSR Supreme Court of 1 July 1966, "On Judicial Practice with Regard to Cases on Inheritance";[73] Decree of the Plenum of the USSR Supreme Court of 26 March 1974 "On the Application by Courts of the RSFSR of Norms of the Civil Code on Inheritance and Fulfillment of the Decree of the Plenum of the USSR Supreme Court of 1 July 1966 "On Judicial Practice concerning Inheritance";[74] and the Decree of the Plenum of the RSFSR Supreme Court of 23 April 1991,

[73] Сборник постановлений Пленума Верховного Суда СССР. 1924-1977 гг. [Collection of Decrees of the Plenum of the Supreme Court of the USSR. 1924-1977] (1978), I, p. 234. This Decree continued to be applied by Russian courts until 29 May 2012 insofar as not repealed or contrary to legislation on inheritance.

[74] Сборник постановлений Пленума Верховного Суда СССР. 1961-1977 [Collection of Decrees of the Plenum of the Supreme Court of the USSR. 1961-1977] (1978), p. 124.

No. 2, "On Certain Questions Arising in Courts with Regard to Cases on Inheritance".[75]

RUSSIAN INHERITANCE LAW (1991-2002)

The former Soviet Union ceased to exist on or about 25 December 1991. On 31 May 1991 the USSR adopted the 1991 Fundamental Principles of Civil Legislation of the USSR and Republics (1991 FPCivL)[76] which were to enter into force on 1 January 1992. The dissolution of the USSR precluded the entry into force from occurring, but in the Russian Federation it was decided to keep the 1991 FPCivL in force as from 3 August 1992.

The 1991 FPCivL operated in a significantly different socio-economic context that attended the transition to a market economy and an exponential increase in the role of private ownership in the national economy. The extent of property which might now pass by operation of law or by will included enterprises as property complexes, stocks and other securities, land plots, private residences, and others. The 1991 FPCivL repealed the special status of savings accounts except those held in the Savings Bank of the Russian Federation, among other minor changes, but the 1964 Civil Code remained in force with respect to inheritance side by side with the 1991 FPCivL. On 11 April 2001 the 1964 Civil Code (Article 532) was amended to introduce third and fourth priorities in the sequence of inheritance, with effect from 17 May 2001.[77]

The contemporary stage of Russian inheritance law commences with Part Three of the Civil Code of the Russian

[75] Бюллетень Верховного Суда РСФСР [Bulletin of the Supreme Court of the RSFSR], no. 7 (1991), p. 10. This Decree continued to be applied until it was deemed to have lost force by a Decree of the Plenum of 26 April 2007. See the Decree of the Plenum of the Supreme Court of the Russian Federation, No. 15, "On Deeming to Have Lost Force Certain Decrees of the Plenum of the Supreme Court of the Russian Federation". Бюллетень Верховного Суда Российской Федерации [Bulletin of the Supreme Court of the Russian Federation], no. 7 (2007).

[76] Ведомости СНД СССР (1991), no. 26, item 733; transl. in W. E. Butler, *The Fundamental Principles of Civil Legislation of the USSR and Republics* (1994).

[77] СЗ РФ (2001), no. 21, item 2060.

Federation, signed by the President of the Russian Federation on 26 November 2001 and in force from 1 March 2002, set out in Section V, "Inheritance Law". These provisions are set out below in an Annex to the present volume.

Chapter 2

General Provisions on Right to Inherit

The 1993 Constitution of the Russian Federation "guarantees" the right of inheritance (Article 35(4)).[1] The Constitutional Court of the Russian Federation has determined that the right to inherit includes the right of the decedent to dispose of his or her property in the event of death and the right of heirs to receive in ownership property inherited.[2] Inheritance in this perception derives from the right of ownership and disposition thereof.

What precisely falls within the law of inheritance continues to be the lively subject of doctrinal discourse in post-Soviet Russia, as indeed was the case during the Kievan, Muscovy, Imperial and Soviet eras of Russian legal history. Some Russian jurists view the law of inheritance as a branch or sub-branch of civil law, others as one of the institutes of civil law. What passes by way of inheritance amounts in aggregate to more than the rights to a thing that belonged to the decedent; rights of obligation, debts, and certain personal nonproperty rights pass by inheritance as well.

This broad understanding of inheritance affects, for example, where inheritance should be placed and discussed in treatises or textbooks devoted to civil law generally. Some follow the structure of the Russian Civil Code; others would place inheritance at the very end, perhaps reflecting the view that inheritance occurs at the end of human life and therefore positioning within the larger framework of civil law

[1] Translated in W. E. Butler, *Russian Law and Legal Institutions* (3d ed.; 2021), p. 456; the 1978 Constitution of the RSFSR provided that the "ownership of citizens and right of inheritance thereof shall be protected by the State" (Article 13) – a formulation well short of a guarantee.

[2] Ruling of the Constitutional Court of the Russian Federation, No. 316-O, 30 September 2004.

should reflect that reality.[1] Yet others would place inheritance immediately behind the sections on the law of ownership, on the grounds that ultimately it is property and property rights that are conveyed primarily by way of inheritance and the general principles affecting ownership also influence approaches to inheriting property.

Principles, in the view of most Russian jurists, determine whether inheritance is an autonomous subdivision of a branch of law. If there are no principles of inheritance law, the rules regulating inheritance cannot lay claim to a solitary or special place and may be subject to the rules of other structural subdivision of civil law or legislation. Principles help eliminate, it is believed, problems and archaisms in legislation and determine the orientation of the development and improvement of inheritance law.

Among the principles of inheritance law identified in Russian doctrinal writings and considered to be expressed in the Civil Code are: the principle of the universality of inheritance succession (Article 1110); the principle of freedom of will (Article 1119); the principle of taking into account the will of the decedent as reflected in determining the heirs by operation of law (Article 1141); the principle of ensuring the rights and freedoms of necessary heirs (Article 1149); the principle of freedom of choice by heirs called to inherit (Article 1157); the principle of protecting an estate against unlawful infringements (Article 1172).[2]

CONCEPT OF INHERITANCE

The Civil Code of the Russian Federation (Article 1110) provided for the first time in Russian legal history a formulation of the concept of inheriting: "In the event of inheriting, the property

[1] At the end of the Civil Code but before the provisions on private international law. See A. P. Sergeev and Iu. K. Tolstoi (eds.), Гражданское право [Civil Law] (1999), III, p. 521.

[2] E. A. Kirillova, Основания наследования в гражданском праве Российской Федерации [Grounds of Inheritance in the Civil Law of the Russian Federation] (2012), p. 25.

of a deceased (inheritance, inheritance property) shall pass to other persons by way of universal legal succession, that is, in unchanged form as a single whole and at one and the same moment, unless it follows otherwise from the rules" of the Civil Code. Inheritance is, according to some Russian authorities, a species, or variety, of legal succession in connection with which the legislator wished to ensure the "stable and uninterrupted functioning of civil turnover by means of preserving property relations with the participation of a certain natural person after his death".[3] This instrumental and economic characterization of inheritance disregards or minimizes the accumulation and disposition of wealth, the possible preservation of family or kinship ties, the duties that individuals may believe they have towards others, related or otherwise, the desires that a decedent may have to promote the public good or what he perceive to be such, The concentration is on the legal status of the property, property relations as such, and the ability to transact with such property: "… if one deems admissible the complete termination of property rights and duties with the death of their possessor, the things belonging thereto prove to be masterless, all contracts to which he was a party – terminated, and so on for a reason not dependent on the will of the participants of such relations".[4]

This view is one long expressed in Russian legal doctrine. Shershenevich wrote as follows: "the aggregate of legal relations in which a person has placed himself with his death do not terminate, but pass to new person … The new person replaces the former and occupies an active or passive position in his legal relations, occupying the place of the deceased. He is a subject of the rights of ownership with regard to all debts of the deceased".[5] Even though Soviet legislation never bothered to define the concept of inheritance, for obvious reasons it would

[3] See M. S. Abramenkov and P. V. Chugunov, Наследственное право [Inheritance Law], ed. V. A. Belov (2013), p. 90.

[4] Ibid., p. 90.

[5] G. F. Shershenevich, Учебник русского гражданского права [Textbook of Russian Civil Law] (reprint ed.; 2005), II, p. 330.

seem, Soviet jurists were known to take analogous positions with regard to property passing by way of inheritance.[6]

The universality of legal succession is significant because the legislator does not seek to differentiate succession by inheritance from other kinds of succession. Under Article 1110, property passing by inheritance goes to the legal successor as a single whole or in that part which is due to the heir. It is immaterial whether the heir knows precisely what the property may consist of; if there turns out to be property in the inheritance of which the heir had no knowledge, there is no reason to accept the inheritance a second time, as judicial and notarial practice have confirmed.

> *Example.* M brought suit against the Inspectorate for Taxes and Charges, indicating that he was the heir by will of his father of property consisting of a motor vehicle. He had allowed the period to accept the inheritance to lapse and requested the court to recognize his right to the vehicle. On 5 August 1994 M had received a certificate of the right to inherit at a notarial office for bonds from his father. By a decision of 15 September 2000 the court satisfied M's suit and established the fact of his acceptance of the vehicle as well as the bonds. In commenting on the case, the Moscow Regional Court and Moscow Regional Chamber of Notaries commented that M did not need to file suit in court; it would have been sufficient to request the notary for a certificate of the right to inherit the motor vehicle.[7]

The unity of inheritance property also is manifest in the fact that it includes not only the assets or rights which belonged to

[6] See, among others, V. K. Dronikov, Наследственное право Украинской ССР [Inheritance Law of the Ukrainian SSR] (Kyiv, 1974), p. 3; P. S. Nikitiuk, Наследственное право и наследственный процесс: проблемы теории и практики [Inheritance Law and the Inheritance Process: Problems of Theory and Practice] (Kishinev, 1973), p. 6; E. B. Eidinova, Наследование по закону и завещанию [Inheriting by Operation of Law and Will] (1984), p. 3.

[7] Example adapted from Case reported in P. V. Krasheninnikov (comp.), Судебная практика по наследственным спорам [Judicial Practice in Inheritance Disputes] (2004), II, pp. 69-71.

the deceased, but also his liabilities or duties. The replacement of a decedent by an heir does not change the running of a period of limitations (Article 201, Civil Code).[8]

Article 1110 of the Civil Code further stipulates that the property of the deceased passes "in unchanged form", likewise a characteristic of universal succession; that is, in the amounts and value which it possessed at the moment the inheritance was opened.[9] The exclusive right to a result of intellectual activity or a means of individualization passes by inheritance (Articles 1229, 1241, Civil Code). Finally, property passed by inheritance at one moment irrespective of the time when the property actually is transferred to the heir, or from the time of State registration of the rights to property, if such rights are subject to registration (Article 1152, Civil Code).

There are exceptions from the general procedure for legal succession by inheritance. These exceptions may be established solely by the Civil Code. Usually the exceptions affect the question of "unchanged form". Article 1176(1) of the Civil Code addresses the issue of the participatory share or share as part of an estate which belonged to a participant in a full partnership, or a full partner in a limited partnership, or a participant in a society with limited or additional responsibility, or a member of a production cooperative. If under the Civil Code, other laws, or constitutive documents of the economic partnership of society or production cooperative the consent of other members is required for the heir to join the said partnership or society and such consent is refused, then contributory compensation in the form of the value of the participatory share or share must be provided. Obviously, in this event the inheritance does not

[8] Decree of the Plenum of the Supreme Court of the Russian Federation, No. 43, 29 September 2015, "On Certain Questions Connected with the Application of Norms of the Civil Code of the Russian Federation on Limitation".

[9] This attribute of universal succession is found in other provisions of the Civil Code; for example, Article 353, which provides that a pledge retains force when the right of ownership to pledged property passes by way of universal legal succession, and the legal successor of the pledgor takes the place of the last and bears all the duties thereof unless provided otherwise.

pass in unchanged form, but rather there is a modification of the property comprising the inheritance.

Not all property belonging to a decedent at the moment of death is subject to being inherited. Certain types of property by operation of law pass to other person(s) and do not constitute part of an estate. Examples include monies accrued but unpaid to the decedent as means of subsistence (Article 1183, Civil Code); State awards (Article 1185(1), Civil Code); or rights and duties of a tenant under a dwelling lease (Article 686(2), Civil Code); or certain pension accumulations.[10]

In a substantial reversal of the position throughout the Soviet era, inheritance by operation of law occurs only when and insofar as inheritance is not changed by a will and in other instances expressly specified by the Civil Code. The will now occupies primacy of place, which in a market system means that the legislator has accorded priority to the wishes of the testator in disposing of his property. Nonetheless, how the testator may give expression to his preferences, in what form, and sometimes under what circumstances are all regulated by law. As some have observed, it would be more proper to speak of "inheritance without a will" and "inheritance by operation of law", the latter occurring when in the absence of a will inheritance occurs in accordance with the prescriptions of legislation.

It is, moreover, the case that inheritance by will and inheritance by operation of law are not mutually exclusive categories. The property of a deceased may pass to others simultaneously by operation of law and by will, for example, when the will disposes of only some of the property of the deceased and the remainder will be inherited by operation of law. Inheritance contrary to a will occurs when the will is deemed to be invalid, or the substance thereof violates the rules on obligatory share, or some such similar shortcoming.

[10] Soviet law rejected the civil-law nature of pensions, a position partly reversed by the present Civil Code, depending on whether the pensions are insurance or cumulative. Pensions which fall outside inheritance law are subject to different legislation and enjoy immunity against creditors of the decedent.

Article 1111 of the Civil Code contains an exhaustive list of the ways of inheriting: by will or by operation of law. This precludes the possibility of inheritance by promise, or inheritance by contract, including any provisions touching upon inheritance in a marriage contract. However, the prohibition against inheritance under a contract does not affect the rules of the Civil Code regulating contracts of personal insurance, pursuant to which the beneficiary under an insurance contract acquires the proceeds not as an heir but as a beneficiary. The exclusion of the possibility of inheritance by contract is normally regarded in Russian legal doctrine as a limitation on the freedom of contract, at least in principle.

OPENING OF INHERITANCE

Inheritance legal relations arise in connection with a particular legal fact which in Russian law is called the "opening of the inheritance". The general rule (Article 1113, Civil Code) is that an inheritance opens with the death of a natural person. From a legal standpoint the death of a natural person is an act of civil status and subject to registration at the ZAGS in the procedure established by the Federal Law on Acts of Civil Status of 15 November 1997, as amended.[11] A death certificate is issued by ZAGS upon the submission of an appropriate medical document; a notary will not open an inheritance other than on the basis of the submission of such evidence. Equated to a death certificate is a judicial decision concerning the declaration of a citizen to be deceased (Article 45, Civil Code).

The opening of an inheritance is the foundation legal fact for inheritance legal relations to arise and occurs at a certain time and place. The time of opening an inheritance is decisive for determining which law will regulate the procedure for the passing of property by way of inheritance; the group of heirs; what the inheritance property comprises; the commencement of the running of the period for acceptance of an inheritance;

[11] СЗ РФ (1997), no. 47, item 5340; transl. in W. E. Butler, *Russian Public Law* (3d ed.; 2013), pp. 945-979.

among other vital issues. The Civil Code provides (Article 1114) that the time of opening an inheritance is a certain calendar day, that day on which the natural person died. That day is indicated on the death certificate. If a citizen is declared to be dead by a court decision, the day of his death will be considered to be the day on which the respective court decision entered into force. If a person is missing under circumstances threatening death or there are grounds to suppose that the person died in a certain accident, the day of death is considered to be the day of supposed death specified in the court decision. Russian law does not recognize temporal gaps in ownership in connection with inheritance nor the possibility of a juridical person opening an inheritance.

The Civil Code (Article 1114) addresses situations when persons died on the same day who under other circumstances would inherit one after the other: spouses, parents and child; and so on. They are considered to have died simultaneously and do not inherit one after the other. The deaths in these situations must have occurred during the same 24-hour calendar day. By way of example, if one spouse died at 23:35 minutes and the other at 00:15 minutes, this rule would not apply because they are considered to have died on different days. An analogous situation would arise if death ensued within the same 24-hour period but in different time zones.[12] If individuals are considered to have died simultaneously on the same day, the heirs of each of them are called to inherit.

When persons inheriting one after the other did not die simultaneously, the rules of inheritance transmission are applied: if an heir dies after the opening of an inheritance without having succeeded in accepting it, the right to accept passes to his heirs (Article 1156, Civil Code).

[12] See point 16, Decree of the Plenum of the Supreme Court of the Russian Federation, No. 9, 29 May 2012, as amended 23 April 2019 and 24 December 2020: The calendar day is determined by the sequential number of the calendar day, number or name of the calendar month, and number of the calendar year; a calendar day is considered to be the period of time of 24 hours between 00:00.00 and 24.00.00 hours calculated according to local time. Available on Consultant Plus.

Example. Z. N. filed suit against a notary who refused to perform a notarial action. On 26 October 1996 her former husband was killed in an automobile accident and their common son died on the same day from injuries sustained in the same accident. The son did not succeed in accepting the inheritance after his father's death; therefore, Z. N. believed his right to accept the share of the inheritance had passed to her; the notary refused to issue a certificate of the right to inherit. At stake was an apartment. Z. N. had sued F. L., now the wife of her former deceased husband, for her share of the apartment. An appeal court determined that the husband was killed immediately in the accident, but the son died one hour later on the same day. The court decided that because the son died after the opening of the inheritance without having accepted it, the right to accept the share of the inheritance passed by way of inheritance transmission to his mother, Z. N. The Judicial Division for Civil Cases of the Russian Supreme Court reversed. The time of opening the inheritance was the day of death of the decedent. Thus, the transfer of the right of to accept the inheritance was possible only in the event of the death of the heir called to inherit after the opening of the inheritance, which is deemed to be the *day*, but not the *hour*, of death of the decedent. The husband and son died on the same day and the inheritance was opened after each of them separately; therefore, irrespective of the hour of death, they did not inherit one after the other and the right to accept the inheritance could not pass to the mother, Z. N.[13]

The Civil Code contains exceptions from the general procedure for inheriting in the event of simultaneous deaths. Article 1146(1) provides for inheriting by right of representation; that is, the participatory share of an heir by operation of law who has died before the opening of an inheritance

13 Adapted from T. I. Zaitseva, Судабная практики по наследственным делам [Judicial Practice in Inheritance Cases] (2007), pp. 63-64.

or who died simultaneously with the decedent passes by right of representation to his respective descendants and is divided between them equally. And in the event of the death simultaneously of a decedent and the person designated by him as his heir in his will, but the decedent has subdesignated an heir, the property bequeathed passes to the subdesignated heir (Article 1121, Civil Code).

The place of opening an inheritance is no less important. The inheritance matters are handled at that place, the heirs make application to accept or to refuse the inheritance, creditors of the decedent submit claims to the heirs who have accepted the inheritance or against the inheritance property, measures are taken to protect the inheritance property, and so on. The Civil Code contains several criteria for determining the place of opening an inheritance: the place of residence of the decedent, or the location of inheritance property. Article 1115 provides that an inheritance is opened at the place of residence of the deceased, that place where he permanently or primarily resided pursuant to Article 20 of the Civil Code. The 1993 Russian Constitution (Article 27) guarantees to each who is legally on the territory of the Russian Federation the right to freely move about and to select a place of sojourn or residence within Russia.[14] The constitutional provision is elaborated in a Federal Law which preceded the Constitution but is widely used in this connection, the Federal Law "On the Right of Citizens of the Russian Federation to Freedom of Movement, Choice of Place of Sojourn and Residence within the Limits of the Russian Federation", of 25 June 1993.[15]

Under the said Federal Law (Article 2), a "place of residence" is a dwelling house, apartment, employment dwelling premise, specialized houses (hall of residence, hotel, house of the maneuver fund, special house for single aged persons, boarding houses for the disabled, veterans, and others), and also other

[14] Article 27, Constitution of the Russian Federation; transl. in W. E. Butler, note 1 above, p. 454.

[15] Ведомости СНД и ВС РФ (1993), no. 32, item 1227, as amended. Available on Consultant Plus.

dwelling premise in which a citizen permanently or primarily resides as an owners, under a contract of rental (or subrental), contract of lease, or on other grounds provided by legislation of the Russian Federation. Citizens of Russia are obliged to be registered at the place of residence (Article 3). As a general rule, the place of opening an inheritance is the registration data of the decedent for the place of residence in Russia, and this is verified by obtaining a reference document issued by the housing operations organizations or agencies of local self-government. The Methods Recommendations for the Formalization of Inheritance Rights, confirmed by the Federal Notarial Chamber on 28 February 2007, provides that "documents issued by registration recording agencies confirming the registration of the decedent at the place of residence shall be submitted for confirmation of the place of opening an inheritance to a notary".[16]

When for various reasons the decedent spent a length period of time away from his place of residence, the respective information may be provided by other organizations and institutions: personnel service at the place of work of the deceased; military commissariats; treatment, educational, or penal institutions, among others. However, these institutions cannot be considered to be either the place of death of the decedent or the place of opening an inheritance. In the case of military servicemen on active duty, students studying away from home, and other persons away from their permanent place of residence, the contractual tenancy relations concluded pursuant to the Housing Code of the Russian Federation (Article 71) may be of assistance.[17]

There is doctrinal support for the view that the fact a deceased was not registered in a particular place should not exclude the application of the general rules concerning the place of opening an inheritance. This view argues that the fact of permanent or

[16] Confirmed by Decision of the Board of the Federal Notarial Chamber, Protocol No. 02/07, 27-28 February 2007. Excerpts are available on Consultant Plus.

[17] S. P. Grishaev, Наследственное право [Inheritance Law] (2014), p. 28.

primary residence may be determined by instituting a judicial proceeding in which the court will take into account the duration of the decedent being in a specific place at the moment of opening the inheritance, the location of inheritance property in that place, and other relevant circumstances.[18]

If the place of permanent or primary residence of the decedent is unknown or is outside the Russian Federation, the place of opening the inheritance in Russia will be the location of inheritance property. The Civil Code structures the relevant rules as follows: (1) if the estate is comprised of immoveable property, the inheritance is opened at the location of the immoveable; (2) if the immoveables are in different places, the inheritance is opened at the place where the most valuable immoveable property is situated; (3) if there are not immoveables which are part of the estate, the location of the moveable property or most valuable part thereof is the place of opening the inheritance. The market value is taken into account when valuing the property (Article 1115, Civil Code). Certain types of inheritance property are valued pursuant to the Tax Code of the Russian Federation (Article 333.25).

INHERITANCE PROPERTY

Article 1112 of the Civil Code treats what may comprise inheritance property and what is an inheritance. An inheritance may be composed of "... the things and other property, including property rights and duties, which belonged to the decedent on the day of opening the inheritance". The Code then proceeds to stipulate what may not comprise inheritance property: "rights and duties ... which are inextricably connected with the person of the decedent, in particular, the right to alimony, the right to compensation of harm caused to the life or health of a citizen, and also rights and duties whose transfer by way of inheriting is not permitted ..." by the Civil Code or other laws, as well as nonproperty rights and other nonmaterial benefits.

[18] Point 17, Decree of the Plenum of the Supreme Court of the Russian Federation, No. 9, 29 May 2012. Available on Consultant Plus.

Some Russian jurists argue that after the death of a person his property acquires special legal qualities transforming it into an object of "civil rights of a local character", meaning various legal relations in which it is involved being intended to achieve only one aim, to ensure that the property passes from the decedent to other persons(s) by way of universal succession. These commentators point to another specific feature of inheritance property: its elasticity – which means that inheritance property may consist of any things or other property, including property rights and duties, in unlimited quantities.

Support for this perception is found in classic Russian civilist writings. Shershenevich observed that "all relations [of the deceased] ... pass to a new person not individually, but as something integral, whole".[19]

From the formulation of Article 1112, it follows that an inheritance principally consists of "things", that is, tangibles. The presumption is that the decedent held these things in ownership, a proposition that has led some Russian jurists to suggest that the formulation of Article 1112 is not correctly phrased and should refer not to "things" as such, but to the "rights to things", having in view the right of ownership.[20] Although there is no special list of things, the rights to which may pass by inheritance, there are special provisions which appertain to certain types of property. Rights to stocks, for example, are inherited "on the general grounds" (Article 1176, Civil Code). So are the rights of ownership or inheritable possession for life to land plots, which are subject to restrictions relating to designated use or purpose, or limitations of alienation, or provisions on division. Things provided to a decedent by the State or municipal formations on special conditions may be subject to inheritance limitations, together with certain State awards.

The reference in Article 1112 to property rights and duties includes intangible elements that are distinctively Russian. The

19 Shershenevich, note 5 above, II, p. 330.

20 See note 3 above, p. 103. To a western observer, a curious observation, because this comment overlooks the role of "title" in ownership.

duties of a donor who promised a gift pass to his heirs unless provided otherwise by the contract of gift (Article 581, Civil Code). Under a Contract of Rent for Life, in the event of the death of one recipient of rent his participatory share in the right to receive rent passes to the recipients of rent who survive him unless the contract provides otherwise (Article 596, Civil Code). The obligation of maintenance of a dependent for life which a decedent assumed also passed to his heirs (Article 605, Civil Code). In the event of the death of a citizen leasing immoveable property, his rights and duties under the contract of lease pass to an heir unless provided otherwise by a law of the contract (Article 617, Civil Code). In the event of the death of a citizen-lender, the rights and duties of the lender under a contract of uncompensated use pass to the heirs (Article 700, Civil Code). Pursuant to the Federal Law "On Participation in Participatory Share Construction of Apartment Houses and Other Objects of Immoveable and Making Changes in Certain Legislative Acts of the Russian Federation" of 30 December 2004, unless provided otherwise by a federal law the rights and duties of a citizen-participant in such construction pass to his heirs (Article 4).[21] Other rights and duties that pass by inheritance may include those connected with the decedent's participation in juridical persons or results of intellectual activity which he created (see Articles 1241, 1283, 1293, and others, Civil Code).

The rights and duties which may not be inherited fall into two categories. First are those which are inextricably connected with the person of the decedent – not a definition of exceptional clarity and precision. Two examples are given: the right to alimony and the right to receive compensation for harm caused to the life or health of the decedent. As regards alimony, the Family Code of the Russian Federation (Article 120) expressly provides that alimony obligations cease with the death of one of the parties. The Civil Code also provides that duties of an author who agrees to create a work of science, literature, or art terminate with the author's death (Article 1288).

[21] СЗ РФ (2005), no. 1(I), item 40, as amended.

Second are those rights and duties whose passing to another by way of inheritance is expressly prohibited by Russian legislation. Among this group are a power of attorney (Article 188, Civil Code); rights of a done to whom a gift was promised under a contract, unless the contract provides otherwise (Article 581, Civil Code); the procedure for the use of donated property in the donor dies (Article 582, Civil Code); the right of a sole or last recipient of rent for life (Article 596, Civil Code) or of maintenance for life of a dependent (Article 605, Civil Code); the right of a tenant to a dwelling premise ((Articles 672 and 686, Civil Code); the right of a citizen loan recipient (Article 701, Civil Code); rights and duties arising from a contract of commission (Article 977, Civil Code); rights and duties of a commission agent (Article 1002, Civil Code) or agent (Article 1010, Civil Code); rights and duties of a trustee manager (Article 1024, Civil Code); and the right of the decedent to receive unpaid amounts granted as means for subsistence (Article 1183, Civil Code). Nor may heirs succeed to a contract for certain telephone services in a dwelling premise; they must conclude a new contract.[22]

Although the logic seems irreproachable that personal nonproperty rights and other intangible benefits belonging to an individual should not pass by inheritance, these are sometimes addressed in other ways. Although, for example, the right to a name, or the right of authorship, or the right to inherit honor, dignity, and business reputation are not inheritable, situations can arise when they require protection after the death of the individual concerned. The Civil Code does permit (Article 152) interested persons, which might include heirs, to defend the honor and dignity of a person after his death; the same applies to authorship (Articles 1267 and 1316, Civil Code).

The inheritance of State awards of the Russian Federation which belonged to a decedent has given rise to concerns. The Edict of the President of the Russian Federation of 7 September

[22] Pursuant to the Federal Law on Communications, of 7 July 2003. C3 PΦ (2003), no. 28, item 2895, as amended.

2010, No. 1099,[23] "On Measures for the Improvement of the State Reward System of the Russian Federation" has established the system of awards. Pursuant to the Civil Code (Article 1185) awards within this system "shall not pass by inheritance" are after the death of the recipient are subject, under the Edict, to keeping by the heirs, and if there are no heirs, to being returned to the Administration of the President of the Russian Federation (point 50, Statute on State Awards of the Russian Federation, confirmed by the said Edict). If the decedent was given a State award posthumously, the State awards and documents pertaining thereto are transferred to the surviving spouse, parent, or child of the awardee (point 47, Statute).[24] Why adoptive parents, brothers, sisters, grandparents, and so on are excluded has been the subject of criticism.

HEIRS

Heirs in Russian law are those persons to whom property of a deceased passes by way of universal succession. Russian legal doctrine traditionally divides heirs into three categories: (1) natural persons; (2) juridical persons; and (3) public-law formations.

Natural persons – citizens of the Russian Federation, foreigners, and stateless persons – may be called to inherit by operation of law or by will if they are alive at the moment of the opening of the inheritance or if they were conceived during the life of the decedent and were born alive after the opening of the inheritance (Article 1116, Civil Code). The Latin expression *nasciturus* is sometimes encountered in doctrinal literature by way of transliteration to describe those heirs who are born in the future after the decedent's death.[25]

[23] СЗ РФ (2010), no. 37, item 4643, as amended.

[24] See O. E. Blinkov, «Наследование государственных наград, почетных и памятных знаков» [Inheritance of State Awards, Honorary and Memorial Marks", Наследственное право [Inheritance Law], no. 4 (2010, pp. 22-27.

[25] See A. L. Makovskii and E. A. Sukhanov (eds.), Комментарий к части третьей Гражданского кодекса Российской Федерации [Commentary to Part Three of the Civil Code of the Russian Federation] (2003), p. 73.

Juridical persons, whether Russian or foreign, may inherit property only by will provided that they exist on the day of the opening of the inheritance. The formulation leaves open the issue of whether a foreign legal entity which is not a juridical person under the personal law of the jurisdiction where it is formed can be an heir by will. A literal reading of Article 1116, "juridical persons ... may be called to inherit by will" would suggest a negative response, although such a reply would seem to be in conflict with the freedom of a testator at his discretion to "... bequeath property to any persons, by any means ..." (Article 1119, Civil Code). "To any persons" might be universally applied, but a legal entity, or subject of law, which lacks autonomous legal personality would seem to lack the legal capacity to be an heir other than as a representative of the natural or juridical person responsible for their creation. In Russia that approach would exclude branches and representations from being heirs, but not necessarily the juridical persons which created and registered them. In the case of foreign subjects of law which are not juridical persons, Russian legislation acknowledges them to be governed by their own personal status, that is, the status conferred on them by the foreign jurisdiction in which they are created. Nonetheless, there is no categorical answer in Russian legislation.

"Public-law formations" is a collective category of which, with respect to inheritance, the Civil Code gives an exhaustive list of examples: the Russian Federation, subjects of the Russian Federation, and municipal formations, which may inherit by will or by operation of law, and foreign States and international organizations, which may inherit only by will.

UNWORTHY HEIRS

Although the concept and category of "unworthy heirs" was discussed by Russian jurists during the preparation of draft civil legislation in 1814 and again in 1906, Russian inheritance provisions did not mention such heirs.[26] Nor did the 1922 RSFSR

[26] The Digest of Laws of the Russian Empire did permit parents whose children

Civil Code.[27] Soviet legal doctrine, however, did not entirely overlook the principle completely. An early and for a lengthy period sole work on the subject favored the introduction of the principle on the grounds that unworthiness constituted "a clear attitude of disrespect of an heir towards the decedent" or the commission by the heir of an act with regard to the decedent that would deprive the heir of the possibility of drawing up or revoking a will (for example, the murder of the decedent) or in "the illegal orientation by the heir of the will of the decedent in the matter of drawing up the will" or in the destruction by the heir of the will "to the prejudice of third persons" or the obstruction after the decedent's death of the discovery of his last will. The consequence of such behavior should be excluding the person from being an heir and the passing of his participatory share to the State.[28]

married against their will to be excluded from inheriting unless the said parents subsequently forgave their children in a will. Article 1566, Digest of Laws, vol 15. As for those who committed serious crimes in prerevolutionary Russia, it was possible to punish those acts by the death penalty or exile accompanied by deprivation of all rights of status, in which event such persons could not be called to inherit. See Article 1107, Digest of Laws, vol. X(1).

27 The Dekret of the All-Russian Central Executive Committee and Council of People's Commissars of the RSFSR of 15 December 1921, "On Deprivation of Rights of Citizenship of Certain Categories of Persons Abroad", in force from 1921 to 1938, was erroneously cited as relating to unworthy heirs. Although this Dekret did deprive relevant persons from the right to inherit, this followed from their loss of general legal capacity, not from actions directed against the decedent or the effectuation of the decedent's last will. See V. N. Gavrilov, «О лишении прав гражданства некоторых категорий лиц, находящихся за границей» [Elimination from Inheriting of Unworthy Heirs: History, Prospects, and Foreign Experience], Правоведение [Jurisprudence], no. 5 (2002), p. 190; cited in O. Iu. Shilokhvost, Наследование по закону в российском гражданском праве [Inheritance by Operation of Law in Russian Civil Law] (2012), p. 14. Soviet doctrine did not support proposals advanced during the 1930s to abolish the right to inherit for persons deprived of citizenship of the USSR. See Zhukov, «О праве наследования» [On the Right of Inheritance], Советская юстиция [Soviet Justice], no. 6 (1937), p. 6.

28 N. N. Tovstoles, «О лишении наследства по Гражданскоиу кодексу» [On Deprivation of Inheritance under the Civil Code], Право и жизнь [Law and Life], no. 6-7 (1927), pp. 52-64; cited in Shilokhvost, note 29 above (2012), p. 15. Nikolai Nikolaevich Tovstoles (1872-19?) was a graduate of the Law Faculty of St. Vladimir University in Kyiv in 1896 who published a number of works on the law of ownership and inheritance. His career was in the Russian judiciary before the 1917 Revolution and from 1920-1926 he taught at the Faculty of Social Sciences in the Kyiv Institute of National Economy. See O. Iu. Shilokhvost, Русские

In the absence of any relevant provisions in the 1922 Civil Code, Tovstoles argued that the rules concerning the consequences of disinheritance should apply by analogy through Article 422(1) of the said Code. But the standard included elements of flexibility: disinheritance should not happen, said Tovstoles, "… in the event the unworthy (or guilty) heir was forgiven by the decedent".

Soviet judicial practice from the 1920s to the end of the 1950s recognized only intentional homicide of the decedent to be grounds for depriving the perpetrator of the right to inherit as an unworthy heir.[29] An Explanation of the Plenum of the RSFSR Supreme Court of 7 June 1926 recognized as the grounds for unworthiness only an "intentional homicide of the decedent punishable under the Criminal Code", which, "proceeding from "the essence and grounds of the right to inherit" deprived "the heir who committed this homicide of the right to inherit the property of the murdered person".[30] Cases of this nature were rarely encountered in Soviet judicial practice. Judging from published accounts of judicial practice, only one other such case was mentioned by 1959,[31] and another in 1962.[32]

This pattern of judicial practice led most Soviet jurists, while making reference to the aforementioned judicial practice, to deny the existence in Soviet law of the institute of unworthy

цивилисты середина XIX – начало XX в.: краткий биографический словарь [Russian Civilists of the Mid-XVIII-Early XX Centuries: Concise Biographical Dictionary] (2005), pp. 146-147.

29 Shilokhvost, note 27 above (2012), p. 17.

30 Protocol No. 9, reproduced in Еженедельник советской юстиции [Weekly of Soviet Justice], no. 28 (1926), p. 885; V. A. Boldyrev (ed.), Вопросы наследования: Справочник по законодательству и судебной практике [Questions of Inheritance: Manual on Legislation and Judicial Practice] (1959), p. 46; cited in Shilokhvost, note 25 above (2012), p. 16.

31 See B. S. Antimonov and K. A. Grave, Советское наследственное право [Soviet Inheritance Law] (1955), p. 70; A. N. Samtsova, Вопросы наследственного права в судебной и нотариальной практике [Questions of Inheritance Law in Judicial and Notarial Practice] (1964), p. 5.

32 See Советская юстиция [Soviet Justice], no. 19 (1962), p. 31.

heirs as such.[33] Serebrovskii was among those who urged that the list of grounds for depriving an unworthy heir should be expanded. He enumerated among the possible grounds: obstructing by means of fraud, threat, or coercion the drawing up or revocation of a will; the malicious destruction or making unfit of any will provided that the testator had no opportunity to reinstate the will; stealing or hiding someone's will – provided that these facts were established by a court.[34]

Although the full story of the preparation of a draft USSR Civil Code which occupied Soviet jurists fitfully during the 1940 and early 1950s remains to be told, the principle of unworthy heirs was incorporated in the draft 1940 USSR Civil Code, as well as in the drafts of 1947, 1948, and 1951 in one fashion or another.[35]

The 1964 RSFSR Civil Code introduced the principle of unworthy heirs (Article 532), depriving citizens of the right to inherit by operation of law or by will if they by their illegal actions directed against the decedent or any of his heirs or against the effectuation of the last will of the decedent expressed in a will facilitates the calling thereof to inherit, provided that these circumstances were confirmed in a judicial proceeding. The scope of this formulation was understood variously in Russian doctrinal writings. Nikitiuk believed that unworthy heirs were not only those who committed criminally-punishable acts abetting their being called to inherit or increasing their share

[33] Antimonov and Grave, note 31 above, pp. 69-70. M. O. Reikhel, «Наследственное право» [Inheritance Law], in Гражданское право [Civil Law] (1938), II, p. 457; and others.

[34] V. I. Serebrovskii, «Наследственное право» [Inheritnace Law], Советская юстиция [Soviet Justice], no. 10-11 (1937), p. 28; republished in Serebrovskii, Избранные труды по наследственному и страховому праву [Selected Works on Inheritance and Insurance Law] (1923), p. 58. Proposals in the spirit of Serebrovskii were advanced by S. A. Dzhaparidze in his kandidat dissertation. See S. A. Dzhaparidze, Наследование по закону в советском гражданском праве [Inheritance by Operation of Law in Soviet Civil Law] (Tbilisi, 1953) (abstract of diss. kandidat iurid. nauk).

[35] Summarized by Shilokhvost, note 27 (2012), p. 18; also citing the Проект Гражданского кодекса Союза ССР: Второй предварительный вариант [Draft Civil Code of the USSR. Second Preliminary Variant] (1940).

of an inheritance, but also individuals who committed acts that were unlawful under civil law: obstructing the drawing up of a will, or concealing from a notary the existence of other heirs, and so on. Nikitiuk would accept not only a court judgment, but also the decree of an investigative or procuracy agency in certain situations.[36]

Gordon construed the provision narrowly. An unworthy heir was solely a person who committed a crime with respect to the decedent, or an attempt on his life, or committed criminally-punishable actions with respect to persons close to the decedent, or by criminal actions attempted to change the sequence of inheritance".[37] Eidinova believed that Article 531 required that the act committed be unlawful and directed against the decedent, or one of his heirs, or against the effectuation of the consequences of the will of the decedent expressed in the testament, and be intentional, as well as be criminally-punishable.[38] Vlasov and Kalinin would have required that the actions of the heir be confirmed by judgment of a court rendered in a criminal case.[39] There was general consensus that other actions of an unworthy heir included obstructing the drawing up of a will, forgery of will or drawing up a fictitious will, concealing a will, or compelling the drawing up of a will or refusal of an inheritance.

Putability was widely considered to be an element of the requisite actions, which meant that a person under the age of 14 or 15 could not be deprived of the right to inherit. Judicial practice in this period required not only "guilt", but guilt in

[36] Nikitiuk, note 6 above, p. 54. The union republic civil codes differed in their formulations of unworthiness, which doubtless contributed to the divergence of doctrinal treatments.

[37] M. V. Gordon, Наследование по закону и по завещанию [Inheritance by Operation of Law and by Will] (1967), pp. 6-7.

[38] Eidinova, note 6 above, p. 8, citing the Decree of the Plenum of the USSR Supreme Court, No. 6, of 1 July 1966, "On Judicial Practice in Cases concerning Inheriting".

[39] See Iu. N. Vlasov and V. V. Kalinin, Наследование по закону и по завещанию [Inheritance by Operation of Law and by Will] (3d ed.; 2001), p. 9.

the form of "intent". A Decree of the Plenum of the RSFSR Supreme Court issued in 1974 expressly excluded depriving a person of the right to inherit who had been convicted of a crime committed through negligence.

Under Article 1117 of the Civil Code, unworthy heirs are divided into two categories: (1) persons not having the right to inherit; and (2) persons removed from inheriting by a court. Turning to the first category, the formulation of Article 1117 suggests that the behavior or conduct of the unworthy heir must be expressed in active behavior, that is, actions; These actions must be of an unlawful intentional character. And these actions must be directed against the decedent himself, or against the effectuation of the last will of the decedent expressed in the will. As a result of such behavior of the unworthy heir he himself must be called to inherit or another person, or the share in the estate must be increased that is due to the unworthy heir or another person.

In practice a number of problems have arisen. The present formulation differs from that of the 1964 Civil Code by a reference to the unlawfulness of the unworthy heir's behavior, rather than, as before, the illegality of that behavior. The term "unlawfulness" in Russian legal thought is traditionally used to designate actions whose commission in view of their special social danger constitute a crime and entail criminal responsibility.[40] This raises the question in doctrinal gloss as to whether Article 1117 has in view any crime or violation of law or an especially grave crime. There is no uniform view in doctrinal writings; some authors seem to have taken both views.[41] Shilokhvost differentiates the grounds for depriving an unworthy heir of the right to inherit as follows: (1) some, such as intentional unlawful acts (crimes) committed with respect to the decedent, family members thereof, or close relatives should results in the unworthy heir being deprived of the right to

[40] Shilokhvost, note 27 above (2006), pp. 30-31.

[41] Zaitseva, note 13 above, pp. 66 and 74, takes the view(s) that the actions of an unworthy heir should be confirmed by the judgment of a court in a criminal case which has entered into legal force or by decision of a court in a civil case.

inherit pursuant to a judicial decision in a criminal case which has entered into legal force; but others (2) which are connected with obstruction of the effectuation of the will expressed in a testament in the broad meaning of such actions (falsification of a will, concealment of a will, compelling other heirs to refuse an inheritance, for example) – which are not crimes – might entail removal of an unworthy heir from inheriting by decision of a court considering a civil case.[42] Such constructions, it has been cautioned, do not follow from a literal interpretation of Article 1117, but merely confirm that the Article has not been drafted as carefully as practice demonstrates is necessary.[43]

The present Civil Code (Article 1117), just as the 1964 predecessor Civil Code, does not precisely indicate the motivation for the actions of an unworthy heir. Does the motive for the commission of the crime have to relate directly and expressly to the purpose of opening an inheritance, or is it sufficient that, for example, the murder of the decedent for whatever reason led to the opening of the inheritance. To take an example discussed in doctrinal writings: suppose two persons who are children of a decedent have a quarrel and one kills the other, which thereby increases his participatory share of the father when he dies in the event of inheritance by operation of law. Two approaches to such a situation are in evidence in doctrinal writings: the first, based on the so-called objective orientation of the actions of the unworthy heir, is based on the fact that the necessary and sufficient condition is the objective link of the son's actions with the result which ensued. Tolstoi has argued that in order to remove an unworthy heir from inheriting the motive for the commission of intentional unlawful actions has no significance.[44]

[42] Shilokhvost, note 27 above, p. 32.

[43] Abramenkov and Chugunov, note 3 above, p. 116.

[44] Iu. K.Tolstoi, in A. P. Sergeev, Iu. K. Tolstoi, and I. V. Eliseev, Комментарий к Гражданскому кодексу Российской Федерации (постатейный). Часть третья [Commentary to the Civil Code of the Russian Federation (Article by Article). Part Three (2002), p. 21. Also see B. A. Bulaevskii, in N. I. Marysheva and K. B. Iaroshenko (eds.), Комментарий к Гражданскому кодексу Российской Федерации, части третьей (постатейный) [Commentary to the Civil Code of

Proponents of what is styled the "subjective orientation" of the behavior of an unworthy heir suggest that only the subject whose intent was directed towards attaining a particular result in the domain of inheritance relations should be removed from inheriting.[45] Abramenkov and Chugunov observe that the text of Article 1117 makes reference to "... facilitated or attempted to facilitate ...", which would suggest that the Russian legislator preferred the "subjective orientation".[46]

Judicial practice supports both approaches, the first with respect to an intentional crime directed against the decedent or persons close to him, and the second directed to other violations of law which do not constitute an intentional crime.

> *Examples.* In 2004 B murdered his wife C, leaving two children, H and K. B was convicted of intentional homicide and sentenced to deprivation of freedom. H and K brought suit to have their father declared an unworthy heir by reason of having committed an act which facilitated the opening of an inheritance connected with her death. No will was found. The court satisfied the suit and declared B to be an unworthy heir. The court attached no importance to the motives that led to the homicide.[47]
>
> Z brought a civil suit against Y to seek the certificate of the right to inherit issued to Y to be invalid and to declare Y to be an unworthy heir. When Y's wife died, Y told his son L that the apartment in which they resided was in State ownership and not part of the estate. Several years later L learned that his father had defrauded him,

the Russian Federation, Part Three (Article by Article)] (2004), pp. 26-27. Zaitseva wrote: "to recognize the right of inheritance, for example, for a son who out of vengeance murdered his mother ... would at least be immoral". Zaitseva, note 13above, p. 69.

[45] Shilokhvost names O. S. Ioffe and M. Iu. Barshchevskii, among others, as being of this persuasion. See Shilokhvost, note 28 above (2005), pp. 37-39.

[46] Abramenkov and Chugunov, note 3 above, p. 117.

[47] Adapted from Zaitseva, note 13 above, pp. 67-68.

the apartment had in fact been privatized, and was in the joint ownership of Z and his mother. The court found that Y failed to properly inform the notary about the existence of Z as an heir by operation of law. Z was deemed by the court to be an unworthy heir because he through his behavior facilitated an increase in the participatory share of the inheritance due to him.

The Plenum of the Supreme Court of the Russian Federation in a Decree of 29 May 2012 would seem to have accepted this position. It also seems to be the position that the relevant criminal judgment or civil decision does not need to expressly deem heir concerned to be unworthy. A notary may exclude the individual from inheriting if the court judgment or decision is submitted to her for this purpose.[48]

Loss of the right to inherit is not irreversible. Article 1117 provides in effect that if after an unworthy heir has lost the right to inherit the decedent draws up a will in favor of the unworthy heir, such heir has the right to receive the property bequeathed to him (sometimes described as the "forgiveness of an unworthy heir"). Nonetheless, the precise operation of the provision is ambiguous in some respects. The phrase "... after the loss of their right to inherit ..." might be understood to mean "after the commission of impermissible actions"

[48] See point 19, Decree of the Plenum of the Supreme Court of the Russian Federation, No. 9, 29 May 2012. In this the Supreme Court is said to have directed judicial practice along a different path than was followed previously. The St. Petersburg City Court on 21 March 2012, two months prior to the Supreme Court Decree had refused to deem an heir unworthy under Article 1117 of the Civil Code if intentional unlawful actions with respect to one heir for which he was convicted were not directed towards increasing his inheritance share or accelerating the opening of an inheritance, but were committed for other motives. See the Ruling of the St. Petersburg City Court, 21 March 2012, No. 33-4074/12, available on Consultant Plus. At about the same time, the Moscow City Court in a Ruling of 21 February 2012, Case No. 33-5512/2012, endorsed a refusal to find an heir to be unworthy because there were no intentional unlawful actions or failure to act on the part of the defendant with respect to the decedent as a result of which the decedent's death occurred. Available on Consultant Plus. Both cases are cited by A. A. Demichev and A. B. Dukhan, Институт наследования в российском праве в XX – начале XXI в. в контексте соотношения интересов государства и личности [Institute of Inheritance in Russian Law in the XX and Early XXI Centuries in the Context of the Correlation of the Interests of the State and the Individual] (2014), p. 128.

with respect to the decedent which served as grounds for the respective judicial decision, or to mean "after the rendering of a judicial act confirming these actions". Both the first[49] and the second[50] constructions have support in doctrinal writings. The question is whether the will itself constitutes "forgiveness", notwithstanding a court judgment or decision whose consequences would deprive an unworthy heir of the right to inherit. The majority of Russian jurists who have expressed a view seem to believe that forgiveness may transpire only after a court decision as confirmed the unlawfulness of the unworthy heir's behavior.

Parents deprived of parental rights and not reinstated in those rights by the day of opening the inheritance are treated as unworthy heirs and may not be heirs by operation of law (Article 1117).

The second category of unworthy heirs is persons who maliciously avoided the fulfillment of duties placed on them by virtue of a law with regard to the maintenance of the decedent. They are removed from inheriting by decision of a court at the demand of interested persons. For the most part the duty to maintain a person is imposed on those obliged to pay alimony, and these individual are determined by the Family Code of the Russian Federation.[51] Among those who may be eligible for alimony are pursuant to the Family Code are: minor children and children who have reached majority but are not capable of working (Articles 80, 85, Family Code); parents who are not capable of working and need assistance (Article 87, Family Code); spouses, brothers, sisters, grandparents, and other relatives (Articles 89, 93, 94, 95, and 97, Family Code). What

[49] See A. A. Bugaevskii, Советское наследственное право [Soviet Inheritance Law] (Odessa, 1926), p. 3.

[50] See R. I. Vinogradova and V. S. Repin , in R. I. Vinogradova, G. K. Dmitrieva, and V. S. Repin (eds.), Комментарий к Гражданскому кодексу Российской Федерации, части третьей [Commentary to the Civil Code of the Russian Federation, Part Three], ed. V. P. Mozolin (2002), p. 22; Abramenkov and Chugunov, note 5 above, p. 122, prefer the second construction.

[51] Translated in W. E. Butler, *Russia & The Republics: Legal Materials* (looseleaf service; 2006-).

constitutes "malicious" avoidance is for the courts to determine. They will take into account how long assistance to the decedent was not rendered, whether the person obliged to pay alimony concealed himself somewhere to avoid enforcement actions, the actual earnings of the person concerned, and similar individual factors.[52]

The "interested persons" who may bring suit may be other heirs. An unworthy heir is obliged to return all property received by him from an estate. The principles of unfounded enrichment apply (Chapter 60, Civil Code). These requirements extend to a testamentary legacy. If the recipient of such a legacy is deemed to be unworthy, he is obliged to compensate the heir for any work performed or service rendered as a variety of unfounded enrichment.

52 Abramenkov and Chugunov, note 3 above, p. 123. See point 20, Decree of the Plenum of the Supreme Court of the Russian Federation, No. 9, 29 May 2012.

Chapter 3

Sources of Russian Inheritance Law

Inheritance law in Russia is widely regarded as a sub-branch of civil law. Therefore, the principal body of legislative and other normative legal acts regulating inheritance relations comprises sources of civil law.

Nonetheless, it is generally accepted in Russian legal doctrine that the legal regulation of relations relating to the inheritance of property is of an integrated, inter-branch character. These enactments consist, first, of those establishing, with the assistance of constitutional and civil-law norms, the very possibility to bequeath and inherit property; second, of norms of civil law determining the powers of citizens to dispose of their property in the event of their death; and third, of those norms establishing legal remedies in the event of an infringement of inheritance rights on the part of third persons.[1] Accordingly, the source of the legal regulation of inheritance is the system of legislative acts (and in some small ethnic groups in Russia, customary rules) and international treaties which regulate relations arising in connection with the opening of an inheritance and with the defense, exercise, and formalization of inheritance rights.[2] Although technically not sources of law, of great practical significance are recommendations of the Federal Chamber of Notaries, particularly the Methods Recommendations on the Formalization of Inheritance Rights.

CONSTITUTION OF RUSSIAN FEDERATION

Inheritance is a constitutionally-protected right. The 1993 Russian Constitution provides in Article 35(4) that the right of

[1] See K. V. Khramtsov, «Обеспечение свободы завещания наследователя» [Ensuring the Freedom of the Will of a Decedent], Российская юстиция [Russian Justice], no. 11 (2009), p. 5.

[2] Khramtsov, Правовое регулирование наследования в Российской Федерации [Legal Regulation of Inheritance in the Russian Federation] (Omsk, 2008), p. 3.

inheritance shall be guaranteed. Russian commentators classify inheritance as an "economic" right of citizens and associations thereof and a corollary to the right of citizens to dispose of property belonging to them by right of private ownership.

Citizens exercise their right of inheritance equally, irrespective of sex, race, nationality, language, origin, property and official position, place of residence, attitude towards religion, affiliation to social associations, and other obligations. Lacking in the Commentaries[3] is any sense of what limitations the State may impose upon the right of inheritance. For example, should the priorities of heirs be so constructed as to satisfy constitutional standards, or should broader considerations of social policy (for example, obligatory shares) be addressed, or is the legislator at liberty to structure the priorities of heirs as he may choose. Having established priorities, are there constitutional standards which would preclude the legislator, for example, from moving someone in the second priority to the third?

Not untypical is the treatment by Professor Baglai, who sees the right of inheriting as a guarantee of the right of private ownership, which it undoubtedly is in Russia. However, no constitutional issues are seen in the existing inheritance regime: "The Civil Code of the Russian Federation regulates all nuances of the transfer of the property of an owner after his death to heirs by operation of law or by will. Inheritance law is called upon to guarantee the fulfillment of the will of the owner with respect to his property and at the same time to ensure justness, especially when one speaks about the protection of the interests of young relatives or those not capable of working".[4]

[3] See N. I. Kosiakova, in O. I. Tiunov (ed.), Конституционные права и свободы человека и гражданина в Российской Федерации [Constitutional Rights and Freedoms of Man and Citizen in the Russian Federation] (2005), pp. 174-175.

[4] M. V. Baglai, Конституционное право Российской Федерации [Constitutional Law of the Russian Federation] (13th ed.; 2018), pp. 291-292.

Inheritance relations are governed principally by Part III, Section V, of the Civil Code (Articles 1110-1185). Article 1110(2) of the Civil Code provides that inheritance is regulated by the Civil Code and by other laws and, in instances provided by a law, by other normative legal acts. "Other laws" in this instance includes family law, the law of taxation, land law, among others.

More specifically, other federal laws regulating aspects of inheritance include the Federal Law of 26 November 2001, "On the Introduction into Operation of Part Three of the Civil Code of the Russian Federation",[5] certain other provisions of the Civil Code itself (for example, Articles 111, 266, 581, 979, 1038, 1224, and a number of provisions regulating intellectual property). There are provisions affecting inheritance in the Federal Law on a Consumer Cooperative Society (or Consumer Societies or Unions Thereof) in the Russian Federation (Articles 13, 14);[6] Federal Law on Production Cooperatives (Article 7);[7] Federal Law on Peasant (or Farmer) Economy (Article 10),[8] Federal Law on an Agricultural Cooperative Society;[9] Federal Law on Housing Accumulative Cooperatives,[10] Federal Law on Limited Responsibility Societies (Articles 21, 23);[11] and Federal Law on Joint-Stock Societies;[12] Federal Law on the Museum Fund and Museums in the Russian Federation,[13] Federal Law

5 СЗ РФ (2001), no. 49, item 4553, as amended.

6 Ведомости СНД и ВС РФ (1992), no. 30, item 1788, as amended.

7 СЗ РФ (1996), no. 20, item 2321, as amended.

8 СЗ РФ (2003), no. 24, item 2249, as amended.

9 СЗ РФ (1995), no. 50, item 4870, as amended.

10 СЗ РФ (2005), no. 1(I), item 14, as amended.

11 СЗ РФ (1998), no. 7, item 785, as amended; transl. W. E. Butler, *Russian Company and Commercial Legislation* (2003), pp. 215-299.

12 СЗ РФ (1995), no. 1, item 1, as amended; transl. in ibid., pp. 165-214.

13 СЗ РФ (1996), no. 22, item 2591, as amended. Article 25 of this Law provides that when inheriting museum articles and museum collections by will or by operation of law an heir is obliged to assume all obligations which the decedent

on Currency Regulation and Currency Control,[14] among others. The Fundamental Principles of Legislation of the Russian Federation on the Notariat contains a number of articles devoted to inheritance matters.[15]

Overall the Civil Code of the Russian Federation contains more than twice as many articles regulating inheritance in comparison with the 1964 Civil Code of the RSFSR. Rather than thrown willy-nilly into a section, as was done in 1964, they have within Section V been systematized into five chapters: General Provisions on Inheritance (Chapter 61); Inheriting by Will (Chapter 62); Inheriting by Operation of Law (Chapter 63); Acquisition of Inheritance (Chapter 64); and Inheriting of Individual Types of Property (Chapter 65). It is worthy of more than symbolic note that the Chapter on inheriting by will has been placed by the architects of the Civil Code ahead of the chapter on inheriting by operation of law.

OTHER NORMATIVE LEGAL ACTS

Inheritance matters are regulated in the Family Code of the Russian Federation (Articles 36, 60);[16] the Merchant Shipping Code of the Russian Federation (Article 70);[17] the Land Code of the Russian Federation (Articles, 21, 22, 40, 53, and others);[18] the Housing Code of the Russian Federation,[19] and the Tax Code of the Russian Federation.[20]

had with respect to these articles. If the heir decides to dispose of these articles, the State has a preferential right of purchase.

14 C3 PΦ (2003), no. 50, item 4859, as amended. Article 14(3) of this Federal Law allows currency valuables to be freely received by way of inheritance (Article 14).

15 Translated in Butler, *Russian Public Law* (2013), pp. 853-890.

16 C3 PΦ (1996), no. 1, item 16, as amended; transl. in Butler, *Russia & The Republics* (looseleaf service; 2006-).

17 C3 PΦ (1999), no. 18, item 2207, as amended.

18 C3 PΦ (2001), no. 44, item 4147, as amended; transl. in Butler, note 16 above.

19 C3 PΦ (2005), no. 1(I), item 14, as amended.

20 C3 PΦ (1998), no. 31, item 3824, as amended (Part 1); transl. in Butler, note 16 above.

SUBORDINATE NORMATIVE LEGAL ACTS

The Civil Code (Article 1110[2]) provides that in instances provided for by a law, inheriting may be regulated by "other legal acts". Within the context of Russian sources of law, these words are understood to refer to "subordinate normative legal acts", which would include edicts of the President of the Russian Federation,[21] decrees of the Government of the Russian Federation,[22] and enactments issued by federal agencies of executive power – a general formulation that embraces ministries, departments, and other State subdivisions.[23] These enactments are detailed and numerous.

JUDICIAL PRACTICE

The relevant decrees of the Plenum of the Supreme Court of the Russian Federation and Constitutional Court of the Russian Federation are an important source for the regulation of inheritance relations, as were any relevant decrees of the Supreme Arbitrazh Court of the Russian Federation (abolished in 2014). Central to matters of inheritance is the Decree of the Plenum of the Supreme Court of the Russian Federation of 29 May 2012, No. 9, "On Judicial Practice with Regard to Cases on Inheriting", as amended.[24]

[21] For example, the Edict of the President of the Russian Federation of 16 May 1997, No. 485, "On Guarantees to Owners of Objects of Immoveable and Acquisition of Land Plots in Ownership beneath These Objects". СЗ РФ (1997), no. 20, item 2240, as amended.

[22] See the Decree of the Government of the Russian Federation of 27 May 2002, No. 351, "On Confirmation of the Rules for Drawing Up Testamentary Dispositions of Rights to Monetary Means in Banks". СЗ РФ (2002), no. 22, item 2097.

[23] See the Order of the Ministry of Justice of the Russian Federation of 15 March 2000, No. 91, "On Confirmation of the Methods Recommendations for the Performance of Individual Types of Notarial Actions by Notaries of the Russian Federation". Бюллетень Минюста Российской Федерации [Bulletin of the Ministry of Justice of the Russian Federation], no. 4 (2000), which lost force on 16 August 2018 and was superseded by Reglament for the Performance by Notaries of Notarial Actions Establishing the Exchange of Information Necessary for a Notary to Perform Notarial Actions, of 30 August 2017, No. 156.

[24] Бюллетень Верховного Суда Российской Федерации [Bulletin of the Supreme Court of the Russian Federation], no. 7 (2012).

Russian jurists experienced in matters of inheritance also follow individual Russian court decisions. These are available online through the judicial system itself or commercial data bases (ConsultantPlus, Garant). Some are the subject of commentary in Russian doctrinal writings, usually as examples, less commonly as having precedential value.

The existence, role, and nature of judicial precedent in the Russian legal system is the subject of continuing discussion, including within the Russian judiciary.[25] Beyond doubt the role of judicial practice in Russian law has transformed almost beyond recognition in comparison with the Soviet era.

INTERNATIONAL LAW

Article 15(4) of the 1993 Constitution of the Russian Federation provides that "generally-recognized principles and norms of international law and international treaties of the Russian Federation" are an integral part of the legal system of the Russian Federation. The "generally-recognized" principles and norms of public international law do not regulate inheritance relations directly, although their operation would ultimately affect inheritance insofar as such relations may fall within the domain of human rights and the realization of treaty rights and obligations. Applicable law provisions contained in inheritance-related documents that choose Russian law would automatically incorporate the general rules of international law and treaties insofar as they constitute part of the Russian legal system.

The term "international treaties" of the Russian Federation encompasses all inter-State, intergovernmental, or interdepartmental documents irrespective of their form and appellation (treaty, agreement, convention, pact, covenant, protocol, exchange of letters, notes, and so on) (Article 1, 1995 Law on International Treaties of the Russian Federation).[26]

[25] An exceptionally well-informed discussion is Alexander Vereshchagin, *Judicial Law-Making in Post-Soviet Russia* (2007).

[26] Translated in Butler, note 15 above, pp. 33-47.

Article 15(4) of the Constitution must now be read in conjunction with Article 125(5^1), which provides:[27]

> 5^1. The Constitutional Court of the Russian Federation shall [added by Federal Constitutional Law, 14 March 2020, No. 1-ФКЗ]:
>
> (a) …
>
> (b) in the procedure established by a federal constitutional law, settle the question concerning the possibility of the execution of decisions of inter-State agencies adopted on the basis of provisions of international treaties of the Russian Federation in a construing thereof which is contrary to the Constitution of the Russian Federation, and also the possibility of the execution of the decision of a foreign or international (or inter-State) court or foreign or international arbitration court imposing duties on the Russian Federation if this decision is contrary to the fundamental principles of public policy of the Russian Federation [added by Federal Constitutional Law, 14 March 2020, No. 1-ФКЗ];

Specific international treaties of the Russian Federation which regulate inheritance relations are discussed in Chapter 10 below.

27 W. E. Butler, *International Law in the Russian Legal System* (2020), p. 227.

Chapter 4

Inheritance by Will

Inheriting pursuant to a will, or testament, drawn up by the decedent is a procedure regulated by law for legal succession upon death. It is the sole means by which a natural person may dispose of property upon his death: "The conclusion of any other transactions providing for the gratuitous transfer of property after the death of the possessor thereof is not permitted".[1] In combination with other circumstances (opening of inheritance, existence of property subject to inheritance, and the like), a will is the basis for inheriting. A will is, in a sense, juxtaposed with inheritance by operation of law (see Chapter 5 below) insofar as the "operation of law" disposes of property in the absence of a will or imposed constraints upon the ability of the testator to exclude statutory heirs completely from inheriting or from reducing their share of the estate below a statutory minimum.

The freedom to draw up a will (Article 1119, Civil Code) is in the view of many legal theorists the fullest possible expression of the right to dispose of private property and, accordingly, enjoys constitutional recognition and protection in the Russian Federation (Articles 35 and 55). Within the conceptual framework of Russian civil law, the freedom and right to dispose of one's property by will is the ultimate expression of the principle of "dispositiveness" in legal regulation – to grant to the party to the transaction (the testator) the discretion to make choices as he or she pleases with respect to his or her property.[2] This is an important observation, for it sets the

[1] A. A. Rubanov, in T. E. Abova, M. I. Braginskii, and A. G. Svetlanov (eds.), Комментарий к Гражданскому кодексу Российской Федерации, части третьи [Commentaries to the Civil Code of the Russian Federation, Part Three] (2004), p. 81.

[2] See V. P. Zvekov, A. L. Makovskii, and O. Iu. Shilokhvost, «Вводный комментарий к проекту Гражданского кодекса Российской Федерации» [Introductory Commentary to the Draft Civil Code of the Russian Federation], in Гражданский кодекс России. Часть третья. Наследственное право. Международное частное право. Текст. Вводный Комментарий [Civil Code

concept of the will within the framework of civil-law relations which, in principle, could range from the complete abolition of inheritance rights (the Bolsheviks came close to achieving this on paper) to no constraints whatsoever upon the disposition of property (which no legal system has accepted). For Russian citizens the present legal regime of inheritance is a marker of how far they have come from an event rare, if not unique, in human experience – an official desire and attempt by the State to eliminate the transfer of property upon death.

The freedom of will (Article 1119) was not provided for previously in Russian civil legislation. Chapter 62 on inheritance by will has been placed ahead in the Civil Code of Chapter 63 on inheritance by operation of law, thereby reversing the sequence and importance of the two ways by which one may inherit in Russia and according priority and preference to the stature of the will.

Although Chapter 62 of the Civil Code, devoted to inheriting by will, plays a central role in regulating testamentary disposition, such disposition is affected by Chapter 61 on general provisions, by the requirements of an obligatory share (which operates to limit the freedom of disposition) and to protect the inviolability of the estate (Article 1149), by the requirements and procedures for acceptance of an inheritance (Articles 1152-1175), and by special provisions regulating particular types of property (Articles 1176-1185).

As general propositions regarding wills, Russian doctrinal writings single out the following: will must be drawn up before the opening of an inheritance, that is, before the death of the testator, because until the moment of death the decedent reserves within himself the legal right and power to make or change his will; the will is a transaction concluded during the life of the testator for the disposition of his property in the event of death; the will is the sole legal means by which a natural person may dispose of his property in the event of his

of Russia. Part Three. Law of Inheritance. Private International Law. Text. Introductory Commentary] (2001), p. 23.

death; the will generates legal consequences after the opening of an inheritance because it is the basis of the inheriting – that is, the will creates rights and duties for the heirs by will and other persons; compliance with and execution of the will is an essential condition for inheriting by will; the limits of freedom of testament are provided by law.

To whom and why a testator has decided to leave property is entirely his or her personal concern. The fate of the property and the choice of successors to it require no explanation or justification. Whatever decisions are made in the will of this nature, and for whatever reason, may be changed at the wish or whim of the testator repeatedly, revoked, reassessed, and so on. Any discussion the testator may have with others about the will is immaterial to what is actually written in the document; the document is binding, not what may have been discussed beforehand or afterwards. Accordingly, the secrecy of a will is protected by the Civil Code.

Secrecy of will. Secrecy and confidentiality have a constitutional foundation in Russian law and are expressly protected by the Civil Code (Article 150), which refers to the inviolability of private life and the personal and family secrecy of a natural person. The secrecy of a will is regarded as an extension of this principle (Article 1123, Civil Code). The secrecy of a will extends to the existence of a will itself, the contents of the will, or any change or revocation of the will. The duty of observing or complying with the secrecy requirement is placed on a notary or any other individual certifying a will, an interpreter, an executor, witness, or any natural person who signs a will in place of the testator. Legislation on the notariat extends the duty of secrecy to any persons working in a notarial office who learned about a will in connection with their employment. Even after leaving their position, they are bound by the duty of secrecy.

Nonetheless, there are substantial numbers of persons to whom the existence or contents of a will may become known in the course of their employment and upon whom a statutory duty to comply with testamentary secrecy is not expressly imposed. These individuals include Russian consular officials, personnel in hospitals and other treatment institutions, the officers and crew of a ship, certain ministry of justice personnel, among others. Suggestions that the scope of Article 1123 of the Civil Code be broadened to encompass these individuals have been made.[3]

On 2 October 2012, Article 1123 of the Civil Code was amended to add paragraph three as part of a larger reform to introduce a centralized register of wills within the unified information system of the notariat. The intention was to enhance the security of wills, but inevitably at the cost of giving other personnel access to the wills included in the register, meaning any personnel of the system, operator, and controller. That broader access in principle is disciplined by a series of subordinate legal acts and departmental instructions. Nonetheless, if there are reasons for testators not to trust the levels of security, commentators recommend either a closed will (Article 1126, Civil Code) or the choice of a foreign jurisdiction where security standards are stricter.[4]

The secrecy of a will endures until the opening of an inheritance, after which there is no reason for secrecy and, indeed, secrecy might obstruct the proper execution of the last wishes of the testator. Any other information relating to the personal or family life of the decedent that became known in connection with drawing up the will remains protected under the general relevant provisions of the Civil Code (Articles 150-152).

The legal consequences of violating the secrecy of a will are addressed in Article 1123 itself. The testator has the right to demand contributory compensation for moral harm and to take advantage of other remedies for the defense of civil rights

[3] M. S. Abramenkov and P. V. Chugunov, Наследственное право [Inheritance Law] (2013), p. 136.

[4] I. G. Rents, in E. Iu. Petrov (ed.), Наследственное право: постатейный комментарий к статьям 1110-1185, 1224 Гражданского кодекса Российской Федерации [Inheritance Law: Article-by-Article Commentary to Articles 1110-1185, and 1224 of the Civil Code of the Russian Federation] (2018), p. 108.

provided by the Civil Code. Such contributory compensation would be sought pursuant to Articles 151 and 1099-1101 of the Civil Code, which address obligations arising out of the causing of harm. Article 1123 is so formulated that the right to compensation belongs solely to the testator during his lifetime and may not be exercised after his death. The situation would be otherwise if violating the secrecy of a will also simultaneously constituted a violation of honor and dignity; this violation and the right to compensation would survive the decedent and could be pursued by interested persons after the decedent's death. Examples are known.

Other remedies for harm caused by a violation of the secrecy of a will, suggested in doctrinal writings, include seeking compensation for property harm caused by conflicts on the basis of a will becoming known if such conflicts involved a deterioration of health, medical costs, related communications or travel costs, and so on.[5] Doubt has been expressed, however, as to whether the victim of a violation of the secrecy of a will might seek restoration of the original position before the alleged violation: that which is no longer confidential presumably cannot become confidential again.[6]

Paragraphs four and five were added to Article 1123 with effect from 1 September 2018 as a response to the introduction of the joint will into Russian inheritance law. A notary may certify such will in the presence of both spouses, although the grounds for exercising this discretion are not specified. When one spouse who drew up a joint will predeceases the other, the notary or executor may disclose to the surviving spouse only information relating to the consequences of the death of the first spouse necessary for them to perform their duties.[7]

[5] Ibid., p. 137.

[6] For the argument in favor of such restoration, see V. V. Piliaeva, Комментарий к Гражданскому кодексу Российской Федерации (постатейный). Часть третья [Commentary to the Civil Code of the Russian Federation (Article-by-Article). Part Three] (2002), p. 25. For the contrary view, see Abramenkov and Chugunov, note 3 above, p. 137.

[7] The rationale of these changes was discussed in P. V. Krasheninnikov,

CONCEPT AND FORMS OF WILL

Following Soviet experience, the Civil Code of the Russian Federation contains no legal definition of a will (unlike, as noted in Chapter 1 above, Article 1010 of the Digest of Laws of the Russian Empire). Russian doctrinal writings extrapolate a legal definition by identifying what are regarded as the "indicia", or special properties, of a will. Under this approach it is observed that a will as a transaction and a will as grounds for inheriting are indistinguishable: "a will generates legal consequences in the form of inheriting in accordance with the will of the testator expressed in a form established by a law".[8]

Transaction of Property Character. A testament is a transaction of a property character and contains dispositions of property belonging to the decedent. This is understood to mean that the dispositions in the will should have "property content", even though some dispositions may be of a nonproperty character[9] – a position long since acknowledged by prerevolutionary Russian legal doctrine. However, dispositions contained in a document of a solely nonproperty character do not constitute a will (for example, instructions on funeral or burial, or appointment of a guardian or trustee over a person): "an act by which nothing at all concerning property is disposed of cannot be deemed to be a will because the law looks upon a will as a means of the acquisition of rights to property".[10]

«Совестные завещания будут востребованы» [Joint Wills Will be in Demand], Закон [Law], no. 1 (2017), pp. 6-22; S. L. Budylin, «Договор с покойником. Реформа наследственного права России и зарубежный опыт» [Contract with the Deceased. Reform of Inheritance Law of Russia and Foreign Experience], Закон [Law], no. 6 (2017), pp. 32-43; E. Iu. Petrov, «Развитие российского наследственного права» [Development of Russian Inheritance Law], Закон [Law], no. 6 (2017), pp. 44-50.

[8] Abramenkov and Chugunov, note 3 above, p. 138.

[9] "... advice, behests, and in general instructions to heirs will not be a testament ... because in these instances there is no disposition of property". See V. I. Sinaiskii, Русское гражданское право [Russian Civil Law] (reprint ed.; 2002), pp. 592-593.

[10] G. F. Shershenevich, Учебник русского гражданского права [Textbook of Russian Civil Law] (reprint ed.; 2005), II, p. 348.

In event of Death. This indicator means that until the death of a natural person occurs or a person is declared to be deceased, no legal consequences arise from a will either for the testator or for anyone mentioned in the will. The testator is not bound in any way in his freedom while alive to dispose of his property, which in Russian doctrine is what distinguishes the will as a transaction from all others. Any will may be revoked or changed as often as the testator may wish. During the days of the Russian Empire, a will was commonly referred to as a "spiritual testament" or a "spiritual will", which was another way of expressing the position that a will did not affect the property status of the testator during his lifetime.

To approach this from another direction, the fact that a will operates in the event, and from the moment, of death means that the will operates when the testator no longer has any legal capacity, or as one Russian jurist aptly expressed the position: a will "is loaded with legal energy for the future".[11] Arguably, this explains why Russian legislation imposes the various requirements that it does concerning the person of the testator.

Dispositive Legal Capacity in Full. Only a natural person having full dispositive legal capacity may draw up a will (Article 1118, Civil Code). This is acquired at the age of eighteen by a Russian citizen (Article 18, Civil Code) as part of general legal capacity, or at age sixteen by a married person (Article 21, Civil Code) or by an emancipated individual (Article 27, Civil Code) and may not be limited other than in the instances and in the procedure established by law (Article 22, Civil Code). Individuals who have not reached majority (Article 21, Civil Code), or who have been limited in dispositive legal capacity by a court (Article 30, Civil Code), or who have been deemed by a court to lack dispositive legal capacity may not draw up a will (Article 29, Civil Code). Wills drawn up by natural persons before being deemed to lack or to be limited in dispositive legal capacity are valid and retain their legal force. If a court decision

[11] Abramenkov and Chugunov, note 3 above, p. 139.

which limited or removed dispositive legal capacity is reversed, testamentary capacity is restored.

Although Article 1118 of the Civil Code is now absolutely clear about the position that a testator must have full dispositive legal capacity to draw up a will, the position under the 1964 RSFSR Civil Code was not categorical and generated considerable controversy in Russian doctrinal writings: "Judicial practice indirectly permitted the possibility of a will being drawn up by a person limited in dispositive legal capacity with the consent of a guardian".[12] Although some consider Article 1118 to have brought an end to the issue,[13] others observe that there is still no uniform view in Russian doctrine on the issue.[14]

The controversy revolves around situations where a will is drawn up by a person who has dispositive legal capacity, that is, such capacity has not been limited or removed by a public act in the form of a court decision, by the individual is not fully aware of the character of his actions and/or able to direct them. Judicial practice in Russia on the point illustrates the complexities and difficulties of sustaining the burden of proof, for an individual drawing up a will may be unaware of the nature of his actions because of mental illness, emotional disturbance, or shock. Such a will might, however, be contested under Article 177 of the Civil Code, which addresses the invalidity of a transaction concluded by a citizen not capable of understanding the significance of his actions or guiding them. The reasons for an individual being in such a position include alcoholic intoxication, consumption of narcotics, and the like. The court may use witness evidence (notary, witnesses to the will, executor) or designate a post-mortem forensic psychiatric examination in order to determine the mental state of the decedent testator.

[12] Rubanov, note 1 above, p. 82, citing point 2, Decree of the Plenum of the Supreme Court of the RSFSR, 4 May 1990, No. 4, "On the Practice of Consideration by Courts of the Russian Federation of Cases on Limiting the Dispositive Legal Capacity of Citizens Abusing Alcoholic Beverages or Narcotic Means".

[13] Ibid., p. 82.

[14] Abramenkov and Chugunov, note 3 above, p. 141.

Personal Character of Will. This principle accentuates that a testament must be solely the express and direct expression of the will of the testator himself. A testament accordingly may not be drawn up by a representative, including a guardian or trustee. For these purposes an executor is not deemed to be a representative; the actions of an executor create no legal consequences for the testator. The executor merely assists the testator in formalizing the will, and may sign for him in his presence if the testator is physically incapable of signing.

This principle reinforces the rule that only one natural person may draw up a will and that two or more individuals may not have a joint will. Although the Civil Code is silent on the point, Russian legal doctrine takes the view that mutual wills also are inadmissible in which the testators assume counter obligations relative to one another. A mutual will, by definition, is a bilateral transaction, whereas the Civil Code requires that a will be a unilateral transaction. Permitting mutual wills would in effect create an inheritance contract. Such contracts were expressly prohibited in prerevolutionary Russian law on analogous, albeit more specific grounds, namely, that an inheritance contract could not be subsequently changed or revoked by one of the parties acting alone, which would violate the freedom of testamentary disposition. Modern Russian civilists have elaborated on the position:

> If an inheritance was opened on the basis of an inheritance contract (irrespective of whether this occurs for each mutual heir in his time or through the confluence of circumstances at one moment common for all), the act of contractual testament or acts of acceptance of an inheritance by each of the mutual testators who survived or act of contractual testament and acts of failure to accept the inheritance in view of the simultaneous death of all mutual testator-heirs proves to be incompatible within the framework of a single multilateral transaction for the origin of whose legal consequences the agreed expression of will of all participants of one transaction is necessary (Article 154,

> Civil Code). In addition, the inadmissibility of drawing up a common will by two or more citizens arises from the personal character inherent to a will of an act of testamentary disposition. In the event of drawing up a will by two or more citizens, the will is transformed form an act of personal will of one person into an act of common will of several persons, and this prevents the free and independent forming and expression of the will of the testator.[15]

The majority view in Russian doctrine accordingly is that an inheritance contract would be contrary to the principles of freedom of testamentary disposition and acquisition of an inheritance and cannot serve as a basis for inheriting.

Will as Unilateral Transaction. Article 1118 of the Civil Code expressly stipulated that a will is a unilateral transaction. This is so notwithstanding the fact that heirs must consent to acquire the property bequeathed to them by the testator. Russian law and doctrine take the view that such acceptance is not a counter act to the testament and that the two acts together – testament and acceptance – do not give rise to mutual obligations and create a mutual (bilateral) transaction. Only the expression of will of the testator is necessary without the prior consent or knowledge of the future heir. In essence there are two expressions of will: the first by the testator when he draws up his will; the second after the inheritance is opened upon the death of the testator by the heirs who accept the inheritance by way of expressing their will to do so. These do not form a single action, and therefore are not a common bilateral transaction.

Moreover, the act on the part of the testator creates no rights or duties for him or for third persons before or until death and can be changed or revoked at any time. After the moment of death of the testator, the heirs acquire the right to accept or refuse to accept the inheritance, and the executor the right to

[15] Abramenkov and Chugunov, note 3 above, pp. 142-143; also see A. P. Sergeev, Iu. K. Tolstoi, and I. V. Eliseev, Комментарий к Гражданскому кодексу Российской Федерации (постатейный). Часть третья [Commentary to the Civil Code of the Russian Federation (Article-by-Article). Part Three] (2002), pp. 26-27.

accept or refuse to accept to perform the duties of executor. These post-mortem rights and duties are part of a larger set of legal facts, which reduce to: unilateral transaction – event of death – consent to accept or act. Russian doctrine distinguishes this unilateral transaction sharply from the gift under Russian law, which is a bilateral contract in the Civil Code based on the expression of will of both parties and is a real or consensual transaction not intended to be performed in the event of the death of the donor (Article 572, Civil Code).[16]

Correlation of Testamentary Succession and Inheritance by Operation of Law. The inter-relationship of these two ways of inheriting is the focal point of the general provisions on inheritance and the provisions regulating inheritance by will. The point of departure is the principle of dispositiveness, which in turn accords priority to inheritance by will. In general an inheritance may be entirely by will if one has been drawn up; or by operation of law unless changed by a will or subject to provisions specially provided by the Civil Code.

Inheritance by will is replaced entirely by intestate succession if: there are no heirs under a will on the day the inheritance is opened (Article 1116, Civil Code); persons conceived during the life of the decedent were born alive after the opening of an inheritance (Articles 1116 and 1166, Civil Code); none of the heirs by will accepted the inheritance or each of them refused an inheritance by will (Articles 1157, 1158, and 1161, Civil Code); none of the heirs by will has the right to acquire the inheritance by reason of being unworthy (Article 1117, Civil Code); the will as a whole is deemed to be invalid (Article 1131, Civil Code).

Inheritance by will is augmented, changes, or otherwise combined with inheritance by operation of law if: the will was drawn up with respect to part of the inheritance property specified in the form of a participatory share in the estate or

[16] Nonetheless, the analysis of the differences between a testament and a contract of gift has generated a large body of doctrinal writings since the mid-nineteenth century in Russia. Among these is M. M. Vinaver, Из области цивилистики. Дарение и завещание [From the Domain of Civilistics. Gift and Will] (St. Petersburg, 1908), pp. 98-100.

individual specific things or rights or part of the property not affected by testamentary dispositions is distributed in the procedure of inheritance by operation of law (Articles 1111 and 1120, Civil Code); the rights of certain categories provided by law to an obligatory share of the estate is violated by the will, in which event the right to part of the property passed by way of inheritance by operation of law outside or despite the will (Article 1149, Civil Code; Article 8^2, Federal Law of 25 December 2018); a will is deemed to be invalid (Article 1131, Civil Code); an heir by will has a right to choose an alternative grounds to inherit (Article 1158, Civil Code); among others.

Amicable agreements of parties to an inheritance are illegal if those agreements establish a correlation between the right to inherit by will and the right to inherit by operation of law that are not consistent with the Civil Code.

Forms of will. Russian law, on the grand spectrum of legal systems measured from the standpoint of emphasis upon formalities, would fall well to the side of those which place considerable emphasis upon compliance with formalities as a precondition of the validity of a transaction. Whatever in the Russian past may have inclined the Russian system in this direction, the heritage of the Soviet planned economy assuredly reinforced any such inclinations and contributed to a Soviet legal consciousness accordingly. In the domain of inheritance, the considerations for and against a formalist approach are important: on one hand there is the expression of will by the testator, which it may be argued should be ascertained and honored without holding the testator to punctilious compliance with a host of formal and procedural requirements. On the other, the imposition of formalities may serve to identify the precise will of the testator more accurately and fully without allowing the inappropriate divulgence of the contents of a will.

The role of the notariat is significant here. Under an extreme formalist approach one could argue that all wills should be notarially drawn up and attested upon pain of invalidity for failure to comply. During the Soviet era, the freedom of will was constrained precisely because of such formalities, and the very presence of formalities (when the notariat was a State monopoly and there were no private notaries) intimidated countless citizens who were reluctant to disclose to a State (and Party) bureaucrat the existence or extent of their personal wealth.

The Russian approach to the forms of a will constitute a rebalancing of the Soviet approach. The Civil Code provides (Article 1124) that (a) a will must be in written form; and (b) attested by an official, usually a notary. Although firm statistics are not available, it would appear that two strong trends are in evidence. First, Russians are increasingly resorting to drafting a will rather than preferring inheritance by operation of law. Second, the notarially-certified will (Article 1125, Civil Code) is by far the most extensively used form of will.

As a rule, wills are certified on the premises of a notarial office. When necessary, a notary will visit a hospital or treatment institution, or home for the aged, or similar institution when the testator cannot attend the notarial office to complete the formalities. When a notary attests a will away from her office, she is entitled to transportation expenses and the notarial tariff increased by 50% over the usual charge (Article 22, Fundamental Principles on the Notariat). A notary may travel outside her notarial district to certify a will if the testator is gravely ill and there is no notary in the notarial district where the testator is located (Article 13, Fundamental Principles on the Notariat).

When a notary draws up a will, the notary will confirm the identity of the testator on the basis of the passport or other document recognized for this purpose.[17] The notary or other

[17] For Russian citizens this is an internal document or appropriate substitute document. See Edict of the President of the Russian Federation, 13 March 1997, No. 232, "On the Basic Document Certifying the Identity of a Citizen of the Russian Federation on the Territory of the Russian Federation". СЗ РФ (1997), no. 11, item 1301. For foreign citizens, a passport issued by their State of citizenship or appropriate document replacing it. See the Article 10(1), Federal Law on the Legal Status of Foreign Citizens in the Russian Federation, 25 July 2002, transl. in W. E. Butler, *Russian Foreign Relations and Investment Law* (2006), pp. 407-442. For stateless persons a document issued that meets the requirements of the Edict of the President of the Russian Federation, 21 December 1996, No. 1752, "On Basic Documents Certifying the Identity of a Citizen of the Russian Federation Beyond

official duly empowered to attest a will is further required to verify the dispositive legal capacity of the testator. The identity documents will disclose the age of the testator; if the testator is a married or emancipated minor, the notary will request a marriage certificate or copy of the relevant court decision on emancipation. However, in other respects the notary can do virtually nothing to verify dispositive legal capacity, including obtain medical documents, or designate expert examination, or otherwise verify the fact of dispositive legal capacity. In practice, therefore, dispositive legal capacity operates as a presumption and a notary would not routinely refuse to draw up a will unless there was some special reason to doubt the existence of dispositive legal capacity.

The text of the will may be either written out by the testator in his own hand or written from the testator's words by the notary or other person certifying the will. If the testator writes out the text, it must be "cleanly written", that is, with no crossings out, corrections, or similar adjustments; a pencil may not be used. If figures, or dates, or the like are used in the text, they must be written out in full, as must be the names of juridical or natural persons and their addresses, without abbreviations (Article 45, Fundamental Principles on the Notariat). The testator affirms the text by a notation which says: "The text of the will has been written by me personally".

If the notary or other attesting person writes out the will from the words of the testator, the same rules apply and the notation is added: "Text of the will was written from my words by the notary", in which case the full text of the document must be read aloud by the testator before his signature is affixed.[18] If

the Limits of the Russian Federation", as amended. СЗ РФ (1996), no. 52, item 5914; (2009), no. 43, item 5049.

[18] Russian commentaries treat this requirement as more than a mere formality; it is intended to ensure that the testator fully understands what is written down and the consequences thereof. The requirement is specifically embodied in standard forms of wills used in notarial practice, and the notary specially notes that this requirement was satisfied in his certification of the will. Standard forms, however, have been encountered in 2020 which quoted Article 1149 of the Civil Code without referring to the introduction from 1 January 2019 of an obligatory

this is impossible because of illness, physical defect, or illiteracy of the testator, the notary is obliged to read out the text of the will aloud to the testator and make a respective notation specifying the reasons why the will could not be personally read out by the testator (Article 1125, Civil Code). If for the same reasons the testator cannot sign the will himself, this may be done by another person, but the reasons must be indicated on the will and information concerning the person who signs for the testator must be given, including data concerning that individual identity document.[19] The language of the signature may be any which is legible and enables the signatory to be identified. Notarial practice encourages the forename, patronymic, and surname to be written out in full in order to reduce possible forgeries and facilitate identification of the testator, although legislation does not so require.

Witnesses. The presence of witnesses when a will is being drawn up and certified is an innovation in Russian law introduced by the Civil Code of the Russian Federation. In some situations witnesses may be present at the discretion of the testator (when a will is notarially certified) or when the law expressly so requires on pain of nullity of the will if this requirement is not observed (will equated to one notarially certified; closed will; will under extraordinary circumstances). A witness signs the will and provides information about himself in accordance with his identity documents (Article 1125, Civil Code). The law is indifferent as to why a particular individual is invited to serve as a witness and requires no explanation.

Irrespective of whether the presence of a witness if obligatory or discretionary, certain individuals as a matter of law may not act as witnesses: the notary or other person certifying the will; a person to whose benefit the will is being

share for women over age 55 and males over age 60. The failure to incorporate this legislative innovation by directly amending Article 1149 was in fact an evasion of the "reading out" practice.

[19] In this event the requirements of Article 1124(2) are imperative and must be strictly followed. Signature by another person is not possible for a closed will, disposition of bank deposits, or a will composed under extraordinary circumstances.

drawn up or a testamentary legacy made; the spouse, children, or parents of a children; natural persons who do not have full dispositive legal capacity; illiterate persons; persons who have physical defects that clearly do not enable them to be full aware of what is happening; persons who do not have a sufficient command of the language in which the will is drawn up unless a closed will is being drawn up. If a witness does not conform to these requirements of legislation, the will is contestable (Article 1124, Civil Code). The notary will caution a witness or a person signing for the testator about the need to comply with the secrecy of the will.

Russian commentators note that because witnessing a will is rather new in Russian practice, where there is discretion to involve witnesses the choice of selecting individuals to act in such capacity should be considered with care. In the Soviet era, the presence of witnesses was regarded by courts as interference in the exercise of freedom of will by the testator and violation of secrecy of the will which may entail invalidity.[20] Witnesses can forget, be confused, or tell falsehoods. If the will is contested, their testimony may strengthen doubts about the true intentions of the testator.[21]

Date and place of certification. The date and place of certification of a will, except for the instance provided by Article 1126 of the Civil Code, are obligatory requisites of a will. The localization of a will in space and time is considered to enable the expression of testamentary will of the testator to be understood and realized. Commentators urge that this requirement be understood expansively as a general rule for any form and type of will.[22] Unless the legislator has specified otherwise, precisely where the date and place are specified on a document is immaterial.

[20] T. I. Zaitseva and P. V. Krasheninnikov, Наследственное право в нотариальной практике [Inheritance Law in Notarial Practice] (5th ed.; 2005), p. 92.

[21] Rents, note 4 above, p. 113.

[22] Zaitseva, in I. G. Medvedev (ed.), Настольная книга нотариуса [Desk Book of Notary] (3d ed.; 2015), III, pp. 137-138.

Language of will. There is no requirement about the language in which a will may be drawn up. It follows that a will may be composed in any language of which the testator has a command. This approach is considered to be consistent with the principle of testamentary freedom and the right of each in Russia to operate in his or her native language. The provisions of the Fundamental Principles of Legislation of the Russian Federation on the Notariat (Article 10) and of the Federal Law of 1 June 2005, No. 53-ФЗ, "On the State Language of the Russian Federation" (Articles 1, 3), however, required that a notary certify a will whose text is in the Russian language and/or the language of the relevant subject of the Russian Federation. If the testator does not have a command of Russian or language of the subject of the Russian Federation, the text of the will may be translated by the notary or a translator/interpreter. Mmost desirable in such a situation is a dual language text in Russian and the respective foreign language.

Explanation of obligatory share. It should be indicated in the will that the rules concerning an obligatory share in an inheritance have been explained to the testator (Articles 1124 and 1149, Civil Code).[23]

[23] In fact this would not be sufficient. On 25 December 2018 by Federal Law No. 495-ФЗ "On Making Changes in the Federal Law 'On the Introduction into Operation of Part Three of the Civil Code of the Russian Federation'", Article 82 was added as follows with effect from 1 January 2019: "Article 82. The rules on inheriting by persons not having labor capacity established by Article 1148, Article 1149(1), and Article 1183(1) of the Civil Code of the Russian Federation also shall apply to women who have reached fifty-five years of age and to men who have reached sixty years of age". The 25 December 2018 change amending the application of Article 1149 represents the most revolutionary change in Russian inheritance legislation since the end of the Soviet era and was introduced in Russia as part of a long-term pension reform to be completed by 2028. Also see Ruling of the Constitutional Court of the Russian Federation of 28 November 2021, No. 76-O, where an obligatory share in an estate was refused because the applicant had neither reached the age of 60 nor lacked the capacity to labor. The data base Consultant Plus, moreover, directs the attention of users reading Article 1149 to the amended version of Federal Law No. 147-ФЗ, as amended 25 December 2018. For a critique of the legislative technique, see E. F. Tsukor, «Обязательная доля в наследстве для лиц предпенсионного возраста в Российской Федерации» [Obligatory Participatory Share in Inheritance for Persons of Pre-Pension Age in the Russian Federation], Наследственное право [Inheritance Law], no. 3 (2021) (available on Consultant Plus).

Certification of will. A will is drawn up, signed, and certified in two examples, of which one is given to the testator and the other remains in the files of the notarial office and is kept in a sequence in accordance with the nomenclature of the files. The will is registered in a register book which indicates the full name of the testator, witness, person who signed for the testator, executor, and interpreter if such were present, and their places of residence. The will also is registered alphabetically in a separate register.

Russia being a vast country in which it is sometimes physically impossible to access the services of a notary, and in the interests of enabling Russian citizens abroad to enter into transactions requiring notarization, officials of agencies of local self-government and consuls have powers to perform certain notarial actions (Articles 1, 37, 38, Fundamental Principles of Legislation of the Russian Federation on the Notariat). This includes the certification of wills when there is no notary on the territory which they respectively serve. Empowered local government officials operate on the basis of departmental instructions issued by the Ministry of Justice of the Russian Federation, but also submit any will certified to the chamber of notaries on their respective territories for inclusion in unified information system of the notariat. With respect to consuls, usually the Consul General acts to certify wills, but he may delegate this power to consuls, vice consuls, or consular agents. Unlike a Russian notary, who may attest wills of anyone on Russian territory, a Russian consul may only act on behalf of citizens of the sending State. Information concerning wills certified or revoked the consul sends to the Federal Chamber of Notaries for inclusion in the unified information system. Russian citizens, of course, also are at liberty to draw up wills in a foreign jurisdiction under the local law, which will be recognized in the Russian legal order.

Certain wills, although not notarially certified, are *equated* to notarially certified wills (Article 1127, Civil Code). The list of such wills (often called surrogate wills in Russian doctrinal sources) in the Civil Code is exhaustive and comprises the following:

(1) wills of citizens situated for care in hospitals, military hospitals, and other in-patient treatment institutions or residing in homes for the aged and disabled certified by chief doctors, their deputies for the medical section or duty doctors of those hospitals, military hospitals, and other in-patient treatment institutions, and also heads of military hospitals, directors, or chief doctors of homes for the aged and disabled;

(2) wills of citizens situated during voyages on vessels sailing under the State Flag of the Russian Federation certified by the masters of those vessels;

(3) wills of citizens on prospecting, arctic, Antarctic, or other similar expeditions certified by the heads of those expeditions, Russian Antarctic stations or seasonal field bases;

(4) wills of military servicemen, and in stationing centers for military units where there are no notaries, also the wills of civilian persons working in those units, members of their families, and members of the families of military servicemen, certified by the commanders of the military units;

(5) wills of citizens in places of deprivation of freedom certified by the heads of places of deprivation of freedom.

Such a will must be signed personally by the testator, person certifying the will, and a witness. Moreover, the list of persons who may attest such wills is strictly construed; substitutions are not permitted. And these persons do not enjoy a general power to perform notarial actions; they may only act with respect to wills. Finally, if instead of using the foregoing persons the testator expresses the wish to invite a notary to draw up and attest the will and there is a reasonable opportunity to honor this request, all measures must be taken to invite a notary (Article 1127(1), Civil Code).

The Civil Code requires that when a will is drawn up and attested that is equated to a notarially-attested will pursuant to Article 1127 of the Civil Code, the will should be sent as soon as possible by the person certifying the will through the territorial agencies of the federal agency of executive power effectuating law-application functions and functions for control and supervision in the sphere of the notariat to the notary at the place of residence of the testator. If the place of residence of the testator is known to the person certifying the will, the will may be sent directly to the respective notary. The failure to comply with this requirement does not prejudice the validity of the will.

Closed will. If a testator wishes no one to know the content of his will, including the person empowered to attest the will, he may draw up what is called a "closed will" (Article 1126, Civil Code), also known as a "secret will". The content of the will is completely confidential. To no one, including the notary, is the testator obliged to divulge what is in the will. The will must be written out and signed in the hand of the testator;[24] the notary will advise the testator of this rule and the consequences of invalidity if the rule is not complied with (Article 1149, Civil Code). The closed will is passed in a sealed envelope to the notary in the presence of two witnesses, each of whom signs the envelope. The envelope signed by the witnesses is sealed in their presence by the notary in another envelope on which the notary makes an inscription containing information about the testator from whom the notary accepted the closed will and the place and date of acceptance thereof, and the full name and place of residence of each witness as indicated of the identity documents of the witnesses. A notation is made on the envelope supplied by the notary that the testator has been familiarized with the rules concerning an obligatory share in an inheritance. The testator is then issued a document confirming acceptance of the closed will: a certificate concerning the acceptance of a closed will. The notary does not recover a fee for keeping the closed will in her files.

[24] This requirement means in fact that a person who for some reason is not capable of writing out a will cannot draw up a closed will because such person is unable to comply with none of the imperative requirements of such a will. See A. N. Guev, Постатейный комментарий к части третьи Гражданского кодекса Российской Федерации [Article-by-Article Commentary to Part Three of the Civil Code of the Russian Federation] (2010), p. 54..

The notary therefore does not certify or attest a closed will; rather, the notary attests the acceptance of a closed will for keeping and the testator assumes the risk that he has complied with all the necessary formalities for drawing up a will without the notary having reviewed the text for possible legal errors. Upon the presentation of a death certificate the notary within fifteen days of such presentation will open the envelope containing the closed will in the presence of not less than two witnesses and other interested persons from among the heirs by operation of law who may wish to attend. After immediately reading out the will aloud, the notary draws up and together with the witnesses signs a protocol certifying the opening of the envelope will the will and containing the full text of the will. The original of the will is kept by the notary. A notarially certified copy of the protocol is issued to the heirs (Article 1126(4), Civil Code). If the document contained in the envelope does not contain testamentary dispositions consistent with law, the inheritance proceeds by operation of law.

When the closed will is unsealed and opened after the death certificate of the deceased is presented, the notary, after reading out the text of the will, draws up and signs a protocol; witnesses to the unsealing and opening of the will also sign the protocol. A notarially certified copy of the protocol is issued to the heirs specified in the will. The Civil Code is silent as to whether heirs by operation of law should receive copies of the protocol, although it is considered desirable that they should have a copy, especially if they intend to contest the will. The original of the protocol is retained by the notary.

Some notaries have criticized the closed will in principle, noting the legal risk assumed by the testator: "The use of the form of a closed will is risky in instances when the testator is not familiar with the rules for drawing up a will. If after the opening of the inheritance it turns out that the will was drawn up with violations of the requirements established by law, it may be deemed to be invalid".[25] No empirical evidence is available

[25] A. B. Blinov and N. Iu. Chaplin, «Очерк по истории законодательства о

to suggest whether a significant percentage of closed wills experience difficulties for this reason; indeed, no such evidence is available with regard to the incidence of closed wills.

With effect from 1 September 2018, Article 1126 of the Civil Code was amended to provide that a closed will which made provision for the creation of an inheritance foundation was void.

Testamentary disposition of rights to money. In addition to the usual ways by which a testator may dispose of his property by will, Article 1128 of the Civil Code permits a person who has money, or "monetary means", in a bank or other credit institution to draw up a testamentary disposition in written form at the branch of the bank in which the account is held , signed by the testator, specifying the date of drawing up the disposition and certified by a bank employee who has the right to execute dispositions of a client with respect to means in his account. This disposition has the legal force of a notarially-certified will. The monies in the account nonetheless are part of the estate, pass by inheritance on the general grounds, and are issued to heirs in accordance with a certificate on the right to an inheritance except as indicated otherwise in the Civil Code. The rules implementing Article 1128 were confirmed by Decree of the Government of the Russian Federation on 27 May 2002, No. 351.[26]

Article 1128 constituted an innovation in Russian inheritance law that did not enjoy universal acclaim in the Russian Federation when it was introduced. The 1922 Civil Code of the RSFSR (Article 436) and the 1964 Civil Code of the RSFSR (Article 561) had permitted the conclusion of a contract between the bank and the depositor which enabled the monies in the bank account to pass to a third person specified in the contract after the death of the depositor. In those times only State banks existed. There were vigorous doctrinal disputes as

наследовании» [Essay on the History of Legislation on Inheritance], Нотариус [Notary], no. 1 (2003), p. 59.

26 СЗ РФ (2002), no. 22, item 2097.

to the nature of the contract, but by 1960 Soviet judicial practice had come to the view that such dispositions were not a will and that the monies passed to the person designated outside the estate, outside the requirement of obligatory shares, and beyond the reach of creditors.

Matters changed when Article 153(4) of the 1991 Fundamental Principles of Civil Legislation of the USSR and Republics abolished this possibility but was declared not to be applicable on the territory of Russia by the Decree of the Supreme Soviet of the Russian Federation (point 9) of 3 March 1993, No. 4604-I, "On Certain Questions of the Application of Legislation of the USSR on the Territory of the Russian Federation" with respect to deposits in the Savings Bank of the Russian Federation.[27]

Because Part III of the Civil Code of the Russian Federation entered into force on 1 March 2002, situations arise when depositors made dispositions under the 1964 RSFSR Civil Code but inheritances opened after 1 March 2002. The provisions of Article 1128, it may be noted, are in direct contrast with the situation prior to their entry into force. Russian jurists continue to disagree whether testamentary dispositions made in banks and credit institutions under the 1964 RSFSR Civil Code are caught by the provisions of Article 1128 of the Civil Code of the Russian Federation.[28]

An individual therefore may dispose of means in a bank account by a notarial will, closed will, will equated to a notarial will, testamentary disposition executed in a bank, or an extraordinary will.[29]

Wills under extraordinary circumstances. The Civil Code provides (Article 1129) that if a person is in a situation clearly threatening his life and by reason of this cannot draw up a

[27] For a full account of the complications, which lasted for years, see Petrov, in Petrov, note 4 above, p. 145.

[28] For the contrasting positions, see Abramenkov and Chugunov, note 3 above, p. 207.

[29] See point 22, Decree of the Plenum of the Supreme Court of the Russian Federation, 29 March 2012, no. 9 (available on Consultant Plus).

will in one of the aforesaid forms, the will may be drawn up in simple written form in his own hand and signed in the presence of two witnesses, both of whom also sign the will. By their signatures or initials the witnesses affirm that they were present when the document was drawn up. The Code does not expressly provide that the word "will" or "testament" appear on the document. What constitute "extraordinary circumstances" is not elucidated in the Civil Code. Doctrinal sources suggest that such circumstances would include a person wounded on the field of combat, or a grave illness, or serious traffic accident. Some have suggested that the definition of "extraordinary circumstances" contained in the Federal Law of 21 December 1994, "On Defense of the Population and Territories against Extraordinary Situations of a Natural or Technogenic Character"[30] be used for testamentary purposes. Judicial practice has determined extraordinary circumstances to be various: one example involved a will written by an ill person in simple written form in a hospital on a day when the notarial office was closed.[31]

The execution of such a will is possible only after the interested persons apply to accept the inheritance within the period established by law to a court for confirmation of the fact that a will was drawn up under extraordinary circumstances. If there is no dispute over this fact, the matter is considered expeditiously in court by way of a special proceeding. If there are disagreements between the interested persons, a suit proceeding is appropriate. If the person who drew up a will under extraordinary circumstances survives, he must within a month draw up the will in the form provided for by law; otherwise the will loses force. Examples of judicial practice are known where a court has deemed to be valid dispositions made by a testator in simple written form but only signed by

[30] СЗ РФ (1994), no. 35, item 3648, as amended.

[31] Cited by A. A. Bogdanova, Завещание как сделка в наследственном праве России [Will as a Transaction in the Inheritance Law of Russia] (2006), p. 3, cited in E. A. Kirillova, Основания наследования в гражданском праве Российской Федерации [Grounds of Inheritance in Civil Law of the Russian Federation] (2012), p. 64.

witnesses after the inheritance was opened, that is, after the death of the testator, sometimes even several days later.

JOINT WILL OF SPOUSES

A will may be concluded by a natural person alone or by natural persons married to one another (joint will of spouses). All provisions of the Civil Code of the Russian Federation applicable to wills also apply to joint wills (Article 1118(4), Civil Code).

In a joint will, the spouses have the right at joint discretion to determine the following consequences of the death of each them, including their deaths which ensued simultaneously: bequeath the common property of spouses and/or the property of each of them to any persons; determine by any means the participatory share of heirs in the respective inheritance estate; determine the property within the inheritance estate of each spouse if such determination does not violate the rights of third persons; deprive of inheritance one, several, or all heirs by operation of law without indicating the reasons for such deprivation; include in the joint will of spouses other testamentary dispositions, the possibility of the performance of which is provided by the Civil Code.

The conditions of a joint will of spouses operate in the part not contrary to the rules of the Civil Code on the obligatory participatory share in the inheritance (including the obligatory participatory share in the inheritance, the right to which emerged after the drawing up of the joint will of spouses), and prohibit inheriting by unworthy heirs (Article 1117).

A joint will of spouses loses force in the event of the dissolution of their marriage or the marriage is deemed to be invalid both before and after the death of one of the spouses.

If the expression of will of one spouse who has concluded a joint will does not correspond to the requirements of a law in the procedure provided by Article 1131(2), paragraph three, of the Civil Code, the provisions concerning contested or void transactions, depending on the grounds of invalidity of the expression of will of one of the spouses, are applicable.

Either spouse at any time, including after the death of the other spouse, has the right to conclude a subsequent will or to revoke the joint will of spouses. If a notary certifies the subsequent will of one of the spouses, accepts a closed subsequent will of one of the spouses, or certifies the instruction of one of the spouses concerning revocation of the joint will of spouses during the life of both spouses, the notary is obliged to send to the other spouse in the procedure provides by legislation on the notariat and notarial activity a notification that such subsequent wills have been concluded or the joint will has been revoked.

The joint will is in essence two individual wills of spouses composed as a single document. The joint will is not irrevocable and may be revoked or changed at any moment by either spouse. If one spouse revokes their will or for any reason that will is defective or invalid, the testamentary disposition of the second spouse continued to be in force. Revocation would presumably take effect from the moment that the second spouse receives notification of the revocation. If the conditions of a joint will relating to the death of the second spouse already have been performed, one can hardly imagine "revocation" with respect to that part of the will.

A joint will does not enable the rights of obligatory heirs to be prejudiced or enable unworthy heirs to inherit. For example, a surviving spouse cannot leave without an inheritance a new spouse who has reached pension age.

A joint will is subject to notarial certification, cannot be a closed will, and cannot be drawn up in simple written form or in a form equated to notarial. It remains unclear whether the joint will can be used in the form employed for the disposition of a bank account. Notarial certification of a joint will, unless the spouses object, is subject to "video-fixation" of the procedure itself (Article 1125, Civil Code).[32]

[32] Russian jurists observe that this provision of the Civil Code provides no direction as to what video devices should be used, where the material should be

The Russian concept of an inheritance contract as introduced in the Civil Code on 19 July 2018 (Article 1140[1]), with effect from 1 January 2019, represents a distinctive combination of various approaches known to other legal systems together with some Russian inventiveness. Russian commentaries suggest the following structure:

(1) the subject-matter of the contract is a testamentary disposition of a future decedent enabling a contracting party of the decedent or a third party beneficiary to count on receiving property by way of inheritance (German variant);

(2) the duty of the contracting party of the decedent is to grant before or after the opening of an inheritance (Ukrainian variant) with the possibility of concluding a contract not providing for any duties of the contracting party of the decedent (German variant);

(3) the means of defending rights, if violated, is compensation of losses if the testator renounces the contract (English variant) in combination with complete freedom of disposition of the property while alive (Russian inventiveness).[33]

When an inheritance contract might be attractive to testators was not an easy question to answer. The commentators suggested three possible scenarios: first, when the decedent needed resources during his or her lifetime (example: pay me monthly rental for my house and upon the my death the house is yours by inheritance); second, the decedent wishes while alive to secure support for someone not capable of managing an inheritance (example: I bequeath my stocks to you and support my children for the remainder of my life); three, the decedent wishes to induce someone to undertake socially-useful activity

kept after the recording, whether the heirs receive a copy, See K. A. Maletina, A. G. Sokolova, and V. N. Gavrilov, «Институт совместного завещания супругов в России и ряде зарубежных стран» [Institute of Joint Will of Spouses in Russia and a Number of Foreign Countries], *Legal Bulletin*, no. 4 (2023), p. 163.

33 E. Iu. Petrov and S. D. Budylin, in Petrov, note 4 above, p. 471.

(example: help me with my garden and I guarantee that you will be my heir).[34]

This model of inheritance contract embodies risks that will deter many from availing themselves of it. The risks to the testator are comparatively low given that the property promised to the other contracting party may be freely alienated at any time, whereas the risks to the other contracting party are considerable – obligatory shares of heirs, rights of creditors, risk of death before the testator, among others. Proponents of the inheritance contract hoped that this institution would reduce disputes among heirs because the inheritance contract would unequivocally disclose the true intentions of the testator; it would be more difficult to argue that the testator did not understand the significance of his or her actions or that a contracting party was an unworthy heir.

The parties to an inheritance contract are the future decedent (still living), the contracting party, and a possible third person beneficiary. Any citizen who has the capacity to draw up a will may enter into an inheritance contract, but representation when concluding such a contract is not permitted (Article 1118). Two or more persons cannot leave a single estate, but they may make a bequest to the benefit of the same persons, or to one another, or to one another with subsequent determination of the fate of the property of the second decedent who survives the first. An inheritance contract in which spouses participate, and also persons who may be called to inherit for each of the spouses (Article 1116), may determine the procedure for the transfer of rights to common property of the spouses or the property of each of them in the event of the death of each of them, including which ensued simultaneously, to the surviving spouse or to other persons; determine the property in the estate of each spouse if this does not violate the rights of third persons, and also may contain other dispositions of spouses, in particular a condition concerning the appointment of an executor or executors acting in the event of the death of each of the spouses.

[34] Ibid.

In the event of the conclusion of such an inheritance contract, the rules on the decedent apply to the spouses.

An inheritance contract loses force in connection with the dissolution of marriage before the death of one of the spouses of if a marriage is deemed to be invalid. Spouses cannot have both a joint will and an inheritance contract. The conclusion of an inheritance contract revokes the joint will of spouses concluded before the inheritance contract.

A decedent while alive may conclude an inheritance contract with anyone who may be called to inherit (Article 1116), which would include a natural person conceived during the lifetime of the decedent but born after the opening of the inheritance, provided that this beneficiary satisfies the requirements for an heir. "Anyone" includes multiple contracting parties, dividing the inheritance between them.

The subject-matter of an inheritance contract is the testamentary disposition of the decedent determined while he or she is alive. The structure of Article 1140[1] suggests that the drafters did not want the inheritance contract to be used as a device or stratagem for the transfer of a decedent's property after death while bypassing inheritance. The inheritance contract may or may not provide for or impose duties upon the contracting party. The rights and duties provided by the inheritance contract arise after the opening of the inheritance, except those which by virtue of the inheritance contract may arise before the opening of the inheritance and have been placed on that party to the contract which may be called to inherit for the decedent (Article 1116). Duties may, when appropriate, be formulated as a condition precedent or subsequent. The rights and duties of a party to an inheritance contract arising from the inheritance contract are inalienable and non-transferable by other means.

Spouses may choose, instead of a joint will, to conclude either an inheritance contract *between* spouses or an inheritance contract *with the participation of* spouses, that is, between the spouses and a third person. An example of the last might be an inheritance contract which provided that common property remains with the surviving spouse and passes after the death thereof by way of inheritance to the third person contracting party.

Unlike a will, which may be unilaterally revoked or changed, the dispositions in an inheritance contract may not be changed or revoked without the agreement of the contracting party and only during the lifetime of the decedent. If after concluding an inheritance contract the decedent wishes to materially change the contract, renunciation thereof will engage the compensation of losses. An alternative course of action might be to request a court to dissolve the inheritance contract and determine the consequences of dissolution. Unilateral revocation of the entire contract, notified through a notary, is possible, but the contracting party may demand compensation for losses.

An inheritance contract may be contested by the parties and, after the death of the decedent, by any persons whose rights or legal interests were violated by the contract – usually heirs by operation of law who were omitted or overlooked. However, the rule that the decedent while alive may freely conclude transactions with this property even though the contracting party to an inheritance contract may be deprived of what was promised is an imperative rule that may not be changed by agreement of the parties. There is no provision of Russian legislation that would prohibit abuse of this right by the decedent while alive.

CREATION OF INHERITANCE FOUNDATION

On 5 May 2014 Federal Law No. 99-ФЗ added the noncommercial unitary organization to the Civil Code of the Russian Federation, defined as an entity "not having membership founded by citizens and/or juridical persons on the basis of voluntary property contributions, and pursuing philanthropic, cultural, educational, or other social, socially-useful purposes" (Article 123^{17}). On 29 July 2017 the category of an "inheritance foundation" was added whose legal status was determined by the same Article and by Articles 123^{18} to 123^{20}, having regard to peculiarities provided by Articles 120^{20-1} to 123^{20-3}: (these Articles repealed and replaced by Articles 12020-4 to 12320-8 on 1 July 2021). Such a foundation is a juridical person (see Articles 50 and 50^1, Civil Code) with its own charter containing the name of the inheritance foundation and the word "foundation", location, subject-matter and purposes of activity, organs, including highest collegial organ and trusteeship council exercising supervision over the foundation activity, procedure for the appointment and release of officials, and the fate of property of the foundation in the event of its liquidation. Reorganization, which means transformation into another type of juridical person, is not permitted.[35]

The inspiration for this innovation in Russian inheritance law was the continental trust, adapted from various jurisdictions with some attention to Anglo-American practices. The Russian word "fond" (фонд) is widely used in sundry contexts and can be translated into English as "fund" or as "foundation". Given the foreign models that were drawn upon, some Russian jurists have chosen to translate the term as "testamentary trust", which is rather more a description than a translation and likely to mislead foreign readers.

Property transferred to an inheritance foundation by the founder(s) thereof, who have no property rights with respect to the foundation, is in the ownership of the foundation. As follows

[35] The introduction of inheritance funds is discussed in M. A. Kartashov, «Наследственный фонд: новое российское законодательство и иностранный опыт» [Inheritance Foundation: New Russian Legislation and Foreign Experience], Современное право [Contemporary Law], no. 10 (2018), pp. 83-90; A. E. Kazantseva, «Создание наследственного фонда» [Creation of Inheritance Foundation], Нотариус [Notary], no. 5 (2020), pp. 63-66; Iu. S. Kharitonov, «Наследственный фонд как инструмент эффективной практики бизнес-планирования» [Inheritance Foundation as Instrument of Effective Business Planning Practice], Хозяйство и право [Economy and Law], no. 1 (2018), pp. 96-105; S. G. Liashko, «Наследственный фонд: проблемы правосубъектности» [Inheritance Foundation: Problems of Legal Personality], Вестник юридического факультета Южного федерального университета [Herald of Law Faculty of Southern Federal University], no. 4 (2018), pp. 90-94; E. V. Turbina, «Правовые предпосылки внедрения института наследственного фонда в гражданское право России» [Legal Prerequisites of Introducing Institute of Inheritance Foundation in the Civil Law of Russia], Молодой ученый [Young Scholar], no. 49 (2018), pp. 180-183.

from its status as a juridical person, the foundation is not liable for obligations of the founders, and *vice versa*. The property of the foundation is to be used for the purposes determined by its charter; annual reports are published by the foundation on the use of its property.

An inheritance foundation is created in execution of the will of a natural person and manages the property bequeathed for that purpose in perpetuity or for a designated period. On the basis of the will of the decedent, the notary files an application with the appropriate State agency (Ministry of Justice) for the creation of the inheritance foundation, appending the decision drawn up by the natural person to have the foundation created, the text of the charter of the foundation duly confirmed by the said natural person and called to inherit, and the conditions for the management of the inheritance foundation – all subject to notarial certification – together with a receipt for the payment of State duty. If the notary fails to perform the duty to create the inheritance foundation, the executor or beneficiary of the inheritance foundation may seek this to be done on the basis of a court decision. The application to create the inheritance foundation must be sent by the notary no later than three weeks after the inheritance case is opened.

Actions of the notary may be contested by beneficiaries of the inheritance foundation, executor, or heirs if the instructions of the decedent relative to creating the inheritance foundation or the conditions for management have been violated as contained in the will or in the decision to found the inheritance foundation.

The inheritance foundation is capitalized when it is created and also by revenues received when carrying out its activity or from the management of the property of the said foundation. Other persons may not transfer property gratuitously to the inheritance foundation. When the inheritance foundation is created and accepts the inheritance, the notary is required to issue to the foundation a certificate on the right to inherit within the period specified in the decision of the testator to create the foundation but no later than as provided in Article 1154 of the

Civil Code (six months). If the notary fails to perform the said duties, the inheritance foundation has the right to appeal the failure of the notary to act.

Management of inheritance foundation. The conditions for the management of an inheritance foundation set out in a will should include provisions concerning the transfer to specified third persons (hereinafter also – beneficiaries of the foundation) or individual categories of persons from an indefinite group of persons (hereinafter – individual categories of persons) all the property of the inheritance foundation or part thereof, including when circumstances ensue relative to which it is unknown whether they will ensue or not.

The conditions for the management of an inheritance foundation may provide that the beneficiaries of the foundation or individual categories of persons to whom the property of the foundation is subject to transfer shall be determined by organs of the foundation in accordance with the conditions of management of the foundation.

The procedure for the transfer by the beneficiary of the inheritance foundation or individual categories of persons of all the property of the foundation or parts thereof, including revenues from the activity of the foundation, should be determined by the conditions of the management of the foundation by indicating the type and amount of property to be transferred or the procedure for determining the type and amount of property, including property right (for example, the right to use property, the right to pay for work, services rendered by third persons to beneficiaries or individual categories of persons), period or periodicity of the transfer of property, and also circumstances in the event of the ensuing of which such transfer is effectuated.

The charter of an inheritance foundation and conditions for the management of the inheritance foundation may not be changed after inheritance foundation is created, except for changes on the basis of the decision of a court at the demand of any organ of the foundation in instances when the management of the inheritance foundation on the previous conditions is impossible for circumstances whose arising during the creation of the foundation could not be supposed, and also if it will be established that the beneficiary is an unworthy heir (Article 1117), only if this circumstance was not known at the moment of the creation of the inheritance foundation.

The conditions for the management of an inheritance foundation are brought by the notary, before sending the application for State registration of the inheritance foundation, to the information of persons designated as members of organs of the foundation and may be disclosed only to beneficiaries and, in the instances provided by a law, to agencies of State power and agencies of local self-government.

An inheritance foundation is managed by a natural or juridical person acting as a one-person executive organ or as a collegial organ; a beneficiary of the foundation may not serve as the one-person executive organ or be a member of the collegial executive organ. If the charter of the inheritance foundation so provides, management may be in the hands of a high collegial organ and a trusteeship council. In this event, beneficiaries may be members of the high collegial organ.

Before the notary sends the application for State registration of the inheritance foundation, those persons specified in the testator's decision to create the said foundation are approached or the procedures specified to select such persons as members of the management organ are implemented, and the relevant State agency is informed about them. Should a person designated in the decision to create the inheritance foundation refuse to accept the proposal to join the management organ, the notary may not send an application for registration. If members of a collegial organ or serving as a one-person executive organ need to be replaced, the charter of the inheritance foundation may provide mechanisms for such, including lists of possible candidates.

The conditions of management may provide for the payment, and amount thereof, to a one-person executive organ or members of the trusteeship council or other organs of an inheritance foundation.

The charter of the inheritance foundation may provide that the consent of a collegial or other organ of the foundation must be obtained as a condition of certain transactions. The activities of an inheritance foundation are subject to being audited as stipulated in the conditions of management or, if a beneficiary so demands, by an auditor selected by him and at his expense.

Unless the charter of an inheritance foundation requires that a notary perform this duty, the one-person executive organ of an inheritance foundation is obliged to keep the charter of the foundation and the changes and additions made therein which have been registered in the established procedure, the decision concerning the founding of the foundation, documents confirming the rights of the foundation to its property, the document containing the conditions for the management of the inheritance foundation, the yearly reports, the bookkeeping documents, the documents of bookkeeping (or financial) reporting, protocols of meetings of collegial organs of the foundation, reports of valuers, opinions of the internal audit commission (or internal auditor) of the foundation, external auditor of the foundation, State and municipal financial control agencies, judicial acts regarding disputes connected with the management of the foundation, other documents provided by the Civil Code, charter of the foundation, and conditions of management of the inheritance foundation.

Unless the conditions of management provide otherwise, the report concerning the use of property of the inheritance foundation is not subject to publication.

Rights of beneficiaries of inheritance foundation. The beneficiary of an inheritance foundation has the right to receive in accordance with the conditions of management of the inheritance foundation all or part of the property of the foundation and other rights so provided specially by the Civil Code. These rights are inalienable and execution may not be levied for obligations of the beneficiary against them. Transactions concluded with a violation of these rules are void.

Any participants of relations regulated by civil legislation, except for commercial organizations, may be beneficiaries of an inheritance foundation. The rights of a citizen-beneficiary of an inheritance foundation do not pass by inheritance. The rights of a beneficiary-juridical person terminate in the event of the reorganization thereof, except for transformation, unless the conditions of management of an inheritance foundation provide for the termination of the rights of such a beneficiary in the event of its transformation.

If the charter of an inheritance foundation so provides, the beneficiary has the right to request and receive information from the inheritance foundation concerning the activity of the foundation. A beneficiary of an inheritance foundation also has the right to demand an audit by an auditor selected by him. In the event of the conducting of such an audit. The expenses of the beneficiary for the services of an auditor may be compensated to him by decision of the trusteeship council at the expense of the foundation.

If a violation of the conditions for the management of an inheritance foundation entailed losses to the beneficiary, the last has the right to demand the compensation thereof if so provided by the charter of the foundation.

A beneficiary is not liable for obligations of the inheritance foundation, and the foundation is not liable for obligations of the beneficiary.

Liquidation of inheritance foundation. The liquidation of an inheritance foundation is undertaken on the basis of a decision of a court on the grounds provided by the Civil Code for the liquidation of a juridical person (Article 61(3), subpoints (1)-(4), Civil Code), or if the period before the expiry of which the foundation was created has lapsed, the circumstances specified in the conditions of management of the inheritance foundation have ensued, or the formation of the organs of the foundation has proved to be impossible (Article 123^{20-4}(4), Civil Code).

Property remaining after the liquidation of an inheritance foundation is subject to transfer to beneficiaries commensurate with the amount of their rights to receive property or revenue from the activity of the foundation unless the conditions of management of the inheritance foundation provide other rules for the distribution of remaining property, including the transfer thereof to persons who are not beneficiaries. If it is impossible to determine the persons to whom property remaining after the liquidation of the inheritance foundation is subject to transfer, such property in accordance with the decision of a court is subject to transfer to the ownership of the Russian Federation.

The creation of an inheritance foundation is undoubtedly among the most legally complex and complicated structures confronting the Russian legal practitioner and requires considerable transactional skill and experience to properly undertake. The formalities are such that such structures will be difficult for provincial agencies of local self-government or Russian consulates abroad to master.

Nonetheless, the idea was attractive, and on 1 July 2021, by Federal Law No. 287-ФЗ, with effect from 1 March 2022, the inheritance foundation was regrouped into a type of socially-useful or personal foundation that might be created not only upon the death of a founder, but during his lifetime. The inheritance foundation became a species of personal foundation. Articles 123^{20-1} to 123^{20-3} were repealed and replaced by Articles 123^{20-4} to 123^{20-8} with respect to the inheritance foundation, which also was addressed in general provisions relating to all personal foundations.[36] The inheritance foundation enjoys a preferential tax status, which may enhance its attractiveness.

Inheritance foundations created prior to 1 March 2022 and meeting the requirements of socially-useful foundations as set out in Article 123^{17} of the Civil Code, as amended, are subject to the provisions of Part One, Chapter 4, §7, as amended, and were not required to re-register. However, such pre-existing inheritance foundations were obliged, if necessary, to bring their founding documents into conformity with the changes in legislation and were exempt from the payment of State duty for doing so.

FREEDOM OF TESTAMENTARY DISPOSITION

The freedom of will contains, as a principle, multiple facets which do not permit exhaustive enumeration in legislation given the individual circumstances to which they may apply. Conceptually, Russian doctrinal writings regard this fundamental principle of the law of inheritance as deriving from the inviolability of private ownership (Article 1, Civil Code) and a sister clause of the Civil Code provisions on the freedom of contract (Articles 421 and 422, Civil Code). Exercise of this freedom is a right, but not a duty, of a citizen. The law does not in this instance tolerate a vacuum; if the freedom to bequeath

[36] See E. A. Bykovskaia, «Правовой статус наследственного фонда в Российской Федерации» [Legal Status of Inheritance Foundation in the Russian Federation], Вестник Сибирского государственного университета путей сообщения [Herald of Siberian State University of Railways], no. 4 (2022), pp. 51-56.

property by will is not taken advantage of, property will pass by operation of law, including, in the complete absence of heirs, by escheat to the State.

Freedom here means the autonomy and independence of a natural person to bequeath his property, or not, and affects the decision to draw up a will as such and the determination of what and who to include in the will. Considerations of equity, justice, advisability, motivation (good or bad), do not enter into the matter. The testator is never obliged, although he may do so, to divulge the reasons for the provisions of his will, or for depriving heirs of an inheritance, or for changing or revoking a will. Consequently, when interpreting a will the purpose is to determine the true will or intention of the testator, but not the reasons for them (Article 1132, Civil Code). If the provisions of the Civil Code designed to ensure the freedom of will were violated, for example, if the will was drawn up, changed, or revoked under the influence of a threat or coercion, the document cannot be deemed to be a proper will and is deemed to be invalid (Article 1131, Civil Code).

Insofar as the freedom of will constitutes the right of the testator at his discretion to draw up a testament, the testator has a number of possibilities, all of which are legitimate choices. First, he has the right to decide whether to bequeath property or not. Second, a promise to draw up a will in favor of a particular individual gives rise to no legal consequences under Russian law for anyone. Third, if a testator makes such an undertaking and performs it with respect to a will, he is at liberty to change or revoke the commitment with respect to a will at any time (Article 1130, Civil Code). The doctrinal substantiation of these manifestations of the freedom of will is regarded as the exercise of a personal intangible absolute right of the inviolability of private life that is defended by Russian civil law. Russian commentators observe that, unlike many Anglo-American jurisdictions where estate planning is undertaken at a relatively early age, under Russian conditions such planning usually ensues during the second half of the life span.[37]

Designation or Sub-Designation of Heir. The freedom of will especially is expressed in the free choice of who should inherit under the testament. Any persons may be heirs: natural persons, including foreigners and stateless persons or juridical persons, including charities or the State or its subdivisions. Natural persons may include individuals who would or would not inherit by operation of law. Moreover, precisely who inherits what and in what share is determined by the testator. There are no limitations on how the shares in the estate are to be determined. One, several, or all heirs by operation of law may be eliminated from inheriting by a will provided this is expressly indicated in the testament without giving any reasons, subject to the provisions for an obligatory share of the inheritance (Article 1149, Civil Code).

A different situation arises when the will does not mention heirs by operation of law at all. They will retain the right to inherit and may do so if there are no heirs by will (there are none alive at the moment of opening the inheritance, or they all refuse the inheritance, and so on), or if there remains property not bequeathed by will which is inherited by operation of law.

Russian legislation does not expressly address the question of whether a foreign organization which is not a juridical person under its own law may be designated as an heir to property by a testator. There is some doctrinal authority for the view that such "subjects of civil turnover" may be heirs by will.[38] It has, moreover, been observed that "… the legal regulation of calling to inherit under a will of juridical persons and other subjects

[37] Rents, in Petrov, note 4 above, p. 123.

[38] See M. S. Abramenkov, «Наследование по завещанию в Российской Федерации и зарубежных странах: сравнительно-правовой аспект» [Inheritance by Will in the Russian Federation and Foreign Countries: Comparative-Legal Analysis], Наследственное право [Inheritance Law], no. 4 (2008), p. 40.

of law which are collective formations is characterized by gaps and contradictions".[39]

The Civil Code is quite categorical in providing that the legal successors of a deceased may be juridical persons existing at the moment of opening an inheritance. Insofar as these are Russian juridical persons, that status would be determined by the entry in the State register of juridical persons (Article 51, Civil Code). Those which may be in the process or reorganization and liquidation but not yet removed from the State register also would fall into this category. That leaves the category of those juridical persons which have gone through the procedures of reorganization. There is doctrinal support for the position that an entity separated from a juridical person or which has acceded to a juridical person should continue to be the proper beneficiary of a will. The same would apply to a juridical person which has changed its name. More controversial is when a juridical person effectively ceases to exist by reason of merger, division, or transformation. A literal interpretation of the legislation would suggest that inheritance by will should not occur in these instances.

A similar issue arises with respect to Russian legal entities which are not juridical persons: branches, representations, sections, chairs of institutes, and so on. Although there is some doctrinal support for the view that the inheritance in these instances should be to the juridical person that has formed these entities, a literal interpretation of the testament here too would dictate a contrary result. It should be noted that although there has been strong judicial support for a more modern approach to the concept of freedom of contract,[40] that view has yet to be accepted in the construction of wills.

An heir may be appointed by way of sub-designation, or substitution. The same freedom of choice is applicable here as in the case of heirs, provided that the sub-designation is made

[39] Abramenkov and Chugunov, note 3 above, p. 149.

[40] See W. E. Butler, "On Freedom of Contract in Russia", *Journal of International Banking Law and Regulation*, no. 11 (2014).

before the opening of an inheritance, that is, before the moment of death of the testator. The rules of sub-designation may be applied with respect to designated heirs or to heirs of the testator by operation of law. In the first instance the testator designates as his heir a certain person and simultaneously indicates in the same will another person who acquires the right to inherit if the designated heir does not take part in the inheriting. In the second instance, the testator, without changing the ordinary court of inheriting of his property by operation of law, designated his heir in place or one, several, or all heirs by operation of law if they turn out not to be participants in the estate. The number of persons appointed by way of sub-designated is unlimited, and, if he so chooses, a testator may create an entire chain of sub-designations.

The Civil Code (Article 1121[2]) associates sub-designation of heirs with certain conditions precedent or subsequent, depending upon the circumstances. Some concern circumstances which occur before the opening of an inheritance and therefore might have been known to the testator, whereas others relate to events after the opening of an inheritance and therefore could not be known to the testator. In either case these are circumstances that cannot be known in advance whether they will occur or not: whether before the opening of an inheritance or simultaneously with the decedent the heir designated in the testament will die; before the opening of an inheritance or simultaneously with the decedent the heir of a testator by operation of law will die; after the opening of an inheritance an heir designated in the testament will die who has not succeeded in accepting the inheritance; after the opening of an inheritance the heir designated in the testament will not accept the inheritance for other reasons not connected with his death before the expiry of the period for accepting the inheritance, or will refuse the inheritance; the heir designated in the testament or heir by operation of law will lose the possibility to acquire the inheritance by virtue of being an unworthy heir.

Russian law recognized what in Roman law was called inheritance by *ordinary substitution*. In this case the testator at his discretion has the right to specify in his will all or any individual conditions for a disposition entering into force concerning the sub-designation of an heir. These will apply only if the basic heir does not become the legal successor or the property rights of the decedent do not pass to him.

Sub-designation in the event of the death of an heir who has accepted an inheritance and become the legal successor of the decedent is not regulated by Russian law, what in Roman law is known as *substitutio fideicomissaria.* Although Russian legal doctrine is divided as to whether this form of substitution is consistent with Russian law,[41] the better view seems to be that such substitution is not consistent with the Civil Code because this form of substitution would operate to limit the powers of disposition of a person who had accepted the inheritance and become the owner of the property. Such a limitation imposed by way of substitution would not be consistent with the Civil Code provisions that civil rights can only by limited by a federal law and only within the limits established by the Constitution (Article 1, Civil Code).

Conditional wills. Russian doctrinal writings exhibit a variety of views on whether so-called "conditional wills" are valid. These are wills which contain dispositions "on condition" that the heir will perform some action (for example, a brother bequeaths his property to his sister on condition that she marry). Shershenevich took the view that such wills were possible,[42] but that, in the example given, the sister would acquire only use of her brother's property until she did marry, whereupon the brother's property would become hers in ownership. It was the indefiniteness of title that concerned Russian and, later, Soviet jurists, some of whom recommended that the legislator resolve the issue. Recent doctrinal publications have in many instances treated this option with approval provided that the "conditions" were consistent with the constitutional rights and freedoms of

41 See, for example, O. S. Ioffe, Советское гражданское право: курс лекций [Soviet Civil Law: Course of Lectures] (1965), III, p. 318.

42 Shershenevich, note 10 above, pp. 365-366.

Russian citizens.[43] Some even proposed categories of admissible and inadmissible conditions. Examples of acceptable conditions included: that an heir receive an inheritance upon reaching a certain age, or that an certain interval of time elapse after the decedent's death, or that the heir cease a parasitic way of life or the use of alcoholic beverages, or that the heir marry, or complete his or her education. Inadmissible conditions were said to be that an heir follow a certain profession or vocation, or choose to live in a certain locality.[44]

Other Russian jurists, however, believe that conditional wills cannot be deemed to be admissible under any circumstances. First, because the "condition" is viewed as a form of limitation on the property rights acquired by virtue of inheriting. This itself is regarded as a violation of the 1993 Russian Constitution (Article 35)[45] and other rights of the heir.[46] The existence of the condition means that the inheritance is not completed for an indefinite interval of time; the inheritance process is not culminated, which in turn interferes with the normal course of civil turnover and may prejudice rights of creditors of the decedent who cannot satisfy their claims because these must be submitted to the heirs, and not against the inheritance property (Article 1175, Civil Code). Russian jurists of this persuasion believe conditional wills should be deemed to be invalid as a whole or in relevant part pursuant to Article 1131 of the Civil Code.

[43] T. I. Zaitseva and P. V. Krasheninnikov, Наследственное право: комментарий законодательства и практика его применения [Inheritance Law: Commentary on Legislation and Practice of Application Thereof] (6th ed.; 2009), p. 56.

[44] See A. A. Novikov, «К истории завещания под условием в отечественном гражданском праве» [On the History of the Will under Condition in Fatherland Civil Law], in B. L. Khaskel'berg and D. O. Tuzov (eds.), Цивилиситческие исследования [Civilist Studies] (2004), I, pp. 349-351.

[45] A. L. Makovskii, «Как лучше гарантировать наследовании» [How to Best Guarantee Inheritance], Законодательство и экономика [Legislation and Economy], no. 3-4 (1997), pp. 37-38.

[46] See M. Iu. Devitsyn, «О недопустимости условных завещаний» [On the Inadmissibility of Conditional Wills], Наследственное право [Inheritance Law], no. 1 (2009), p. 15.

Disinheritance. Pursuant to Article 1119 of the Civil Code, the freedom of will includes the right to deprive one, several, or all heirs by operation of law of an inheritance without any explanations or reasons for doing so. Russian legislation does not require that heirs by operation of law who are being deprived in a will be specifically named. The need to name others follows from the simple logic of the position; they must be named in order to know who they are. The formulation used in a will commonly is the following: "I deprive of inheritance {...)". If specific individuals from among the heirs by operation of law are to be disinherited, they must be designated by precise name or by some other means that enables them to be identified with accuracy.

The question is whether a document is a will if it contains only a list of those who are deprived of the right to inherit without naming specific heirs. Neither the 1922 nor the 1964 Civil Codes of the RSFSR expressly required that a will had to name heirs and could not contain solely a list of those who were disinherited. Nonetheless, some Soviet jurists took the position that designating an heir was an essential condition for a valid will and if heirs could not be determined one way or another from the document, it was not a will.[47] Although the Civil Code of the Russian Federation does not expressly so indicate, the meaning of Articles 1119 and 1121 suggests that a testator has the right to confine himself to depriving legal heirs of an inheritance without specifying heirs. This would follow from the principle that the basic purpose of a will is to dispose of property in the event of death, and the means of such disposition are not limited to precisely designating heirs.[48]

Russian jurists point out that a will which designates a certain person as the heir to part or all of the inheritance property automatically disinherits all other persons who would fall into the group of heirs by operation of law. Silence about other heirs

[47] See B. S. Antimonov and K. A. Grave, Советское наследственное право [Soviet Inheritance Law] (1955), p. 141.

[48] Abramenkov and Chugunov, note 3 above, pp. 156-157.

by operation of law accompanied by a designation of an heir by will, however, has other legal consequences. If, for example, the will is not subject to execution because the designated heirs are no longer alive, or those heirs refuse the inheritance, or fail to accept the inheritance, the heirs by operation of law who were not specifically deprived of the right to inherit but with regard to whom the testator was silent. are called to inherit. The consequence can be that silence of the testator is a weak means of eliminating individuals from inheriting.

The right to bequeath any property extends to things which by law are limited in circulability. The relevant principle is that the existence of a special regime for a particular thing may not serve as grounds for limiting the freedom of will or obstruct the inclusion of such a thing or property right from being part of an estate or accepted as an inheritance.

A testator may bequeath property duties, or debts, as well as property and property rights. If this is done in such a way that the debts fall upon one or some heirs and not others, the testamentary disposition is in violation of the rule that heirs are responsible for debts of the decedent (Article 1175, Civil Code) and, therefore, invalid on the grounds not only that some heirs are favored over others improperly, but also that creditors may be disadvantaged, to whom all heirs are jointly and severally liable for debts of the decedent (Article 323, Civil Code).

A testator may identify property in a will by any means convenient to him, and if he simply indicates participatory shares in property, these shares may be specified in the will by any means (Article 1122, Civil Code). Equally, however, the testator may not identify any specific property or shares of all or any of the estate. Russian notarial practice long since formed the convention that if a testator was silent about the procedure for the distribution of property among designated heirs, the property would be distributed in equal shares. When the 1964 RSFSR Civil Code was being drafted, proposals were advanced to incorporate a provision expressly stipulating equal distribution in such instances. This approach was analogous at the time to the way in which the shares of heirs by operation of law were determined. Ultimately, however, the proposal was not accepted and the 1964 RSFSR Civil Code was silent on the point. Article 1122 of the Civil Code of the Russian Federation specifically addressed this "gap" and provides that property bequeathed without indicating the procedure for distribution among designated heirs is considered to be bequeathed in equal shares.

It has been justly observed that this approach to equal division of shares rests upon a presumption about the expression of will of the testator,[49] which in itself would create grounds for contesting the division of property equally. However, because the testament is the only basis for determining what the intention of the testator was and no other documents except the testament may be used as a source to ascertain such intention, contesting the will is unlikely to succeed. However, the assumption of the testator's intention is not a general one, but must always relate only to a specific will.

The presumption underlying Article 1122 concerning equal distribution could, in certain cases, operate inappropriately if, for example, the real intention of the testator was to leave the distribution of property to the discretion of his heirs or to encourage a distribution among them based on the actual use and possession of his property. Considerations of this nature have persuaded some Russian jurists to support changes in Article 1122 that would recognize the possibility of the heirs after the opening of the inheritance agreeing to a distribution of property other than on an equal share basis.

The inheriting of indivisible things is the source of considerable discussion in Russian legal doctrine. Difficulties would obviously arise when a testator bequeaths an indivisible thing in parts to two or more persons in kind. Although, for example, it is unlikely that a testator would bequeath the motor of a vehicle to one heir, the wheels to another, and the steering mechanism to a third, it can and does happen that a testator bequeaths a room in a building to two or more individuals. The

[49] Abramenkov and Chugunov, note 3 above, p. 179.

better view is that bequeathing parts of an indivisible thing in kind is physically impossible because the division of the thing is impossible without changing the nature of the thing (Article 133, Civil Code).[50] However, the legislator did not deem such a bequest to be invalid.

Testamentary Legacy or Imposition. Article 1119 of the Civil Code permits dispositions in the form of a testamentary legacy (Article 1137) or testamentary imposition (Article 1139). These types of disposition are a combined expression of the freedom of will and the principles of civil law in accordance with which civil rights and duties may be established.

The *testamentary legacy* is a type of disposition that enables the testator to transfer property to heirs as his direct legal successors and simultaneously transfer property benefits to other persons at the expense of the estate; these other persons do not acquire the status of heirs. The term itself is rather odd; literally translated in means "testamentary refusal", which does not begin to convey what this legal provision does. The legislator, it should be observed, preserved the traditional term also used in the 1964 Civil Code of the RSFSR (Article 538), notwithstanding searing criticism over the years in Russian doctrinal writings.

The "legacy" enables the testator to establish a unilateral transaction in the form of an obligation by virtue of which the heir is obliged to perform a determined duty at the expense of the inheritance to the benefit of one or several persons, and these recipients of the testamentary legacy have the right to demand the performance of this duty from the heir. The legacy thus also is a legal fact by virtue of which legal relations arise between the heir and the recipient of the testamentary legacy. The obligation satisfies all the requirements for the indicia and properties of a civil-law obligation (Article 307, Civil Code). The category of persons who may receive a legacy under a will is broadened in the Civil Code in comparison with the 1964

[50] Rubanov, in note 1 above, p. 87.

RSFSR Civil Code and may be any of the heirs, irrespective of the grounds of inheriting.

The heir who is encumbered by a testamentary legacy becomes the debtor in the obligation provided that he accepts the inheritance, which follows because in order to perform the legacy at the expense of the inheritance, he must have accepted it. The beneficiary of the legacy is the creditor in the obligation. Any natural or juridical persons may be designated as beneficiaries in this context, including the State and municipal formations or any heirs by will or by operation of law.

If a will is exhausted by the testamentary legacy an heir by operation of law must be indicated as the executor of the testamentary legacy because only that person has the right to inherit in the absence of designated heirs by will and only he can perform the legacy at the expense of the estate. It would follow that if a will is exhausted by a testamentary legacy placed on an outside person who is not designated to be an heir, that will is invalid.[51]

The testamentary legacy operates differently for the debtor and creditor to the obligation. Although the debtor may refuse the legacy, he may not do so if he accepts the inheritance (Article 1152, Civil Code) and the refusal of one must occur simultaneously with the refusal of the other. The creditor, however, is not obliged to accept or take advantage of the legacy; that is, he may refuse to accept the legacy. Should that occur, the testator would be wise to foresee the possibility and appoint a substitute recipient of the testamentary legacy.

The subject-matter of a testamentary legacy, set out in general form by Article 1137(2), Civil Code, operates as an encumberment upon the right to inherit and accordingly should not be a form of concealed limitation on an heir's right to dispose of property received under an inheritance. If a testamentary legacy requires an heir to transfer a thing to the recipient of the legacy, the right of ownership in the said recipient arises from

[51] Discussed in T. I. Zaitseva, Судебная практика по наследственным делам [Judicial Practice in Inheritance Cases] (2007), p. 165.

the moment that the legacy in the form of a thing is transferred to him. Although the reasons for creating a testamentary legacy vary from one situation to the next, Russian jurists observe that a common reason for establishing such a legacy is uncertainty on the part of the testator over whether the recipient will accept the legacy or not. Should the recipient refuse or for other reasons be unable to accept, the property remains with the heir in ownership and its fate is certain.

The testamentary legacy may be used to make provision for what Anglo-American law would call a form of life interest in immoveable property. Article 1137(2) of the Civil Code allows a thing to be transferred in possession and use, but not title – a possibility that can affect natural persons as well as State enterprises and institutions who hold property by right of economic jurisdiction or economic management. The Civil Code expressly mentions a dwelling house, apartment, or other dwelling premise[52] in the ownership of the testator which may be encumbered by the duty of the heir to provide such premise, or designated part thereof, to the recipient of a testamentary legacy for the lifetime of the recipient or other period of use. It is recommended to those who take advantage of this possibility that they indicate in the will the precise conditions for exercising the right to use the testamentary legacy, including the duration of use and whether the use is gratuitous or otherwise. If such details are lacking, they will be determined through an interpretation of the will.

Although precise data are not available, the encumberment of an inheritance with a testamentary legacy is regarded as the most widely used form of such a legacy. In practice the recipients of a testamentary legacy in the form of use of a dwelling premise are the tenants of the premise before the inheritance was opened and represent individuals for whom the testator had special concerns or responsibilities. The encumberment follows any transfer of ownership of the premise by the heir and therefore

[52] The concept of a "dwelling premise" is defined in the Housing Code of the Russian Federation (Articles 15, 16).

burdens the property without limiting the right of the owner to dispose of the property – although, just as any encumberment, its very existence may affect the value and desirability of the property.[53]

Testamentary legacies sometimes take the form of the transfer of a property right, such as a right of demand for the payment of a debt or the right to demand the performance of a specified duty. This can result in the creditor and debtor being combined in one person, which under the Civil Code (Article 413) will extinguish the debt, or may entail a change of persons in an obligation and engage Article 387 of the Civil Code.

A testamentary legacy may require the transfer of property which is not part of the testator's estate but to be acquired at the expense of the inheritance. An example would be the duty of the heir to acquire property and transfer this to the recipient of the testamentary legacy, or to perform certain work or to provide a certain service, or even to make periodic payments to the legacy recipient. These need not necessarily be performed personally by the heir, for otherwise this would limit his personal freedom and violate the legal requirement that performance come at the expense of the estate. Accordingly, the heir may enter into contracts for the performance of the necessary actions or transfer of the necessary property. The Plenum of the Supreme Court of the Russian Federation has drawn attention to the fact that whether an heir needs the property which is the subject of a testamentary legacy does not influence the right of the recipient of the legacy to demand performance.[54]

A testamentary legacy in the form of period payments by an heir to the legacy recipient can pose difficulties. Such payments

[53] This aspect of the testamentary legacy has been classified in various ways by Russian doctrinal writings. See Iu. S. Povarov, «К вопросу о юридической природе права пользования жилым помещением в силу завещательного отказа» [On the Question of the Legal Nature of the Right of Use of a Dwelling Premise by Virtue of a Testamentary Legacy], Наследственное право [Inheritance Law], no. 3 (2009), p. 29.

[54] Point 24, Decree of the Plenum of the Supreme Court of the Russian Federation, 29 May 2012, No. 9.

may be made for any designated period: weekly, monthly, quarterly, and so on. They are an attractive option, for example, if the testator had a bank account from which payments are to be made, say, to cover private school tuition for a minor child until he completes schooling. Such payments would continue until the legacy was performed or the funds in the estate exhausted.

Controversial in Russian doctrine is the question of whether wills which do not specify heirs but contain instructions regarding funeral, burial, religious rites, and the like constitute a testamentary legacy or variants thereof.[55] The fact that no transfer of property or property rights from the estate occurs under such arrangements is reason for some jurists to reject such a characterization.[56] On the other hand, the Federal Law "On Burial and Funeral Matters" (Article 5) grants to a person the right to leave instructions concerning the procedure for burial and the commemoration of his memory.[57] A person may in the presence of witnesses or in simple written form leave instructions: concerning consent or nonconsent to the removal of organs and/or tissue from his body; be burial in a particular place or according to particular customs or traditions, or beside other persons; be cremated; or entrust these matters to a particular person. This list is exhaustive, but leaves the issue of why this type of instruction may not be contained in a will if this is permitted by legislation in less formal form than a will requires.

The obligation embodied in a testamentary legacy is, for the recipient of the legacy, purely personal in nature which may be accepted or not, but may not be transferred to someone else. If the recipient of the legacy dies before the performance of the legacy, the legacy does not form part of the estate of the recipient or otherwise pass by succession (Article 1137(4), Civil Code). The matter is otherwise for the heir; his duty to perform the legacy passes to other heirs unless provided otherwise by

[55] See Zaitseva, note 51 above, p. 165.

[56] Abramenkov and Chugunov, note 3 above, p. 164.

[57] СЗ РФ (1996), no. 3, item 146, as amended.

the will or by law. Indeed, because the testamentary legacy falls within the law of obligations, the general provisions on obligations in the Civil Code extend to such legacies. For example, the general Article of the Civil Code regulating the performance of obligations in accordance with the conditions thereof and the requirements of law would extend to testamentary legacies, but the formulations of the same Article concerning the interpretation of the will in accordance with the "usually presented requirements" (Article 309) would not be applicable to a will. If the heir does not perform the testamentary legacy properly, the general provisions of the Civil Code on responsibility for violation of an obligation (Article 393) would be applicable, or if money was involved, Article 395.

Limits of Testamentary Legacy. The Civil Code imposes limits on the performance of a testamentary legacy (Article 1138). First, the heir performing the legacy is obliged to do so solely within the value of the estate and from the estate. If the expenditures necessary to perform the legacy exceed the value of the estate, the heir is limited to the amount of the estate which he received; any balance outstanding does not pass to the other heirs. The doctrinal rationale for this position is that the recipient of the testamentary legacy is not a creditor of the decedent, but of the heir and unlike creditors of the decedent, may not seek satisfaction of his demand from the estate itself but only the participatory share of the heir. On this premise, the recipient of the testamentary legacy cannot proceed against the entire estate insofar as it has passed to other heirs.

It follows that if an heir is aware that a testamentary legacy cannot be performed from his inheritance because the amount of this portion of the estate is insufficient, he has the right to refuse the inheritance or, having accepted it transpires that the estate is insufficient, to refuse to perform the testamentary legacy pursuant to the Civil Code provisions concerning the impossibility of performance of an obligation (Article 416). However, the heir and the recipient of the legacy might agree that the recipient will provide sufficient funds for the legacy to be performed.

Second, the substitution of an heir on whom a testamentary legacy has been placed by another heir is permitted by way of the transfer of a duty when this is permitted by a law (Article 1140, Civil Code). The basis for such a transfer from one heir to others is found in the provisions concerning the sub-designation of heirs (Article 1121), inheritance transmission (Article 1156), refusal of an inheritance (Article 1158), increment of inheritance (Article 1161), among others. These are examples not of the substitution of a debtor in an obligation, but the transfer of an inheritance share encumbered by a legacy by an heir who has fallen away to other heirs. The debtor under the legacy obligation is the heir to whom the encumberment has passed unless it follows otherwise from the will or a law. The provisions of the Civil Code concerning the change of persons in an obligation do not arise in this connection.

Third, creditors of the decedent enjoy priority in the settlement of their demands before a testamentary legacy may be performed at the expense of the estate (Article 1138, Civil Code). This rule prevents a decedent from avoiding debts by transferring property in the form of a testamentary legacy and attempt to avoid levy of execution against such property. Other expenses of the inheritance fall into this category of priority (Articles 1136, 1174, Civil Code), among them expenses caused by the illness and burial of the decedent, expenses for the protection or management of inheritance property, remuneration to the executor of the will, expenses to perform the legacy, and the like.

Fourth, a testamentary legacy may not be performed in violation of the freedom of will. Under Russian law, the freedom of will, as observed above, is limited by the obligatory shares in an inheritance. Such obligatory shares may not be reduced by placing duties on an heir to perform a testamentary legacy. If an heir receives inheritance in excess of his obligatory share, he is obliged to perform the legacy within the limits of such excess, but not from the obligatory share itself. This rule protects the integrity of the obligatory share.

If a testamentary legacy is placed on two or more heirs, the procedure for performing the legacy is subject to Article 1138 of the Civil Code and the provisions on obligations generally. The general principle in the law of obligations is that if several persons have a duty to perform, that duty as between them is equal unless determined otherwise by a law or by the obligation. If the will does not determine the precise share for each heir to perform a testamentary legacy, then each heir is encumbered by the legacy in a proportion commensurate with his share in the estate.

Similarly, a testamentary legacy may be to the benefit of several recipients. Russian legislation does not specifically address this situation with respect to inheritance; therefore, the general rules apply to an obligation with several creditors. Depending on the provisions of the testamentary legacy, the obligation may be joint and several or on the basis of participatory shares. Unless the will or rules on testamentary legacies provide otherwise, Articles 321 and 326 of the Civil Code are applicable. If one of the creditors to the legacy refuses to accept his share of the legacy, the heir is released from the respective encumberment.

If the subject-matter of the testamentary legacy is indivisible (for example, a one-room apartment to the use of two individuals who comprise a single family), and one of them refused to accept the rights granted under the legacy, the heir must nonetheless perform the entire testamentary legacy at the demand of the other joint and several creditor (Article 326, Civil Code), who is not obliged to compensate in any way the legacy recipient who declined to accept his portion of the legacy. If the heir performs a testamentary legacy to one joint and several creditor, he is released from the legacy; how the several recipients address the performance made is a separate obligation of their own pursuant to the Civil Code.

Termination of Testamentary Legacy. Article 1138(3) of the Civil Code permits the termination of a testamentary legacy for reasons connected with the recipient. These are circumstances that, if they ensue, the legacy is left without a recipient: death of the recipient before the inheritance is opened or simultaneously with the decedent; unconditional and unreserved refusal to receive the legacy (Article 1160, Civil Code), to which a three-year period of limitations is applicable from the date of opening the inheritance; actual failure to exercise the right to receive the testamentary legacy within the three-year period of limitations; deprivation of the right to receive the testamentary legacy on the grounds of unworthiness of the recipient (Article 1117, Civil Code). The liquidation of a juridical person which received a testamentary legacy before the opening of the inheritance would terminate the legacy.

Other circumstances of impossibility of performance arise under the general provisions of the Civil Code on obligations (especially Article 416). Examples would include the destruction of the physical objects of the testamentary legacy by reason of natural calamities (floods, earthquakes, and so on), or by reason of being lost.

The *testamentary imposition* is a species of disposition which enables a decedent to pass property to heirs as his direct legal successors and simultaneously place on them the duty to perform certain actions of a property or non-property nature for a generally useful purpose (Article 1139, Civil Code). Such an imposition has certain features of the testamentary legacy: it is established solely in a will; it may be the sole content of a will; it encumbers the heirs to perform certain actions. If the imposition has as its subject-matter the performance of actions of a property character, the rules concerning the performance of a testamentary legacy apply.

Usually a testamentary legacy has two main features: (1) the actions comprising the subject-matter of the imposition may be of a property or a non-property character; (2) the imposition is directed towards the achievement of a generally-useful purpose and not the benefit of a specific individual, as in the case of the testamentary legacy. There is no legislative definition of a "generally-useful" purpose. Doctrinal writings mention actions performed for the benefit of the State or society as a whole, or to satisfy the material or spiritual needs of various social groups or institutions, social movements, scientific, cultural, or educational institutions, or to achieve other purposes not connected with giving advantage to a specific individual. Examples cited include the disposition by a testator of his royalties for a book to societies for the blind, or by a collector of his valuable collection of artifacts to an organization for periodic exhibitions open to the general public, or a collection of rare books to a public library. Examples are known of an heir being instructed to systematically care for the burial place of the decedent, which is considered to be of sufficient public benefit to be classified as a testamentary imposition. So too is the duty of an heir to care for pets or animals, which are not regarded as having a specific individual interest in the disposition and the performance of the imposition is believed to contribute to the moral satisfaction of a society which believes in the humane treatment of living things.

Performance of a testamentary imposition is at the expense of the inheritance property which passes by will or by operation of law. However, unlike the testamentary legacy, the testamentary imposition is not an obligation, but rather a unilateral duty of the debtor or executor of the will. This is evident from Article 1139(3) of the Civil Code, which addresses the remedies available to demand performance of the imposition in a judicial proceeding. Any interested person may sue for performance of the testamentary imposition. The testator can mitigate the exposure of the heir by stipulating in the will that performance of the imposition is at the discretion of the heir in light of the social and other conditions to which the testamentary imposition is directed.

OBLIGATORY SHARES IN ESTATE

Freedom of will is limited by the statutory requirement creating obligatory shares in an inheritance for certain persons (Article 1149, Civil Code). The obligatory share (Latin: *portio legitima*) is intended as a form of "social defense" of persons who, as a rule, are insufficiently provided for materially and who, by reason of the death of the decedent, have been deprived of the means for subsistence. In Russian legal doctrine these individuals are often called "necessary" or "obligatory" heirs. That term has been criticized as inappropriate because these persons enjoy the freedom and discretion not to accept an obligatory share; they cannot be compelled to do so.

In the twentieth century the notion of an obligatory share became what Russian jurists consider to be an imperative norm of inheritance law. The family operated as the principal source of personal wealth; an individual received the property of his or her deceased relatives and in due course passed that wealth on to descendants. Family ownership and the need to preserve the family underlay the obligatory share as a constrain on the unlimited freedom of disposition. Soviet Russian legislation from April 1918 onwards pursued the notion of providing security for those in need. The initial version of the 1922 RSFSR Civil Code made no provision for the obligatory share but rejected freedom of disposition by permitting a deceased to bequeath property only from among heirs by operation of law. In 1928 the RSFSR Civil Code was amended to require that minor heirs had to receive no less than ¾ of the participatory share due to them by operation of law, and further adjustments were made in 1945.

The Civil Code of the Russian Federation (Article 1149) reduced the obligatory share in comparison with the 1964 RSFSR Civil Code from two-thirds to one-half of the share which would be due to each heir in the event of inheritance by operation of law. The reduction itself has been the subject of controversy in Russian doctrinal writings. Some consider the original two-thirds share in the 1964 RSFSR Civil Code to have been more socially just to the family; the present allocation allows the testator to place his personal interests ahead of those of his family and dependents and reduces the function of the family as a provider of material security.[58]

[58] See E. V. Vavilin, «Принцип справедливости как основа осуществления наследственных прав» [Principle of Justness as Foundation for the Exercise of Inheritance Rights], Юрист [Jurist], no. 1 (2007); N. B. Demina, «Гарантии прав родственников наследователя в наследственном праве РФ» [Guarantees of

Among those who have the right to an obligatory share in an estate are persons who are minors and children who lack labor capacity on the day of opening of the inheritance, including adopted children, or a spouse, parents, and dependents who lack labor capacity (Article 1148, Civil Code). With effect from 1 January 2019, all female persons aged 55 or above and males aged 60 or above, by virtue of the addition of Article 8^2 to Federal Law of 25 December 2018, No. 495-ФЗ, "On Making Changes in the Federal Law 'On the Introduction into Operation of Part Three of the Civil Code of the Russian Federation'" have the same right; being disabled or lacking labor capacity is no longer a consideration for them. Being a spouse, parent, or dependent is sufficient. Irrespective of the content of the will, they inherit not less than half the share due to each of them in the event of inheritance by operation of law. Minor children have the right to an obligatory share even if they have labor capacity, are married to a minor, or were emancipated. The list of persons in the Civil Code (Articles 1142, 1147, and 1148) who have the right to an obligatory share is exhaustive and not subject to expansive interpretation. The right to an obligatory share does not pass to descendants of a deceased heir by right of representation.

Under the Family Code of the Russian Federation, property of spouses may be part of an inheritance estate after the death of one of them only if the surviving spouse has declared that he or she does not have a participatory share in the property acquired during the marriage. Property belonging to each spouse before marrying and property received by one spouse during the marriage as a gift, by way of inheritance, or on other gratuitous grounds is in the ownership of that spouse and not part of the estate of the other spouse (Article 36, Family Code). If family relations have *de facto* terminated but a marriage remains formally in force, the spouses no longer keep a common household, and did not acquire joint property, such property is not in their common ownership (Article 38, Family Code).

Rights of Relatives of Decedent in Inheritance Law of the Russian Federation], Юрист [Jurist], no. 5 (2005). Both available on Consultant Plus.

The general approach for determining an obligatory share is as follows. One first calculates the ideal shares in an estate for each legal heir and then establishes the amount of the obligatory share. For example, if a testator bequeathed all his property to a brother (who would as a legal heir be in the second priority), but at the moment the inheritance was opened, the testator had a son who lacked labor capacity, in the absence of a will all property would go to the heir of first priority (Article 1142, Civil Code). Consequently, the obligatory share may not be less than his legal share, which would be one-half of the inheritance. If the son of the decedent wishes to take advantage of his right to an obligatory share, the notary must formalize two certificates of the right to inherit: one for the brother, who receives one-half of the inheritance by will, and a second certificate for the right to inherit by operation of law for the son, who likewise receives half of the inheritance.

In the preceding example, the son was entirely overlooked by the testator. Situations can arise when the statutory heir receives less than the obligatory share. Assume that in a will the property of the decedent is so divided that the surviving son receives a 7/8 share and the surviving spouse, a 1/8 share. The spouse lacks labor capacity at the time of opening the inheritance and requests her obligatory share in the estate. The ideal calculation would be: in the absence of a will the property would have been divided equally between the spouse and the son, which means her obligatory share may not be less than one-fourth of the estate. The notary will issue certificates of the right to inherit to the son for ¾ of the inheritance by will and to the spouse for 1/4 of the estate by operation of law. If the will had divided the estate in those proportions, both heirs would have received a certificate of the right to inherit by will for 3/4 and 1/4 of the estate accordingly.

The obligatory share (Article 1149(2), Civil Code) is first satisfied from the unbequeathed portion of an estate even if that may lead to a reduction of the property received by those who inherit by will. If the unbequeathed portion of the estate is not sufficient to satisfy the obligatory share, the heirs by testament experience a reduction of the property they are designated to receive. If an heir entitled to a testamentary legacy also is entitled to an obligatory share, the value of the testamentary legacy is set off against the obligatory share (Article 1149(3), Civil Code). Some Russian jurists are of the view that the obligatory share should include items of an estate that are inherently difficult to determine or value, such as articles of household use, expensive furniture, and the like. Commonly in these situations the notary will suggest to the heirs that they have recourse to a Russian court for a valuation and division of the property, probably enlisting valuers and experts for this purpose. The 1964 RSFSR Civil Code, admittedly in a different economy where such items had a different value, explicitly included domestic household items in the value of an obligatory share.

Although Russian doctrinal writings widely share the opinion that the obligatory share operates as a limitation of the freedom of will, that is not necessarily so. Insofar as the freedom of will constitutes the right and ability of a decedent to incorporate in his will the most diverse of dispositions, the obligatory share does not impinge upon this range of possibilities. Moreover, the law merely provides for the right of appropriate individuals to demand an obligatory share, but for various reasons they may prefer not to exercise that right, particularly in light of the possible consequences of doing so: a reduction of the claims of other legal heirs if the property in the estate is insufficient to cover what has been bequeathed to them, in which event it is not the freedom of will that is constrained but the ability of the named heirs to receive all of the property designated for them in the will; or the unbequeathed property is sufficient to cover the obligatory share, in which event the last wishes of the decedent were satisfied and there is no issue of the freedom of will. In view of these considerations some Russian jurists suggest that rather than speaking of limitations on the freedom of will, it would be more accurate to speak of a competition for the right to inherit amongst the heirs by will and heirs entitled to an obligatory share in which Russian legislation plays a role.[59]

With effect from 1 September 2018, an heir having the right to an obligatory participatory share and who is the beneficiary of an inheritance foundation loses the right to an obligatory participatory share. If such heir during the period established for acceptance of an inheritance declares to the notary conducting the inheritance matter the renunciation of all rights of the beneficiary of an inheritance foundation, he has the right to an obligatory participatory share in accordance with Article 1149. If an heir renounces the rights of a beneficiary of an inheritance foundation, a court may reduce the amount of the obligatory participatory share of this heir if the value of the property due to him as a result of the inheritance materially increased the amount of the means necessary for the maintenance of a citizen, taking into account his reasonable requirements and obligations he has on the date of opening the inheritance to third persons, and also the average amount of expenses and standard of living before the death of the decedent.

REVOCATION OR CHANGE OF WILL

The freedom of will means that a testator may at any time change or revoke a will previously drawn up (Article 1130, Civil Code). In exercising these options, the testator is constrained by nothing – not the time which has elapsed since the previous will was drawn up, or the date, or the place of drawing up the will, or the purposes of testamentary dispositions, or the reasons why the testator changed his mind, or the form in which the will is changed or revoked.[60] A *change* of a will means drawing

[59] See Abramenkov and Chugunov, note 3 above, pp. 195-196.

[60] The Constitutional Court of the Russian Federation has rejected the view that Article 1130(1) and (2) of the Civil Code are unconstitutional because they allow a testator to draw up a new will without informing the notary who attested the

up a new document or testament with the inclusion thereof of dispositions that completely or partially differ from the dispositions contained in the previous will(s). It is impossible to change a previous will without revoking all or some of its dispositions and without indicating other dispositions in the new will. The *revocation* of testamentary dispositions is either an integral part of changing a will and is embodied in the overall result – the new will – or is in "pure form", that is, the will is revoked without being accompanied by other new dispositions. To put it otherwise, in the first instance a new will is drawn up by way of change, whereas in the second, the revocation is performed by actions which are not a will.

There are two ways by which a will may be changed under Russian law. The first is by means of drawing up a new will in which there is an express indication that the preceding will(s) is revoked as a whole or in part by certain disposition and new specific testamentary dispositions on heirs, property bequeathed, or the distribution thereof, and so on are set out in accordance with the Civil Code. The second is by drawing up a new will in which there is no express indication concerning the revocation of an earlier will(s) as a whole or in part, but the specific testamentary dispositions in substance replace those of the previous will(s) in whole or in part.

The legal consequences of a change of a will depends upon what the new will provides. If the will does not expressly revoke previous will(s), it revokes those will(s) insofar as provisions do not remain in the earlier will that are unrevoked. It is possible, therefore, that the new will may prove to be operative side by side with an earlier will insofar as the earlier remains in force with respect to unrevoked or unchanged provisions. If the new will categorically revokes or in essence revokes earlier wills, the earlier wills lost force as a whole or in respective part (Article 1130, Civil Code). There is doctrinal support for revocation

previous will about the revocation thereof and they allow any notary to attest the new will, and not merely the notary who attested a previous will. See Ruling of the Constitutional Court of the Russian Federation, 21 April 2011, Re: G. G. Sokolov. Available on Consultant Plus.

occurring by the by the restoration into force of a will previously drawn up.[61]

There is a residual nuance with respect to revocation in Russian inheritance law that requires comment. Under the 1922 RSFSR Civil Code (Article 426) and the 1964 RSFSR Civil Code (Article 543), the way to achieve a "pure" revocation of a will not connected with a "change" of the will was to submit a "statement of the testator concerning the revocation of a will", whereas the current term is a "disposition concerning the revocation of a will". Russian doctrine treats both formulas as completely identical in essence and in legal consequences. Nonetheless, the new terminology is considered to be preferable because the old term "statement of the testator concerning revocation of a will", read literally, seems to suggest it amounts to a request to perform some action with regard to revocation of the will. The modern phrase leaves no doubt that the disposition concerning the revocation of a will is a categorical volitional action, a transaction, of the testator himself and that the revocation is an integral component of this action.[62]

Being a transaction, the disposition concerning the revocation of a will is subject to all the requirements for the validity of a transaction. If the revocation proves to be an invalid transaction, the inheritance will proceed pursuant to the will which was not effectively revoked (Article 1130, Civil Code). On this analysis, however, the disposition to revoke the will is not a testamentary disposition, that is, is not itself a will. The Civil Code is not entirely consistent in drawing this distinction, for pursuant to Article 1130(5), any act revoking an "extraordinary" will is called a will, although in substance it is a pure instruction to revoke unaccompanied by any change of testamentary dispositions.

There are certain requirements of form applicable to revocations of wills. If a disposition to revoke is regarded as a testamentary disposition, the general rules concerning the form

61 Petrov, in Petrov, note 4 above, p. 153.

62 Abramenkov and Chugunov, note 3 above, p., 213.

of such dispositions would apply. If the revocation is a "pure" or "clean" revocation, pursuant to Article 1130(4) of the Civil Code the revocation should comply with the form established for drawing up a will. There are two exceptions. The first relates to the form of wills drawn up under extraordinary circumstances; while wills may be composed under those circumstances, there is no provision for changing or revoking wills previously drawn up and notarially certified or will equated to those notarially certified, or closed wills, or testamentary dispositions arranged in banks and credit institutions by means of wills made under extraordinary circumstances. Moreover, wills concluded in the proper forms which predate a will that was drawn up under extraordinary circumstances will always take precedence over the last.

The second exception relates to testamentary dispositions given to banks or credit institutions with respect to deposits held in those banks or credit institutions. These may be changed or revoked only by testamentary dispositions given to those institutions in the form and in the procedure provided by special rules provided by the Decree of 27 May 2002.

INTERPRETATION AND PERFORMANCE OF TESTAMENTARY DISPOSITION

Interpretation of will. The purpose of interpreting a will is to determine or elicit the will of the person expressed by him in the testament which he drew up. Where there is no proper interpretation of a will, there is no genuine testamentary freedom. The proper interpretation enables the testamentary dispositions to be most precisely performed and the rights of all the heirs to be most fully guaranteed.

The rules regulating interpretation of a will are set out in Article 1132 of the Civil Code and had no predecessor in the 1964 RSFSR Civil Code. The provisions of Article 1132 combine the approach to interpreting a contract (Article 431, Civil Code) with that taken in the Model Civil Code of the Commonwealth of Independent States (Article 1167), which required one proceed from the literal meaning of words and expressions and, in the event of ambiguity, to confine oneself to contrasting the parts of the will. Article 1132 thus gives priority to literal interpretation, and a notary or court cannot go around the literal and clear meaning of the words and expressions by trying to reconstruct the true will of the testator that seems to be the most likely.[63]

Three persons are mentioned in Article 1132 as encountering the task of interpretation: the notary, the executor of the will, and the court. The notary or other person certifying the will is involved in interpretation at the stage when the document submitted for certification is still a draft. Pursuant to the Fundamental Principles on the Notariat (Article 54), the notary must explain the sense and meaning of the draft will to the testator and verify whether the content of the draft is consistent with the true intention of the testator and the requirements of Russian legislation. If the sense of individual dispositions in the draft will are not clear or are contrary to other dispositions, the notary will recommend to the testator that these problems with the text be eliminated, explain the relevant rules of inheritance, and caution what the consequences may be if the problems are not rectified. If the notary is not content with the changes made by the testator to address the problems, the notary may refuse to certify the will, in which case the testator may apply to a court to seek redress against the notary's refusal to certify or turn to another notary.

When the time comes to execute the will and issue a certificate on the right to inherit to individual heirs, the notary pursuant to the Fundamental Principles on the Notariat (Article 73) must interpret the dispositions in the will in the strict sense of the word. The ultimate outcome of the notary's interpretation is reflected in the attendant documentation, especially the issuance of the certificate of the right to inherit by will and by

[63] Petrov, in Petrov, note 4 above, p. 170, who points out that the Methods Recommendations for the Formalization of Inheritance Rights (point 33) provide that when eliciting the literal meaning (or sense) of words and expressions contained in a will their generally-accepted meaning is ascertained, and when interpreting legal terms, their meaning given by the legislator in respective legal acts is applied. Russian law contains no special norms devoted to determining the content of a will.

operation of law or the reasoned refusal of the notary to issue a certificate, although such refusal might be appealed to a court.

Judicial interpretation of a will occurs when a suit or other applications have been made in connection with inheritance. The interpretation is made pursuant to a determination to recognize or not a right to inherit. There is no independent means of instituting a proceeding purely for a judicial interpretation of a will.

An executor, notary, or court may not use any direct or indirect external evidence to assist with interpretation, such as letters or other correspondence of the testator – an approach even stricter than prerevolutionary Russian practice, where the Ruling Senate had authorized letters of the testator to be examined, if necessary. The literal approach has generated its own problems in post-Soviet Russian practice. Testators of the older generation, for example, who bequeathed a dwelling said nothing of the land plot on which the dwelling was sited because land, at the time, was in the sole ownership of the State or the whole people and not theirs to bequeath. A literal approach to interpretation excluded the land plot from the dispositions of the will even though the legal context had changed, juxtaposing the literal reading and the presupposed will of the testator and leading Russian courts to determine that the dwelling passed under the will and the land plot by operation of law, with the possibility of different heirs or different shares in the ownership of the dwelling and the land plot.[64]

The will of the testator is ascertained first by interpreting the literal meaning of the words and expressions used in the will (Article 1132, Civil Code), which echoes the approach to the Russian interpretation of contracts (Article 431, Civil Code). This in practice is understood to mean the interpretation should not disclose what the testator wanted to say, but what he said. This has led many Russian jurists to reject an expansive or

[64] See the Ruling of the Division for Civil Cases of the Supreme Court of the Russian Federation, 1 August 2017, No. 18-КГ17-116 (available on Consultant Plus).

limited interpretation of wills as being inappropriate and not consistent with Article 1132.

Execution or performance of will. The term "execution" can be ambiguous in English insofar as in connection with contracts or wills "execution" can be the process of negotiating and concluding or drawing up the document or refer to the implementation of the document after it enters into force. The Russian terminology makes clear that we are here referring to the latter stage. Here execution or performance means undertaking actions which lead to succession in accordance with the will of the testator. The purpose of "performance" is sometimes said in Russian doctrine to be the protection of the freedom of will after the testator's death, the protection of the estate as a complex of property rights and duties, and the protection of the rights and interests of persons acquiring property benefits from the inheritance or persons having claims to the estate.[65] The concept of execution under Russian law encompasses those who execute the will, the powers and rights of the executor.

As a rule, the heirs execute a will. Although they have no special authority or powers under Russian legislation to do so, the heirs perform execution actions in the process of exercising their rights as heirs, such as: acceptance of the inheritance; recourse to the notary for measures to be taken to protect the inheritance property, notifying other heirs about the opening of an inheritance, giving consent to the acceptance of an inheritance, applying to a court to remove the executor of a will, among others.

A will may, however, appoint an executor (Articles 1133 and 1134, Civil Code). This person, strictly speaking, is not a representative of the testator or of the heirs. Any person who has dispositive legal capacity, including a foreigner or stateless person, may act as an executor; an heir may act in this capacity, whether an heir by will or by operation of law. Prior to 1 September 2018, only a natural person could be an executor; thereafter, the executor might be either a natural or a juridical

[65] Abramenkov and Chugunov, note 3 above, p. 222.

person, presumably either a commercial or noncommercial juridical person whose legal capacity allows that entity to act in this capacity.

Essentially the executor is acting in the interest of others by virtue of powers based on the will and recognized by law. If the heirs are carrying out the testamentary dispositions, the executor operates as an additional supervisory and controlling presence. If disagreements arise between the heirs or between the executor and the heirs, recourse to a court is always available.

If a testator has appointed an executor in his will, he is not obliged to explain why a particular person was chosen as the executor. Irrespective of whether an individual knew he was designated as executor or learned of this after the opening of the inheritance, he must give consent to be the executor. Several methods of giving consent are available under Article 1134 of the Civil Code. The first two involve the executor giving written consent on the will itself or in a statement appended to the will. Otherwise, the person may express consent to acting as executor by sending a statement to the notary within a month from the day of opening of the inheritance or by means of actually executing the will. No data is available as to how frequently Russian testators appoint executors in their wills. One may expect this to happen increasingly as Russian continues to move in the direction of a market economy: heirs are more likely to encounter a complex aggregate of moveable and immoveable property or property rights which require immediate attention to manage and protect or family situations that need legal and professional support on the part of an entrusted individual in whom the testator had confidence. A testator may appoint more than one executor if he wishes.

The appointment of an executor in a will is a unilateral disposition of the testator. If an executor does not give consent to acting in that capacity within the month allowed for this by the Civil Code, the question arises: what consequences follow. The Civil Code does not address the issue. Some suggest that if the executor appointed declines to act, the duty to execute the will, based upon a systematic interpretation of Articles 1133 and 1134 of the Civil Code, falls upon the other heirs in the will.[66] Russian doctrine does not regard the lapse of the period as depriving the executor of the right to act if his consent to do so was given late, and judicial practice would appear to accept that position.

The appointment of more than one executor is not prohibited. If two or more executors were appointed, Russian legislation does not expressly address what the consequences might be for them and for the heirs. The duties of co-executors of a will are assumed to be joint and several only if the subject-matter of the obligation is indivisible (Article 322, Civil Code). In all other cases the co-executors are obliged to equally perform the instructions of the deceased, each being liable only for his own actions (Article 321, Civil Code).[67] This approach has been challenged: the likelihood would be that the co-executors would come to an agreement among themselves as to who should do what, but that leaves the issue of whether their agreement is consistent with the will of the testator.[68] Although Article 1134 of the Civil Code is silent on the issue, Russian commentators support the proposition that a will may designate sub-executors who would act if the individual first named as executor is unable or refuses to act, or pre-deceases the testator.[69]

The provisions concerning the execution or performance of a will do not fix a period of time during which the executor acts. The only date certain is that the executor may not act before the inheritance opens, that is, before the moment of death of the testator (Article 1113, Civil Code), but the moment of death and the moment of an executor commencing his activity may coincide. Depending upon the substance of the will and

[66] Guev, note 24 above, p. 90.

[67] V. V. Plekhanova, «Исполнение завещания душеприказчиком» [Execution of a Will by an Executor], Закон [Law], no. 4 (2001), p. 62; cited in Kirillova, note 21 above, pp. 69-70.

[68] Kirillova, note 21 above, p. 70.

[69] Petrov, in Petrov, note 4 above, p. 176. Prerevolutionary Russian legislation so permitted. See K. P. Pobedonostsev, Курс гражданского права [Course of Civil Law], ed. V. A. Tomsinov (2003), II, p. 587.

complexity of tasks to be performed by the executor, the executor may act until the inheritance of accepted by the heirs or well beyond. In general the executor of a will can expect to act for the period reasonably necessary to fulfill the tasks set out in Article 1171 of the Civil Code – that is, to take measures to protect and manage the estate until the property is transferred to the heirs. However, an executor could cease to act in that capacity if, for example, all the heirs by will refused the inheritance, or if a court released an executor of his duties pursuant to Article 1134 of the Civil Code.

Article 1134(2) of the Civil Code provides that an executor is released from his duties by notification of the notary conducting the case after the opening of an inheritance when there are circumstances preventing the individual from properly performing the duties in accordance with the conditions and expression of will of the testator. The notary may consider the issue of release upon the application of the executor himself or the request of the heirs. Circumstances which may justify releasing an executor from his duties include grave illness, the executor not having or being limited in dispositive legal capacity, or missing, or away for an extended period, or similar reasons which are believed to be important. One controversial issue is whether an executor may be released from duties upon the demand of others besides the heirs – creditors of the estate, participants of organizations in which the deceased had participatory shares, legatees, or other interested persons. Russian commentators support a broad understanding of the right to demand recusal.[70]

An executor has the right under the Civil Code to perform certain actions and to demand reciprocal actions in connection with executing the will on the part of heirs, other persons, State agencies, and the like. Not only does the executor have the right to act before third persons, but he must do so in order to execute the will. The will is the legal basis for the executor to act except for a situation when apart from appointing the executor the will

[70] E. A. Ostanina, in Petrov, note 4 above, p. 179.

contains no other dispositions about heirs or the inheritance (although if there are other earlier wills still operative, they would form the basis for the executor to act). Moreover, there must be grounds for an inheritance; in the absence of such, the basis for the executor to act also falls away.

The powers of an executor are certified by a certificate issued by a notary (Article 1135(1), Civil Code). The certificate officially confirms the powers of the executor of the will and releases third persons from the duty to verify the basis for and limits of those powers. The procedure for the issuance of a certificate to an executor is not regulated by the Fundamental Principles on the Notariat – an odd omission. Article 1135(2) gives an exemplary list of the powers of an executor:

(1) ensure the transfer to the heirs of inheritance property due to them in accordance with the will of the testator expressed in the will and by a law;

(2) take in the interests of the heirs in his name all necessary legal and other actions for the protection of the inheritance and management thereof in the interests of the heirs, and if it is not possible for him to take such actions, to apply to the notary for measures to be taken to protect the property;

(3) receive monetary means due to the testator and other property for transfer thereof to heirs, if this property is not subject to transfer to other persons (Article 1183[1]);

(4) perform a testamentary imposition or demand from heirs the performance of a testamentary legacy (Article 1137) or testamentary imposition (Article 1139).

These are regarded as outlining the general tasks of an executor and the principles by which he should be guided. The executor in order to perform his duties has the right to obtain information about all wills of the testator from the notary and other empowered officials, is obliged to search for heirs under the will or those who have received a testamentary legacy, may place a notice in the mass media concerning the search for heirs, inform heirs and other interested persons about the content of the will, determine what is part of the estate and the location and physical condition thereof, and so on. The powers of an executor to himself or through the notary protect and manage property in the interests of the heirs are addressed in Articles 1171 to 1174 of the Civil Code.

Monies received by the executor which were due to the testator are placed on deposit with the notary as part of the executor's duty to protect estate property.

Expenditures made by the executor are subject to being compensated from the estate in the procedure established by law. Such expenses might include those associated with searching for heirs, publishing notice of the opening of the estate and calling for heirs, paying a custodian to protect or manage estate property, a trustee manager, court costs, and the like. They expenses are subject to compensation if they were necessary by their nature and amount. The duty to prove the expenses and the need to make them rests on the executor. An executor is paid for his services from the estate if this has been provided by the will (Article 1136, Civil Code).

Since 1 September 2018 an executor is considered to have been greater powers to act in the interests of the heirs, but issues of an executor acting *ultra vires* have received little attention in Russian doctrine.

Russian doctrinal writings refer to the "fiduciary character" of acting as an executor. The Civil Code does not elaborate the nature of this fiduciary relationship; it would be imprudent to read into the term the Anglo-American equivalent of a fiduciary, even though Article 1135 after 1 September 2018 refers to an executor also as a trustee manager.

INVALIDITY OF WILL

The invalidity of a will arises when the will fails to correspond to express provisions of legislation with respect to the expression of the testator's wishes or to requirements of form. Russian legal doctrine emphasizes that the issues of validity are not a dispute about the interests of heirs, but rather about the law protecting the private wishes of the testator after his death as a principle of private law. When the validity of a will is challenged by an interested person, one of the fundamental presumptions of the law of inheritance is being challenged: any testament is presumed to be valid so long as not proved otherwise. The burden of proof with respect to validity therefore rests upon those challenging validity. The presumption in effect means that the document drawn up by the testator and containing instructions regarding the disposition of his property is valid without any other expert assessment, legal or otherwise, by the person empowered by law to certify the will, especially the notary.[71]

Neither prerevolutionary Russian law nor Soviet law contained general provisions concerning the invalidity of wills. The 1964 RSFSR Civil Code took the approach that general rules concerning the invalidity of transactions applied to wills. Article 1131 of the Civil Code of the Russian Federation in effect makes the general rules concerning the invalidity of transactions (Articles 166-181) relevant to wills and introduced an analogous classification of the grounds of invalidity: defects relating to the subjects of wills (Articles 171, 172, 175, 176); defects of the expression of will of the testator (Articles 177 to 179); defects of form (Article 1124); and defects of content (Articles 169 and 170). To these general grounds of invalidity, Article 1135 adds special grounds peculiar to wills. These rules are concentrated in the Civil Code; however, the procedure for testamentary dispositions in a bank was confirmed by a Decree of the Government of the Russian Federation; Russian judicial practice does not regard this as an obstacle to deeming invalid testamentary dispositions made in violation of the rules established in that Decree.

Article 1135(1) textually reproduces Article 166(1) of the Civil Code and provides that a will may be a null, or void, or a

[71] One commentator has observed: "In Russia, unlike European countries, the contesting of a will is no rarity. The reasons are the advanced age of the typical testator and the absence of a culture of respect for the last will of the deceased". Petrov, in Petrov, note 4 above, p. 155.

contestable transaction. The will is void if by the nature of the violations it is invalid irrespective of being deemed to be such by a court. It is contestable if it is deemed invalid solely by virtue of a judicial decision. In reality, however, because the grounds of invalidity of a will are not usually obvious on their face and the acquisition of the right to an estate is of an official nature, a judicial decision is commonly essential in both instances, of nullity and of contesting. Russian judicial practice recognizes the possibility of filing a suit to deem null transactions to be invalid.[72]

A will is null, or void, if: the rules concerning written form of the will or certification thereof have not been complied with (Article 1124[1]), including the failure to comply with the rules on notarial form or form equated thereto or the group of persons having the right to certify a will (Articles 1125, 1127, 1128), or the failure to draw up and sign the text of a closed will in own hand (Article 1126), or failure to comply with the obligatory presence of witnesses when drawing up a will (Article 1124[3]); failure to comply with requirements concerning the full dispositive legal capacity of the testator (Articles 21, 168, 1118);[73] failure to comply with the requirement that the testator must personally draw up the will and inadmissibility of doing so through a representative (Articles 182(3), 1118); the disposition by the testator of someone else's property (Article 1118); or the refusal of a court to confirm the fact that a testament was the last will of the testator in extraordinary circumstances (Article 1129).

A will may be contested if: the witnesses present do not conform to the requirements of law (Article 1124[3]); a will was drawn up by a person not capable of understanding the significance of his actions or directing them (Article 177); the

[72] Point 32, Decree of the Plenum of the Supreme Court of the Russian Federation and Plenum of the Supreme Arbitrazh Court of the Russian Federation, 1 July 1996, No. 6/8, "On Certain Questions Connected with the Application of Part One of the Civil Code of the Russian Federation".

[73] Russian doctrinal writings, and judicial and notarial practice are quite categorical on the point: "Persons deemed to lack dispositive legal capacity may not conclude any transactions, including drawing up a will". E. A. Sukhanov, Гражданское право [Civil Law] (2005), I, p. 204.

will was drawn up under the influence of delusion having material significance (Article 178) or under the influence of fraud, coercion, or threat (Article 179); or the failure to comply with requirements concerning an obligatory share for persons who have the right to such (Article 1149).

Any person whose rights or legal interests have been violated by a will may bring suit in court concerning invalidity. This rule follows from Article 166(2) of the Civil Code. Whether an executor may be a plaintiff in suits concerning invalidity is not addressed by Russian legislation expressly. Doctrinal writings support this possibility, although it has been observed that if the executor is not an heir under the will, he does not have the same interest. The right of an executor to be a plaintiff with regard to invalidity is believed to flow from his powers as executor and his duty to perform the will of the testator. It is possible that in order to fully execute what the testator wished to happen, individual provisions of a will or the entire will may require a judicial determination.

Who is the respondent or defendant when the validity of a will is challenged? The testator obviously cannot so act. It has been suggested that by analogy with Article 1175(2) of the Civil Code the defendants would be the heirs by will who were such before the proceedings in the inheritance were suspended by the filing of the civil suit.[74]

A will cannot be contested before an inheritance is opened (Article 1131(2), Civil Code), which follows from the special properties of a will as a transaction to be performed upon death (Article 1118, Civil Code). Until the inheritance is opened, there is no subject-matter of a dispute, no individuals who may by plaintiffs or defendants in a civil proceeding pursuant to law. Given the right of the testator to change or revoke his will at any time, whatever putative parties there might be to a suit prior to the opening of an inheritance are, at best, purely theoretical.

[74] Abramenkov and Chugunov, note 3 above, p. 233.

The classification of invalid wills into the categories of void or contestable has significant implications for the application of periods of limitation and the rules for calculating them. A suit to apply the consequences of a void transaction (Article 181, Civil Code) may be brought within three years from the day when the execution or performance thereof commenced. That day would be the day of opening the inheritance. A suit to deem a contestable transaction to be invalid may be brought within one year from the day when the plaintiff knew about the circumstances which are the grounds for deeming the testament to be invalid. Because contesting the will of a testator during his lifetime is not permitted, this day might be the day of opening the inheritance if the circumstances were known to the plaintiff earlier but he could not bring suit, or some other day after the inheritance was opened when the plaintiff discovered the circumstances.

In response to difficulties experienced by Russian courts, given their long-standing tradition of taking usually a highly formalistic approach to applying the law, when dealing with "technical" lapses of drafting a will, the Civil Code provides that "Slips of the pen and other insignificant violations of the procedure for drawing up thereof, signature, or certification, if it is established by a court that they do not influence the understanding of the expression of will of the testator, may not serve as grounds for invalidity of a will" (Article 1131[3]). The court in applying this provision needs to analyze the circumstances and the will itself to determine whether these insignificant violations influenced the expression of will of the testator. The legislator was not of great assistance in formulating the provision. Instances of Russian courts refusing to deem a will invalid because of violations occurring when the will was drawn up were known.[75]

[75] See, for example, the Survey of Judicial Practice of the Supreme Court of the Russian Federation for the Fourth Quarter of 1999. Бюллетень Верховного Суда Российской Федерации [Bulletin of the Supreme Court of the Russian

Examples of "technical" slips include slips of the pen when indicating the number of a house being bequeathed by the testator, or drawing up the will in pencil without any evidence of erasures or other corrections, or placing the registration number of a notarial action only on one example of the will and omitting to place it on the other, or omitting one element of the full name of an heir. On the other hand, "material" slips are those which do not enable the will to be accepted as a fact or as an expression of the testator's wishes; examples would be the absence of the date of certifying the will[76] and a respective entry in the notarial register of wills; the absence of the testator's signature on a document; or the signature of the will by a person other than the testator.

> *Example.* The question has been raised in connection with slips of a "pen" what should happen when a testator has submitted a will to a notary that has been prepared by a typewriter or computer. The following scenario is offered: K brings to a notary a typewritten will. The notary has no other evidence that the testator prepared the will in his own hand other than the oral confirmation of the testator himself, and the notary cannot otherwise confirm this. The notary certifies the will. After the death of the testator, persons appear who prove by way of witness testimony that the text of the will was not written by the testator, but at his request by another person. Is the will valid? If the Civil Code is read literally, the answer must be no. But in good reason when the testator in the presence of the notary expressly said that the text expresses his last will, does not the

Federation], no. 7 (2000).

[76] The absence of the date is regarded as a material slip because it is not possible to determine whether the testator had dispositive legal capacity at the time, or whether a particular will was drawn up before or after another will. Some Russian jurists recommend that not only the place and date be specified on a will, but also the time of day at which the will was drawn up and signed.

question of who typed the will, that is, who performed a technical function, no longer have legal significance?[77]

A will may be deemed to be invalid in whole or in part (Article 1131[4]), which is consistent with the general provisions of the Civil Code on transactions (Article 180). Whether the will is invalid in whole or in part will depend upon the grounds of invalidity. If a court determines that the will was drawn up under circumstances, for example, when the testator did not understand the significance of his actions or violated formalities that result in the will losing its significance as such, the will is likely to be deemed to be invalid as a whole.[78] Partial invalidity is likely to be the outcome when individual testamentary dispositions are concerned, such as the need to provide an obligatory share to an heir that is less than provided by the law, or the will purports to dispose of property that is, in fact, in common ownership rather than solely that of the testator.

The consequences of invalidity are determined by Article 1131(5) of the Civil Code. A will deemed to be invalid in whole or in part creates no legal consequences and falls away in whole or in part as grounds for inheritance in accordance with that will; it does not create a right to inherit for which compensation may be sought .

Example. "G". brought suit in court against agencies of local self-government seeking compensation for lost advantage in the amount of the value of a one-room apartment in connection with the invalidity of a will.

[77] The example was given by a critic of the practice of allowing "technical means' to be used for drafting wills. See Ch. Sulaimanova, «Порочное завещание» [Defective Will], Журнал «Домашний адвокат» [Journal "Home Advokat"], no. 9 (2009), p. 12.

[78] An example from judicial practice was the decision of the Ramensk District Court, Moscow Region, in Case 2-38 (2008) declaring a will to be invalid which had been attested by a treating doctor of the district hospital, whereas this right is given by the Civil Code only to chief doctors, deputies thereof for the medical section, or duty doctors. Нотариус [Notary], no. 3 (2009), p. 13.

> "F" while on holiday drew up a will which was attested in agencies of local self-government and bequeathed the apartment to "G". That will was later deemed to be invalid because it was attested by a person not empowered to do so. "G" argued that if the will had not been deemed invalid, he would have received the one-room apartment and therefore suffered lost advantage. The trial court satisfied the suit, but was reversed by the Judicial Division for Civil Cases of the Moscow City Court on appeal.[79]

However, invalidity does not eliminate the other legal grounds of inheriting pursuant to those dispositions of the will which are valid, or pursuant to another valid will, or by operation of law. The general consequences of the invalidity of a transaction (Article 167, Civil Code) are relevant insofar as they are applicable to a will. For example, if a will deemed to be invalid has already been performed and bequeathed property passed to the ownership of the persons specified in the will, restitution of the property would be the outcome pursuant to the Civil Code provisions on unfounded enrichment (Articles 1102-1108, Civil Code). The Civil Code does not create special consequences for the invalidity of a will, but merely clarifies some of them.

The notion of invalidity of a will is not relevant to wills which do not operate for reasons unconnected with violations of the requirements established for a valid will as transactions. Examples of such would be wills that contain no defects but cannot be performed because the testator revoked them, or none of the heirs are alive, or the heirs refused to accept the inheritance, or the heirs

[79] Reported from archival sources in Iu. F. Bespalov and A. Iu. Bespalova, Дела о наследовании [Cases concerning Inheritance] (2013), p. 7. The trial court overlooked the fact that declaring the will to be invalid meant that the will never existed and did not create for "G" a right to inherit. Consequently, lost advantage never happened.

were unworthy, and the like. Wills composed under extraordinary circumstances that lapse a month after the circumstances have abated would fall into this category. In effect, such wills lost force or become redundant.

Chapter 5

Inheritance by Operation of Law (Intestacy)

Inheritance by operation of law (intestacy) is the general procedure for the inheriting of property which proceeds not by the will of a testator but in the absence of such a will pursuant to rules established by legislation, principally in the Civil Code of the Russian Federation. During the Soviet era, most estate property passed to heirs by operation of law. Wills were the exception. In the post-Soviet era, the situation has been reversed, but nonetheless substantial numbers of estates continue to be acquired by heirs on the basis of intestacy for various reasons: poverty, indifference, superstition, lack of estate-planning culture, and general effectiveness of the legislative provisions regulating inheritance by operation of law.

CONCEPT OF INHERITANCE BY OPERATION OF LAW

Given that a natural person has decided to leave no instructions regarding the distribution of his property upon death, inheritance by operation of law relies upon the legislator to determine who should inherit and in what priority. In this the legislator is guided by what might be called general social notions and values as to what would be a just and proper distribution of an individual's property based on ideas of marriage, kinship, and material security or prosperity of those persons close to the deceased. Russian legal doctrine often sees inheritance by operation of law as a form of "tacit will". On this premise the testator, presumed to know the consequences of his passivity with regard to not drawing up a specific testament, is content with the order of distribution established by the legislator. Although this view is widely shared in one formulation or another in Russian legal doctrine, recent works have undertaken a more detailed and considered approach.

The suggestion is that two basic principles underlie inheritance by operation of law: individual and social. The individual approach is reflected in the fact that property of the decedent passed to those persons closest to the decedent by virtue of marriage, kinship, adoption, dependency, and so on. Blood relatives are preferred as among these categories. Of the two basic systems for determining kinship between the decedent and heirs, Russian law accepted what is called the classical Roman law system, based on the number of births separation the decedent and the heir, usually known as the degree of kinship. The birth of the decedent himself is not counted. The sequence of degrees constitutes a line. Lines may be direct, combining persons who emanate one from the other (descending – from the decedent to his progeny, or ascending from the decedent to his ancestors), or indirect, combining persons who have a common ancestor.

The social principle in inheritance by operation of law is the aspiration of the State, society, or collective to free itself from the burden of supporting indigent relatives of the decedent. This principle finds expression in requirements that relatives of the decedent who lack labor capacity or are indigent should enjoy an early priority in the distribution of the estate. The social principle also is reflected in the principle that the State should inherit property by escheat when there are no other heirs. Although escheat was prominent during the Soviet era, it enjoyed support in prerevolutionary Russia, where the draft Civil Code provided that escheat property "should pass to establishments engaged in public assistance in that locality where the inheritance was opened".[1]

Inheritance by operation of law occurs unless it is changed by a will or in other instances established by a law (Article 1111, Civil Code). This means that inheritance by operation of law will operate: if the testator left no will; the testator revoked his will(s) and precluded them as serving as the grounds of

[1] See G. S. Limanskii, Наследование по закону: вопросы теории и практики [Inheritance by Operation of Law: Questions of Theory and Practice] (Samara, 2003), p. 10.

inheriting; the will(s) was deemed by a court to be invalid as a whole; testamentary dispositions affect only part of the inheritance with the balance passing by operation of law; the will contains other dispositions which do not preclude inheritance by operation of law; among others.

In fact, under Russian law two domains of inheritance coexist. On one hand, priority is given in the Civil Code to inheritance by will as the leading, some would say preferred, means for a natural person to dispose of his property upon death. The will may change what otherwise would by inheritance by operation of law. In this sense, inheritance by will is the exercise by a testator of a dispositive opportunity to determine the fate of his property. However, that domain is constrained by imperative rules of Russian law which place limits upon the testator and his capacity to determine the future fate of his property. The Civil Code expressly provides for individual instances of inheritance by operation of law irrespective of the presence or content of a will. They are not numerous and seem to be dictated by overriding social and moral considerations or other public interests. These instances would include the obligatory share (Article 1149, Civil Code, and Article 8^2, Federal Law on Introduction of Part 3 of Civil Code into Force), the transfer to heirs by operation of law of property which an heir by will is deprived of because of unworthiness (Articles 1117, 1161); the absence of heirs by will or their failure to accept the estate bequeathed to them (Article 1151).

Certain legal features or characteristics of inheritance by operation of law differ from inheritance by will. These features are, as a rule, found in imperative norms and may not be changed by a will or by agreement of the parties to an inheritance.

PRIORITY OF HEIRS

The group of heirs by operation of law is determined on the basis of personal links between the decedent and the heirs: marriage, kinship, adoption, and family relations (of the relatives of one spouse to relatives of the other spouse), and by the provision of maintenance to the heir by the decedent. Heirs by operation of law connected with the decedent by kinship are persons who fall into the direct ascending, direct descending, or indirect lines of kinship with a limited degree of kinship by blood – not more than the fifth degree of the indirect line of kinship. Article 1141(1) of the Civil Code provides that heirs by operation of law are called to inherit by way of priorities consisting of the closest relatives of the decedent. Determination of the priorities of heirs in accordance with the degree of kinship is one of the principles of inheritance by operation of law.

Russian inheritance legislation makes provision for eight priorities of heirs by operation of law, as follows. The *first* priority comprises the children, spouse, and parents of the decedent and grandchildren of the decedent and their descendants by right of representation (Article 1142, Civil Code). The *second* priority consists of full and half brothers and sisters of the decedent, grandfather and grandmother on the side of the father and mother, and children of both categories of brothers and sisters of the decedent (Article 1143, Civil Code); the *third* priority comprises the full and half brothers and sisters of the parents of the decedent (uncles and aunts of the decedent) and first cousins of the decedent by right of representation (Article 1144, Civil Code); the *fourth* priority consists of the relatives of the third degree of kinship, the great-grandfather and great-grandmother of the decedent.[2] The *fifth* priority is made up of relatives of the fourth degree of kinship – children of full cousins of the decedent (grandchildren once removed) and own brothers and sisters of his grandfather and grandmother (grandfathers and grandmothers once removed). The *sixth* priority comprises relatives of the fifth degree of kinship – children of grandchildren once removed of the decedent (great-grandchildren once removed), children of his brothers and sisters once removed (nephews and nieces once removed), and children of his grandfathers and grandmothers once removed (uncles and aunts once removed). The *seventh* priority does not consist of relatives, but of relations of the decedent: stepchildren,

[2] These four priorities fully coincide with those provided for by the 1964 RSFSR Civil Code (Article 532, as amended 14 May 2001).

stepdaughters, step-father, and step-mother of the decedent. The *eighth* priority comprises dependents of the decedent who do not have the capacity to work; when there are other heirs by operation of law they inherit together and equally with heirs of that priority which is called upon to inherit. In the absence of other heirs by operation of law dependents not having labor capacity of the decedent inherit autonomously as heirs of the eighth priority (Article 1148, Civil Code).

The fifth through the eighth priorities were added to heirs by operation of law as part of the civil law reforms of the late 1990s. Each priority inherits in succession. If there are no heirs of the first priority, the heirs of the second priority inherit, and so on. The existence of even one heir in an eligible priority excludes all lower priorities from inheriting. As provided in Article 1141 of the Civil Code, the grounds for calling a subsequent priority of heirs to inherit arises when at the moment of opening an inheritance there are no heirs alive of the preceding priorities, or all heirs have proved to be unworthy, or heirs of preceding priorities were deprived of the right to inherit by a will, or none of the heirs of the preceding priority accepted the inheritance, or all heirs of the preceding priority refused the inheritance without indicating to whose benefit the refusal was made (Article 1157 and 1158, Civil Code).

The heirs of one priority receive the property due to them in equal shares except for inheritance by right of representation (Article 1141(2), Civil Code).

Heirs of first priority. Children, spouse, and parents of the decedent are heirs of the first priority (Article 1142(1), Civil Code). Children inherit from their parents on the basis of biological origin as certified by information concerning the parents on the birth certificate of the child issued by the Registry for Acts of Civil Status. The procedure for entering such information is regulated by the Family Code of the Russian

Federation (Chapter 10)[3] and by the Federal Law 'On Acts of Civil Status" (Chapters 2 and 6).[4]

The origin of a child from the mother is established without reference to the fact of whether she was married to the father or to the means of conception (natural or artificial insemination). Motherhood or maternity under the Family Code (Article 48) is determined on the basis of documents confirming the birth of the child in a medical institution, and if the child is born outside a medical institution, on the basis of medical documents, witness testimony, or other evidence. The Federal Law on Acts of Civil Status contains more detail on the requisite documentation and signatures on the documents.

In instances of surrogate motherhood, by agreement between the surrogate mother and the spouses the mother has the right to keep the child born and make an entry concerning her motherhood in the register of acts of civil status (Article 51, Family Code). A child born to the registered surrogate mother as a result of the implantation of an embryo will later, if called to inherit, by an heir by operation of law of the surrogate mother (Article 53, Family Code).

The procedure for determining the origin of a child from the father differs, depending upon whether the mother was married to the father or not. If she was married, the paternity of the husband is presumed and information concerning the father of the child is entered in the birth register on the basis of the marriage certificate of the child's mother. If the child was born within 300 days from the moment of dissolution of the marriage or from when marriage was deemed to be invalid, or from the moment of death of the spouse, the father of the child is deemed to be the spouse of the mother. If the mother of the child at the moment of the birth thereof was not married, information concerning the child's father is entered on the basis of an act establishing paternity, such act being based on the joint declaration of the father and mother of the child, or by

[3] Translated in Butler, *Russia & The Republics* (looseleaf service; 2006-).

[4] Translated in Butler, *Russian Public Law* (3d ed.; 2013), pp. 945-979.

the father of the child under certain designated circumstances, or by decision of a court (Article 49, Family Code). The judicial procedure for determining paternity differs depending upon whether the father of the child is alive or not at the moment the judicial decision is rendered.

If paternity is established in the procedure established by law, a child born of parents who were not married to one another and the father have the same mutual rights and duties as when a child is born of persons who are married to one another (Article 53, Family Code), including the right to inherit after one another as heirs of the first priority. If paternity is not established, then the child and the man who is his father are not called to inherit by operation of law in this capacity.

Children are not eliminating from inheriting after the death of parents whose marriage was subsequently deemed to be invalid (Article 30, Family Code) or who were deprived of parental rights (Article 71, Family Code).

The surviving spouse inherits together with children in the first priority as heirs by operation of law. The spouse of the decedent is the person who at the moment of opening the inheritance is married to the decedent. The general rule in the Russian Federation is that only a marriage concluded at the Registry for Acts of Civil Status is recognized (Article 1, Family Code). A person is deemed to be married from the day of State registration of the marriage (Article 10, Family Code). State registration of a marriage is confirmed by a marriage certificate. The rights of a spouse to an inheritance do not depend upon the duration of the marriage or whether the spouse remarried after the opening of the inheritance. If the day of opening the inheritance coincided with the day of State registration of the marriage, the spouse of the decedent would be considered to be an heir. When necessary, the fact of State registration of a marriage may be established by a court.

Citizens of the Russian Federation abroad may conclude a marriage at diplomatic missions or consulates of the Russian Federation (Article 157, Family Code). Marriages of Russian citizens with foreigners or stateless persons or marriages of foreigners between themselves are recognized in Russia provided that they are in compliance with the legislation of the State on whose territory they are married and do not violate the rules of the Russian Family Code that would prevent marriage (Article 14). Marriages between foreigners concluded in Russia at the diplomatic mission or consulate of a foreign State are deemed to be valid in Russia on the basis of reciprocity provided these persons are citizens of the State which appointed the ambassador or consul (Article 157, Family Code).

De facto marriage relations, that is, cohabitation, does not give rise to rights of inheritance, subject to certain exceptions prior to 1944 pursuant to Soviet legislation. Although Russian doctrine has pursued the discussion of whether it would be advisable to recognize cohabitation as creating the right to inherit, noting in so doing the experience of some foreign jurisdictions, this is not supported in Russian legislation. The best means for cohabiting individuals to inherit from one another would be to draw up wills accordingly or to be able to prove that one such person was dependent on the other as someone who did not have labor capacity (Article 1148, Civil Code).

A person who divorced the decedent cannot be called to inherit as a surviving spouse. The moment of termination of a marriage is the day on which the dissolution was registered at the Registry for Acts of Civil Status or the day on which a judicial decision granting a divorce entered into force (Article 25, Family Code). If the day of opening an inheritance coincides with the day of termination of a marriage, the person with whom the marriage was terminated will not be deemed to be an heir. Russian law does not know inheritance by contract, which precludes spouses who conclude a marriage contract from including any conditions that affect inheritance. The Family Code (Article 40) provides that a marriage contract determines property rights of spouses in a marriage "and/or in the event of the dissolution thereof". This formulation excluded the possibility of spouses including provisions intended to address other situations such as termination of marriage in the event of death of a spouse.[5]

On the other hand, although the surviving spouse is a first priority heir, he or she does not within that priority have any privileges or limitations with respect to the property of the decedent spouse. The preferential right to receive ordinary household articles, for example, belongs to any heir who resided on the day of opening the inheritance with the decedent and not merely the spouse who lived with the decedent (Article 1169, Civil Code). However, when determining what the surviving spouse should receive, the regime of spousal property at the moment of opening the inheritance needs careful consideration. Property acquired by spouses during marriage becomes their common joint ownership (Article 34, Family Code), which means they have equal rights to possess, use, and dispose of this property. The earnings of the spouse are immaterial. One spouse may not be employed anywhere and occupy herself or himself with household matters and raising the children, but nonetheless will have equal rights to the property of the marriage.

Russian legislation expressly mentions types of property acquired during marriage: revenues of each spouse from labor or entrepreneurial activity and results of intellectual activity, pensions or benefits received and other payments of money not having a special targeted purpose. Moveable and immoveable things acquired from the common revenues fall into this category: securities, deposits, shares in capital, deposits in credit institutions, or any other property acquired by the spouses during marriage irrespective of in whose name the property is held (Article 34, Family Code). Moreover, by the marriage contract this regime of common ownership may extend to other property (Article 42, Family Code).

In addition, each spouse may have his or her own personal property, which would include that acquired before marriage, property received by one spouse by way of inheritance, gift,

[5] See L. Maksimovich, Брачный договор [Marriage Contract] (1997), p. 40.

or other gratuitous transaction; of property acquired during marriage, including from common assets, that was intended for one of the spouses (clothing, footwear, articles for professional use), awards, and others. These regimes have different consequences. Personal property of the decedent passes by inheritance to heirs in the usual procedure, including the proper share to the surviving spouse. As for property in common joint ownership of husband and wife, the right of the surviving spouse to inherit is not eliminated or reduced by the right of this spouse to part of the property acquired during marriage (Article 1150, Civil Code). The right belonging to each spouse to part of the property which is in their common joint ownership is not counted when the inheritance is opened after the death of one of the spouses in the inheritance share of the surviving spouse. The procedure works as follows: first the share of the surviving spouse in property held by common joint ownership is calculated for the surviving spouse as owner; this portion does not pass by inheritance. The balance is part of the estate, and the surviving spouse inherits this portion together with all other eligible heirs.

To clarify the position, the surviving spouse will seek a certificate from the notary of the right of ownership to a participatory share in common property acquired during marriage. This might be obtained before an inheritance is opened, or after by the surviving spouse. An application for such a certificate from the notary will need to be accompanied by evidence confirming, first, that the spouses are married to one another; second, the act of acquiring the property during the marriage; and third, the fact that particular property is in their common joint ownership.

If a marriage is deemed to be invalid from the day it was concluded (Article 27, Family Code), the former spouse loses the right to inherit. Russian law, however, does recognize the status of a "good-faith spouse" (Article 30) whose marriage a court deemed to be invalid. Although the status of a good-faith spouse will not give rise to inheritance rights, such a spouse may demand an apportionment of property jointly-acquired during the marriage pursuant to the rules for the division of common property of spouses (Articles 34, 35, and 38, Family Code). That right of a good-faith spouse can be exercised after the death of the decedent, in which event such property would be deducted from the property forming part of the estate of the decedent.

The parents of the decedent are the individuals from whom the decedent originated. The evidence of this origin is the birth certificate of the child or other documents confirming parentage. The mother inherits after the death of any of her children; the father inherits after the death of children on the same grounds that the children inherit after him. Parents deprived of parental rights and not reinstated in those rights at the moment an inheritance is opened do not have the right to inherit after the death of the children. This provision of the Civil Code (Article 1117) is consistent with the Family Code (Article 71), according to which parents deprived of parental rights lose all rights based on the fact of kinship with a child with respect to whom they were deprived of parental rights.

Heirs of second priority. The heirs of the second priority are the full and half brothers and sisters of the deceased and the grandfather and grandmother thereof on the side of the father and mother (Article 1143, Civil Code). The brothers and sisters of the decedent are relatives along the indirect line of kinship having a common ancestor. As a rule, birth certificates establish the necessary kinship, although such legal facts may also be established by a judicial decision. Brothers and sisters of the decedent whose relationship is more distant than second degree are not called to inherit in the second priority.

The grandmother and grandfather of the decedent are the primogenitors of the decedent. They are related to the decedent along the direct ascending line. Kinship is established on the basis of birth certificates of the parents of the decedent. The grandparents on the side of the mother are always heirs, and the grandparents on the side of the father inherit only if the father was in a registered marriage with the mother at the moment of the birth of the child or the paternity thereof was recognized in the established procedure (Articles 49 and 50, Family Code).

Heirs of third priority. The heirs of the third priority are full or half brothers and sisters of parents of the decedent (uncles and aunts) – relatives along the indirect line of the third degree of kinship. Their origin is identical to that of the father and mother of the decedent. Proof of kinship is established by the kinship link between the heir and his brother or sister and then by the link between the last and the decedent. Russian doctrine assumes that those who fall into this priority comprise separate solitary family groups that maintain stable periodic ties and contact with one another and, when necessary, assist one another. There is, or believed to be, a sense of family responsibility of brothers and sisters for the fate of children born to each unit – all of which serves to justify these individuals comprising the third priority in the event of inheritance by operation of law.

Heirs of fourth to sixth priorities. Article 1145 of the Civil Code combines the heirs of the fourth to the sixth priorities. These are relatives of the third, fourth, and fifth degrees of kinship to the decedent who do not fall into higher priorities. It would be unusual at this distance from the decedent for all these relatives to be personally acquainted with one another or with the decedent. Although birth certificates will be helpful to some extent in establishing kinship with the decedent, they will in all likelihood need to be supplemented by other documents, such as marriage certificates confirming a change of surnames. The legal fact of kinship may be confirmed by a court in the procedure established by a law. In practice relatives of the decedent at this distance of kinship are unlikely to know one another at all, which limits the actual possibilities of their being called to inherit by operation of law.

Heirs of seventh priority. The seventh priority represents the first time in Russian legal history that stepsons, stepdaughters, stepfathers, and stepmothers of decedents have been mentioned in the law of inheritance (Article 1145(3), Civil Code). There is no legal definition in Russian legislation of these concepts, even though they are mentioned in the Family Code (Article 97).

The sole definitions are doctrinal or lexicographical in nature. These individuals are sufficiently remote from the decedent in priority that their actual exercise of the right to inherit will be uncommon, notwithstanding the fact that they may have closer personal contacts with the decedent than persons in the fourth through sixth priorities. The absence of legal definitions makes it difficult to determine what evidence they would need to submit in order to establish their status.

RIGHT OF REPRESENTATION

Article 1146 of the Civil Code makes provision for a special mechanism for calling heirs to inherit by operation of law called inheritance by right of representation: "the participatory share of an heir by operation of law who has died before the opening of an inheritance or simultaneously with the decedent shall pass by right of representation to his respective descendants in the instances provided for by Article 1142(2), Article 1143(2), and Article 1144(2) of the present Code, and shall be divided between them equally".

The term "representation" has long been criticized in Russian legal doctrine as not being apt: in fact the heir who replaces the principal "represents" no one. Those eligible to inherit by right of representation are the grandchildren of the decedent and descendants thereof in the first priority (Article 1142, Civil Code); nieces and nephews of the decedent in the second priority (Article 1143); and first cousins of the decedent in the third priority (Article 1144). No other heirs or their children may inherit by right of representation.

The right of representation is regarded as an embodiment of the individual principle in inheritance by operation of law. Persons who died simultaneously with the decedent do not inherit after the decedent (Article 1114); the same follows if they died before the opening of the inheritance (Article 1141).

The fact that inheritance by right of representation is addressed in the provisions of the Civil Code regulating priorities is perceived variously in Russian legal doctrine. Some have argued that a person who inherits by right of representation does not do so within a priority because such individuals are called to inherit even though other heirs exist in the same priority. [6]The contrary view sees no inconsistencies in the formulation of the relevant provisions in this respect.[7] Questions persist, however, as to what should be the consequences if an heir is removed from the right to inherit by reason of unworthiness or analogous grounds: should this deprive eligible relatives from the right to inherit by right of representation. In other words, is proximity of kinship the operative principle, or should the behavior of the heir being represented influence the outcome. A literal interpretation of Article 1146(2) and (3) of the Civil Code is not consistent with the model of inheriting by right of representation.[8]

RIGHTS OF DEPENDENTS AND ADOPTED PERSONS

Dependents. The notion that indigent individuals who do not have the capacity to work should constitute a special category of heirs and inherit by operation of law (Article 1148, Civil Code) first appeared in Russian law in the Dekret of 27 April 1918 "On the Abolition of Inheritance". The 1922 Civil Code of the RSFSR (Article 418) made reference to the category of heirs by operation of law including "indigent persons not capable of working completely dependent on the deceased for not less than one year before his death". This category of individuals was retained in the amendments to inheritance law introduced in 1945 and again in the 1961 Fundamental Principles of

[6] See A. L. Makovskii, in A. L. Makovskii and E. A. Sukhanov (eds.), Комментарий к части третьей Гражданского кодекса Российской Федерации [Commentary to Part Three of the Civil Code of the Russian Federation] (2003), p. 183; B. L. Khaskel'berg, «Наследование по праву представления и переход права на принятие наследства» [Inheritance by Right of Representation and Transfer of the Right to Accept an Inheritance], in Цивилистические записки [Civilist Notes (2004), III, pp. 228-229.

[7] O. Iu. Shilokhvost, Наследование по закону в российском гражданскгм праве [Inheritance by Operation of Law in Russian Civil Law] (2012), p. 95.

[8] Ibid., pp. 131-132.

Civil Legislation of the USSR and Union Republics (Article 532). Doctrinal writings in Russia sometimes referred to this category of heirs as a "floating priority".[9] Accordingly, from 1922 onwards the indicia of lacking the capacity to work and indigency were used not to limit the group of heirs by operation of law but to enlarge that group by including within it not only blood relatives, but any such dependents.

The doctrinal gloss is of particular interest here. The "social" principle doubtless was predominant in the decision to include such dependents within the group of heirs by operation of law: the State would otherwise be obliged to support such individuals, whereas if they were intestate heirs, a source of primary support was not only immediately at hand, but already established. But a second and perhaps more powerful line of reasoning developed in justification of this approach: it was appropriate to regard this category as heirs by operation of law because they were *de facto* part of the family[10] and to so recognize this was to give further recognition of the wishes of the decedent:

> Inasmuch as the decedent maintained them when living, one may assume that when drawing up a will he would have left something to them after death. The law thus attempts to assume and fulfill the orientation of the will of the decedent with respect to dependents.[11]

The Civil Code of the Russian Federation clarified and imposed more severe requirements for indigents as heirs by operation of law, arguably weakening the "social" principle present in these policies. First, the Civil Code created different conditions for indigents not capable of working to inherit, depending upon whether they qualified as heirs by operation

[9] Z. G. Krylova, in L. P. Anufrieva (ed.), Комментарий к Гражданскому кодексу Российской Федерации. Часть третья (постатейный) [Commentary to the Civil Code of the Russian Federation. Part Three (Article-by-Article)] (2004), p. 129.

[10] M. V. Gordon, Наследование по закону и по завещанию [Inheritance by Operation of Law and Will] (1967), p. 23.

[11] M. V. Teliukina, quoted in M. S. Abramenkov and P. V. Chugunov, Наследственное право [Inheritance Law] (2013), p. 276.

of law in the sixth and subsequent priorities or whether they qualified as being in the second to the seventh categories or not. In the first instance in order to be called to inherit they had to satisfy the same conditions as in the 1964 RSFSR Civil Code: to lack the capacity to work on the day of opening the inheritance for not less than a year before the decedent's death (Article 1148(1), Civil Code). In the second instance a dependent who is not within any of the seven priorities must in order to be called to inherit, in addition to lacking the capacity to work and being dependent on the decedent for a year, also live jointly with the decedent (Article 1148(2), Civil Code). Absent meeting those requirements, such a dependent would not qualify as an heir and the property of the decedent would escheat to the State.

The capacity to work is established under Russian law by social security legislation, most especially the Federal Law of 17 December 2001, "On Labor Pensions in the Russian Federation"[12] and of 15 December 2001, "On State Pension Security in the Russian Federation".[13] Russian notarial and judicial practice consider persons to lack capacity to work if they are women who have reached the age of 55 or males, aged 60; disabled persons of the I, II, and III categories irrespective of whether these persons have been assigned a pension for old age or disability; individuals who have not reached the age of 16 or, if they are studying, the age of 18.

There is no definition of "indigent" or "indigency" in the Civil Code. The Federal Law on Labor Pensions in the Russian Federation provides that indigency occurs when the assistance of a decedent is the principal source of existence of a person who does not have the capacity to work. Even if a person lacking the capacity to work received a pension but it was insufficient to exist and the decedent regularly supplemented the pension without which the recipient could not subsist, indigency would exist. Whether the decedent supplied subsistence as his moral

[12] СЗ РФ (2001), no. 52(I), item 4920, as amended.

[13] СЗ РФ (2001), no. 51, item 4831, as amended.

duty or did so through compulsory alimony payments is immaterial.

However, the recipient of a citizen who lacked labor capacity but received maintenance for life under a contract of rent (Article 601, Civil Code) would not qualify as an heir by operation of law. The reason is that the rent encumbers the estate of the decedent and the duty to pay passes on to his heirs.

Given the evidentiary issues in establishing the fact of dependence on a decedent, the matter is likely to be best confirmed by a judicial decision establishing the legal fact of dependence. Russian courts have been instructed how to address the issue.[14]

Adopted persons. Adoption is defined in Russian legal doctrine as a special legal act of accepting another's minor child into the family of the adoptive person in order to provide to that child complete maintenance and proper physical and spiritual upbringing. Adoption is recognized by legislation as a basis for the inclusion of the adopted person among heirs by operation of law. A person is adopted pursuant to a judicial decision (Articles 269-275, Code of Civil Procedure of the Russian Federation).[15] The adoption of brothers and sisters by different persons is not permitted. The fact of adoption is confirmed by the judicial decision to establish the adoption and/or by a certificate of adoption issued by the Registry for Acts of Civil Status. These documents are deemed to be the sole evidence of adoption if the adoption was performed on the territory of the Russian Federation after 29 September 1996.

An adopted person and his descendants, on one side, and the adoptive person and his relatives, on the other, are equated to relatives by origin (blood relatives) (Article 1147(1), Civil Code). The Family Code of the Russian Federation (Article 137) provides that "adopted children shall lose personal nonproperty

[14] See point 31, Decree of the Plenum of the Supreme Court of the Russian Federation, 29 May 2012, No. 9.

[15] See W. E. Butler, *Russian Civil and Arbitrazh Procedure* (2012), pp. 109-112.

and property rights and shall be relieved from duties with respect to their own parents (or own relatives)". With respect to inheritance, this provision is made more explicit: "An adopted person and his descendant shall not inherit by operation of law after the death of the parents of the adopted person and others of his relatives by origin, and the parents of the adopted person and others of his relatives by origin shall not inherit by operation of law after the death of the adopted person and his descendant", save for instances specified in point 3 of Article 1147.

Russian legal doctrine long supported the view, which also found reflection in Russian family legislation, that "when in accordance with the Family Code of the Russian Federation an adopted person retains by decision of a court relations with one of the parents or other relatives by origin, an adopted person and his descendant shall inherit by operation of law after the death of these relatives, and the last shall inherit by operation of law after the death of the adopted person and his descendant" (Article 1147[3]).

Inheritance legislation in the Russian Federation does not address the consequences that follow if an adoption is revoked or cancelled. Ioffe argued that if an adoption is revoked "it loses the significance of a legal fact also in the domain of inheritance".[16] An adoption is revoked in a judicial proceeding (Article 140, Family Code). The result is that the "mutual rights and duties of the adopted child and adoptive persons terminate and the mutual rights and duties of the child and his parents or relatives are restored if the interests of the child so require (Article 143, Family Code). The phrase "if the interests of the child so require" indicates that when an adoption is revoked, the rights and duties of the child and the parents thereof are not automatically restored. If the child involved in the revoked adoption is still a minor, one might anticipate that the rights and duties of the original parents would be restored. The same

[16] O. S. Ioffe, Советское гражданское право: курс лекций [Soviet Civil Law: Course of Lectures] (1965), III, p. 300.

would not necessarily follow if the adopted child reached majority. The implication is compelling that the provisions of the Family Code concerning the revocation of an adoption were formulated without any thought being given to the implications for inheritance. Likewise unregulated is the issue of what transpires if a judicial decision to revoke an adoption enters into force after the opening of an inheritance of the adoptive person.

ESCHEAT PROPERTY

The concept, if not the terminology, of escheat was known to Russian doctrine and practice before the 1917 revolutions and in the 1922 Civil Code of the RSFSR, as well as later legislation. The 1964 RSFSR Civil Code and earlier enactments preferred the expression "transfer of inheritance property to the State"[17] or "transfer of an inheritance to the State". This term is broader than "escheat", for property may be transferred to the State through inheritance by will or by operation of law.

Under the Civil Code of the Russian Federation, property becomes escheat if there are no heirs with respect to that property by operation or law or by will. As expressed in Article 1151 of the Civil Code: "If heirs are lacking both by operation of law and by will, or none of the heirs has the right to inherit, or all heirs have been removed from inheriting (Article 1117), or none of the heirs had accepted the inheritance, or all the heirs have refused the inheritance and in so doing none of them has specified that he is refusing in favor of another heir (Article 1158), the property of the deceased shall be considered to be escheat".

Under this approach, escheat property ensues by way of inheritance to the ownership of the Russian Federation. Legal succession is the very essence of this approach and determines the fate of the property as a whole in the estate, including things,

[17] See, for example, the Rules for the Transfer of Inheritance Property to the State, confirmed on 28 December 1943 by the Council of People's Commissars of the USSR.

rights, duties, and so on belonging to a natural person. Succession operates only in the event of the opening of an inheritance. Some Russian jurists within the context of inheritance law theory characterize escheat as a default situation in which the norms regulating the procedure for inheritance "did not work".

The grounds for escheat are almost never evident at the moment when an inheritance opens and can be determined only after the period elapses for ascertaining whether there are any heirs and to search for them, or to confirm that any possible heirs are unworthy, or do not accept or refuse to accept the estate. The reasons that heirs may prefer not to accept an inheritance are sundry: the estate is too minimal to be worth the bother; there are no heirs; or ignorance that an inheritance has been opened and the period for acceptance has lapsed.

The duration of this period for seeking heirs, however, is not precisely indicated in Russian legislation. Nor is there a special procedure for declaring inheritance property to be escheat. That status is acquired from the moment the inheritance is opened until ownership of the property passes to the State; throughout this period of indeterminacy, the property must be protected and managed. The question remains what consequences flow from the interval of time between the opening of an estate and the completion of procedures to identify and seek possible heirs: in effect the State acquires *de facto* title to the property when those procedures are completed, but legal title vests from the moment the inheritance was opened – in effect, an element of retroactivity.

It is possible for only part of an estate to become escheat. This might occur when only part of an estate was bequeathed, there were no heirs by operation of law to the balance of the property, and this unbequeathed part did not fall under the operation of rules concerning an increment of unbequeathed property. Russian doctrine is divided on the subject. Some writers deny the possibility of partial escheat in the case of intestate succession, taking the position that in principle this is impossible and in practice does not arise. The suggestion that if a testator has devised only an individual thing or part of his property to a sole outside heir, in the absence of heirs by operation of law the testament should be read as "ambiguous" and not operate to prevent all the estate property passing to the sole heir, including, if necessary, by analogy the application of rules relating to an increment to the estate.[18]

This approach constitutes an expansive interpretation of the will and the attribution to it of dispositions that the testator did not in fact make or apparently have any intention to make. The alternative view reads the will more literally, consistent with long-standing Russian approaches, and would recognize partial escheat.[19]

The Russian Federation, subjects of the Russian Federation,[20] or municipal formations thereof may receive property by way of escheat. However, municipal formations may only receive immoveable property physically located on the territory of the Russian Federation. The operation of escheat differs from the usual inheritance. First, the State must accept the property passing by escheat and has no choice to accept or not. Second, the State need not perform any special act to accept the estate. The acceptance of escheat property is accomplished by virtue of a law. Third, when inheriting escheat property, the State assumes responsibility for the debts of the decedent within the limits and in the procedure as established for other heirs who have accepted an inheritance and for creditors (Article 1175, Civil Code).

If, however, the Russian Federation, subjects of the Russian Federation, or municipal formations are heirs by will, they

[18] See, among others, B. S. Antimonov and K. A. Grave, Советское наследственное право [Soviet Inheritance Law] (1955), pp. 240-241.

[19] Among the writers sharing this view, see K. B. Iaroshenko, Наследственное право [Inheritance Law] [2005), p. 157.

[20] Article 1151(2) of the Civil Code was amended on 23 July 2013 to provide that a dwelling premise, land plot, including the buildings, installations, and other objects of immoveable property situated on such land plot, and participatory share in a right of common participatory share ownership to a housing premise or objects of immoveable property, if situated on the territory of the cities of federal significance Moscow or St. Petersburg, shall pass to the ownership of those subjects of the Russian Federation. СЗ РФ (2013), no. 30(I), item 4056.

have the right just as any other heirs to accept or to refuse to accept the inheritance. The exception to this principle would be if the Russian Federation were the sole heir by will and there were no heirs by operation of law. In this event the Russian Federation, most Russian jurists concur, cannot refuse to accept the inheritance because such a refusal would be tantamount to refusing to accept escheat property. On this premise, if the Russian Federation, for example, refused to accept an inheritance as the sole heir and the property proved to be escheat, the decision refusing the estate should be formally annulled (and thereby constitute an exception to the principle of Article 1157(3) of the Civil Code that a refusal to accept an inheritance cannot be reversed).

The procedures for the Russian Federation and other relevant State entities to record, value, and realize the use of inherited or escheat property were for many decades regulated by the Decree of the USSR Council of Ministers of 29 June 1984, No. 683, "On Confirmation of the Statute on the Procedure for Recording, Valuation, and Realization of Confiscated and Masterless Property and Property Which Passed by Right of Inheritance to the State, and Treasure".[21] The Statute does not address the transfer of property to the ownership of subjects of the Russian Federation or municipal formations and regards tax agencies as the competent authorities to receive escheat property, although Russian tax legislation does not include this duty within their jurisdiction.[22]

[21] СП СССР (1984), no. 24, item 127, as amended 29 June 1989, 14 July 1990, 3 September 1990, 21 December 1990, 25 July 1991, and 15 January 2007. Available on Consultant Plus as amended; lost force 3 February 2020. Also see the Letter from the Ministry of Finances of 21 June 2006, No. 08-01-02/6-23, and the Letter of the Federal Tax Service of the Russian Federation, 19 February 2007, No. 02-3-04/3@, "On Escheat Property"; Letter of the Federal Tax Service of the Russian Federation, 4 December 2008, No. ШС-6-3/892, "On Escheat Property", both available on Consultant Plus and otherwise unpublished.

[22] The duty to receive escheat property was imposed by Decree of the Government of the Russian Federation of 27 November 2004, No. 691, "On the Federal Agency for the Administration of Federal Property", whose Statute was confirmed by the said Decree and provides in point 5.30 that this agency should act in this capacity. СЗ РФ (2004), no. 49, item 4897. The 2004 Decree was repealed by the Decree of 5 June 2008, No. 432, "On the Federal Agency for the Administration of State Property" (point 5.35), as amended. СЗ РФ (2008), no. 23, item 2721.

Consistent with the values of a market economy, it would be reasonable to conclude that the scope and structure of heirs by operation of law are designed to reduce instances of the escheat of inheritance property to the minimum – a policy reflected in the establishment of eight priorities of inheritance, a greater emphasis upon family units rather than blood relationship, and the modification of the social principle to embrace situations in which a person is actually dependent upon a decedent rather than necessarily related to the decedent. Russian jurists report that escheat, given the existence of eight priorities of heirs in the Civil Code, is encountered "significantly rarely".[23]

The Supreme Court of the Russian Federation has consistently taken the view that property, the rights to which were not formalized or were improperly formalized, is nonetheless part of an estate. If, for example, a citizen died after filing an application to privatize his dwelling premise but did not succeed in formalizing the contract for the transfer of the dwelling premise into ownership or to complete the State registration of this contract, the court nonetheless considered that the decedent had expressed his will to privatize the dwelling and incorporated the dwelling within the estate.[24] This position is reflected in the Decree of the Plenum of the Supreme Court of the Russian Federation, No. 9, of 29 May 2012 (points 8 and 9).

Russian judicial practice has encountered situations where a public formation acquired property by escheat which, by way of fraud, subsequently was acquired by a good-faith purchaser and the public formation, having later discovered the transaction, sought return of the escheat property from the good-faith acquirer. The Constitutional Court of the Russian Federation considered as follows: in 2007 some schemers succeeded in defrauding a notary and obtained a certificate of the right to inherit an escheat apartment which they sold in 2008. The public formation in 2014 filed suit to recover the

[23] T. I. Zaitseva, Судебная практика по наследственным делам [Judicial Practice with Regard to Inheritance Cases] (2007), p. 206.

[24] See Zaitseva, Нотариальная практика: ответы на вопросы [Notarial Practice: Replies to Questions] (2008), II, pp. 282-291.

apartment from the illegal possession of another; the apartment was duly registered in the good-faith acquirer's name as the true owner, having failed to undertake due diligence when the escheat apartment was sold to the new owner. The Court found in favor of the good-faith owner.[25]

[25] Decree of the Constitutional Court of the Russian Federation, 23 June 2017, No. 16-П (available on Consultant Plus).

Chapter 6

Acquisition of Inheritance

Although modern Russian civil law prefers the term "inheritance property", which in the present volume is sometimes referred to as the "estate" of the decedent, there was a period when doctrinal writings in Russia spoke of the "inheritance mass" – not a term that translates well, although it may convey better that the inheritance property may include not only things, but rights and duties and thereby give a better impression of the larger integral nature of what passes by way of inheritance. Russian inheritance law is founded on the long-established Roman-law principle of *hereditas jacens*, that an inheritance must be accepted and that such acceptance by an heir is voluntary. An heir may not accept, or may refuse to accept, an inheritance.

LEGAL REGIME OF PROPERTY AFTER OPENING AND BEFORE ACCEPTANCE OF INHERITANCE

The question arises: is there not an interval of time between the moment of death of the decedent (when the inheritance opens) and the decision to accept (or not) an estate by the heirs, whether by will or by operation of law. During this interval, what is the legal status of the inheritance property? Russian legal doctrine recognizes that the inheritance property during this interval is ownerless, masterless, abandoned, and so on. The inheritance property is *hereditas jacens*, or "lying" or in "abeyance"; that is, existing in expectation of an heir taking or accepting ownership of it.

The Digest of Laws of the Russian Empire proceeded from the "system of acceptance": "An heir may accept or not accept an inheritance, and until acceptance of an inheritance he does not have any rights to a thing" (Article 1255); the failure of an heir to act was considered non-acceptance of the inheritance (Article 1355); a ten-year period of limitations was established to receive an inheritance, calculated from the moment of the summons of heirs (Article 1246).[1] The 1922 RSFSR Civil Code likewise remained true to a system of accepting by proceeding from various presumptions, depending upon whether an heir was present at the place of opening the inheritance:

(1) tacit acquisition of an inheritance by an heir present who within three months did not declare a refusal thereof;

(2) tacit refusal of an inheritance by an heir absent who did not accept the inheritance within six months (Articles 430 and 431).[2]

These periods initially were calculated from the moment of taking protective measures. The opening of an inheritance was introduced in 1930.

The 1964 RSFSR Civil Code unified the system of accepting an inheritance. The distinction between heirs present and absent was abolished; silence was not recognized as acceptance; a common period of six months was introduced for acceptance of an inheritance, which might be prolonged by a court if there were justifiable reasons or the other heirs agreed; and additional periods would apply if other priorities of heirs were involved.

The Civil Code of the Russian Federation reinforces the perception of the status of the inheritance property being in abeyance in its approach to the filing of claims by creditors of the decedent. Such demands are filed against the heirs who have accepted the inheritance, against the executor of the inheritance, or against the inheritance property. In the last two instances a Russian court suspends the consideration until some heir accepts the inheritance or the property is deemed to be escheat and passes to the State (Article 1175(2), Civil Code). Demands concerning compensation for expenses encumbering the inheritance are submitted in an analogous manner (Article 1174(2), Civil Code). It follows that the Russian legal system

[1] I. G. Rents, in E. Iu. Petrov (ed.), Наследственное право: постатейный комментарий к статьям 1110-1185, 1224 Гражданского кодекса Российской Федерации [Inheritance Law: Article-by-Article Commentary to Articles 1110-1185, and 1224 of the Civil Code of the Russian Federation] (2018), p. 259.

[2] Ibid.

acknowledges that the inheritance property is itself not a subject of law and that the executor does not own the inheritance and accordingly is not liable for the debts of the decedent or of the inheritance property. As the court awaits the appearance of an heir, the property has no owner, no bearer of the rights and duties that attend ownership.

This view has been dismissed as a chimera, as fundamentally erroneous, as "absurd".[3] These epithets are applied because of the consequences of such an analysis, even the notion that for a fraction of a second an estate could be without a subject of the right of inheritance. On this view succession occurs instantaneously upon the death of the decedent and thereafter it is a matter of precisely determining who the heirs are and who the valid creditors are. As a "property complex", an estate is never without a subject even while the precise identity of that subject is under determination.

ACCEPTANCE OF INHERITANCE

Concept of accepting. Heirs by operation of law or by will do not automatically become the owners of the inheritance property once an inheritance is opened. They must express their will to accept the inheritance property, that is, they must accept the inheritance. This legal principle extends well back into prerevolutionary Russian law. Shershenevich wrote:

> at the moment of opening an inheritance the person designated in the will or specified in a law acquires the *right to inherit*. This right is conferred on him contrary to his wish irrespective of an intention expressed by him by virtue solely of the legal event of death ... But this right to inherit ... is not identical with the inheritance itself. The right to inherit is only a right to enter into those legal relations which in aggregate comprise inheritance.[4]

[3] M. S. Abramenkov and P. V. Chugunov, Наследственное право [Inheritance Law] (2013), p. 323.

[4] G. F. Shershenevich, Учебник русского гражданского права [Textbook of

There is an imperative element in this: not that the heir must accept the inheritance because he has no choice, but that he must make a choice to accept or not or he will have been deemed to have not accepted and does not acquire the inheritance. The acceptance is a unilateral transaction on the part of the heir. The exception is the escheat of property to a State, subject of the Russian Federation, or municipal agencies, in which event, as noted above, acceptance is not required.

Acceptance of an inheritance is attended by certain features arising from the nature of inheritance as a species of universal succession. The Civil Code provides that acceptance of part of an inheritance means the acceptance of everything due to the heir wherever located and of whatever it may consist (Article 1152(2)(1), Civil Code). This means that an heir is not required to specify exactly what inheritance property is being accepted, the more so because when the inheritance is opened the likelihood is that no one knows precisely what the estate comprises and this is subject to further empirical investigation. Acceptance, therefore, is sometimes said to have an expansive outcome, subject to the proviso that the acceptance relates only to the property due to the individual heir by way of succession and not to the entire inheritance unless the heir is the sole heir.

The Civil Code further provides that if an heir has the right to claim property within several priorities of legal succession – by will, by operation of law, by way of inheritance transmission, or as a result of the opening of an inheritance, the heir may at his choice accept the inheritance due to him within one, several, or all of the said procedures (Article 1152[2]). The fact that an heir expresses a wish to inherit to one of the said grounds does not automatically extend to the other grounds; for example,

Russian Civil Law] (reprint ed.; 2005), II, p. 402. Also see Serebrovskii, who wrote: "the opening of an inheritance does not mean that the ... person within a group of heirs ... has entered into those property rights of which the deceased was a subject. To become the successor in property rights of the decedent something else is required ... that he have expressed his consent to the acquisition of the inheritance". See V. I. Serebrovskii, Избранные труды по наследственному и страховому праву [Selected Works on Inheritance and Insurance Law] (2d ed.; 2003), p. 169.

if an heir accepts property due to him by a will, this does not automatically make him the owner of property that he would receive by operation of law nor affect the decision of any other heirs in regard to their participation in the succession (Article 1152[3]). However, there is doctrinal support for the view that an heir entitled to inherit on several grounds who refuses to inherit on one or several of those grounds is regarded as having accepted the inheritance on those grounds not rejected.[5]

With regard to the property which an heir has accepted, the heir becomes the owner thereof as a whole, at once, and at the same time (Article 1110, Civil Code) and cannot impose any conditions or reservations upon his acceptance (Article 1152, Civil Code). Contrary to mathematical logic, pursuant to which a part is never equal to the whole, the acceptance of any part of an inheritance constitutes acceptance of the entirety of the estate due thereto . As Chepig aptly expressed the position:

> "The acceptance of an inheritance is regarded by the law as a carefully thought out decision of the heir to accept it as made up of any rights and duties of the decedent of whatever they consist, whatever they constitute, and wherever they are situated".6

The inheritance property is considered to have passed to the ownership of the heir from the moment of opening the inheritance irrespective of whether the heir has actual possession of the property and irrespective of whether the property is subject to State registration (Article 1152(4), Civil Code). This is the case even though the heir could not dispose of property subject to State registration before completing that formality; some Russian jurists have described the heir's interest in the property as a "sleeping" or "latent" interest under these circumstances. A discussion is underway as to whether an

[5] See T. D. Chepig, in L. P. Anufrieva (ed.), Комментарий к Гражданскому кодексу Российской Федерации. Часть третья (постатейный) [Commentary on the Civil Code of the Russian Federation. Part Three (Article-by-Article) (2004), p. 207.

[6] Ibid., p. 158.

heir could alienate an inherited non-dwelling premise before State registration pursuant to a contract subject to a condition subsequent (registration) or whether the right to register the rights to the inherited property might itself be transferred by way of universal succession.[7]

Means of accepting inheritance. The expression "means of accepting inheritance" refers to the behavior of an heir expressing his intention to accept a share in property of a deceased due to him. The term originates in the Civil Code (Article 1153). A distinction is traditionally drawn between "formal" and "*de facto*" means of accepting. Formal acceptance occurs when the heir expresses his wish to accept the inheritance in writing before competent authorities. This may take the form of filing a statement to accept the inheritance or an application for the issuance of a certificate of the right to inherit at a notary. A statement of acceptance or application for a certificate may be delivered personally, sent by post or by courier, or filed through a representative on the basis of a power of attorney (not required for legal representatives, such as parents, adoptive parents, trustee, guardians).

Russian legislation does not exhaustively define or determine what may constitute *de facto* acceptance, but merely gives examples: taking possession and managing inheritance property; taking measures to preserve inheritance property and defend it against the claims or infringements of third persons; making expenses on own behalf to maintain inheritance property, payment of debts of the decedent and receipt of monies due to the decedent (Article 1153(2), Civil Code). These actions are all presumed to express the will of the person to be an heir and can be rebutted.

Taking possession and managing property of the decedent means establishing actual dominion over things which are part of the estate and which the heir regards as belonging to

[7] See V. A. Alekseev, «Наследование недвижимости и государственная регистрация прав» [Inheritance of an Immoveable and State Registration of Rights], Наследственное право [Inheritance Law], no. 2 (2011), pp. 21-24.

him, appropriates them, and joins them to his own property. The appropriation may take various forms, including physical possession, or relocating them to a particular place, or continuing to reside in the dwelling premise in which the heir resided jointly with the decedent. Notarial practice considers a document on the registration of the heir and decedent at the same address to be sufficient evidence of accepting the inheritance.[8] However, merely taking possession of property of a decedent may not suffice to prove the intention to accept an inheritance; it is desirable to accompany the possession with management of the property, by maintaining it in a proper state and ensuring its normal use to satisfy own requirements and needs. Management may be expressed in current maintenance or repairs, care for a garden plot, using the personal archive and papers of the deceased to locate all necessary right-establishing and financial documentation, and so on. In some instances the actions of an heir to dispose of property, for example to discard property that is subject to spoilage or is perishable, may be evidence of acceptance of an inheritance.

Actions taken to preserve and protect inheritance property against potential dangers and/or third persons may be regarded as being tantamount to the acceptance of an inheritance. These may take the form of requesting a notary to take such measures by an heir or of the heir acting independently to do so. Examples include the installation of an alarm system, replacement of a door or locks, entering into contracts with protection firms or agencies, or filing demands against other persons for the demanding and returning of the decedent's property.

The payment of the decedent's expenses for the maintenance of property may be taken as the acceptance of an inheritance. Such expenses might include the costs of housing or municipal services, taxes, urgent repairs, and the like. Acceptance of an inheritance may be evidenced by payment of the decedent's debts or the recovery of payments due to the decedent, such as repayment of a loan, payments for work or services which the

[8] Abramenkov and Chugunov, note 3 above, p. 330.

decedent ordered, receiving lease payments for property leased by the decedent to a tenant, and so on.

If the heir cannot prove by appropriate documentation to a notary the fact of performing such actions, the alternative would be to request a court to do so by way of a simplified proceeding pursuant to the Code of Civil Procedure. Although Russian law considers actions of the above nature to reflect a presumption that the heir performed them with the intention to accepted the inheritance, that presumption can be rebutted. On the other hand, Russian doctrine and judicial practice are reluctant to accept the position of a notary who rejects the claim of an heir to be such because the heir's actions did not result in the actual taking possession of property or did not fall within the period of limitations for doing so.

Russian legislation provides no specific mechanism for the acquisition of an inheritance by an inheritance foundation. In this connection there is merely a reference to the duty of a notary to issue a certificate of the right to inherit, which is in fact the next step in the formalization of the inheritance. Russian commentary suggests that because the inheritance foundation is, in effect, a forced, or necessary, heir, the fact of creation of the foundation is tantamount to accepting the inheritance.[9]

Periods for accepting inheritance. The reasons for a legislatively established period for the acceptance of an inheritance are presumed to be several. The heirs of the deceased require time to cope with the emotional stress of the death and to come, when necessary, to the place where the inheritance is opened and assemble the essential documents and information about the property concerned. The notary and/or executor may need to take measures to identify and seek the whereabouts of heirs and notify them of the opening of the inheritance.

Prerevolutionary Russian legislation took a liberal approach and fixed a general period for accepting an inheritance of ten years from the moment of being called to inherit (Article

[9] Rents, in Petrov, note 1 above, pp. 276-277.

1242, Digest of Laws of the Russian Empire), with a briefer period applicable to heirs who appeared after the estate was opened. Members of a University and officials of an educational department were given one year to accept an inheritance (Article 1251, Digest of Laws). The 1922 RSFSR Civil Code offered a six-month period, by which time the items subject to be ing inherited were significantly reduced in scope.

The Civil Code of the Russian Federation makes provision for general and special periods of limitation (Article 1154). The procedure for calculating the periods is technical and can be complex; the Plenum of the Supreme Court of the Russian Federation has offered explanations, guidance, and examples of how the periods should be calculated.[10]

The general period for accepting an inheritance is six months from the day of the opening thereof. The period begins to run from the moment of opening and relates to those heirs who become such by virtue of this legal fact. Examples of heirs who fall within this category are those by will or substitution; those by operation of law if there is no will, or there are no heirs by will, or there are unworthy heirs; and heirs of the first and/or subsequent priorities if heirs of the preceding priority are absent, were deprived of the right to inherit, or are unworthy heirs. If the precise moment of opening the inheritance cannot be determined and a court decision is necessary for this purpose, the six-month period commences to run from the moment such judicial decision enters into force.

Special periods of limitation exist for so-called special cases or situations. These arise, for example, for individuals whose right to inheritance arises as a consequence of another heir refusing to inherit or being eliminated from inheritance as being unworthy. In this event the period of limitation runs for six months from the moment their right to inherit arises (Article 1154[2]). For persons whose right to inherit arises solely because another heir has refused to accept an inheritance, the period

[10] See point 38, Decree of the Plenum of the Supreme Court of the Russian Federation, 29 May 2012, No. 9.

of limitations is three months from the day of the end of the general period for acceptance of an inheritance (Article 1154[3], Civil Code).

In practice situations arise when an heir for one reason or another failed to accept an inheritance within the established period. The legal consequences of such failure differ, depending upon the reasons. If the heir did not and should not have known about the opening of the inheritance or for other justifiable reasons allowed the period for acceptance of the inheritance to lapse, a court may upon the application of this heir restore the period of limitations and deem the heir to have accepted the inheritance provided that the heir concerned filed such an application within six months from the period when the reasons for the period lapsing fell away (Article 1155, Civil Code). Under these circumstances, the application of the heir must satisfy two criteria: (1) the reasons for the original period of limitations having lapsed must be justifiable, sometimes translated as "important", and (2) the heir must have applied to a court within not later than six months from when the reasons for the lapse "fell away" (sometimes translated as "disappeared", which is the present writer's preferred version, albeit not without controversy). Cases of this nature are considered by way of a suit, rather than a simplified proceeding, because the matter concerns the right of a person to possess part or all of the property of the decedent. The respondents would be other heirs who accepted the inheritance or public formations in the person of competent agencies who may claim escheat property. During the proceeding, the plaintiff would need to prove the circumstances which served as the reason for allowing the period to accept the inheritance to lapse and the objective impossibility of the heir accepting the inheritance in the established procedure (grave illness, serving in the Armed Forces, failure to have reached legal age at time when acceptance should have been made and parents, guardians, or trustees did not or could not properly perform their duties to defend the interests of a minor; extended period on business trip, and so on).

The very filing of an application by an heir under these circumstances is regarded by the Civil Code as evidence that the applicant wishes to accept the inheritance due thereto. Accordingly, the Civil Code does not "restore" the lapsed period pursuant to a court decision, as was the approach under the 1964 RSFSR Civil Code, but rather proceeds directly to recognizing the heir as entitled to inherit or not.

The Civil Code permits an extra-judicial procedure to resolve the dispute when an heir fails to accept an inheritance within the established period. If the heirs who have accepted an inheritance within the established periods give their consent in written form to the heir who allowed the period for acceptance to lapse to his become an heir, that extra-judicial procedure will operate to enable the said heir to inherit, provided that: (1) all heirs who accepted the inheritance must give consent, and any heir who does not consent need not give reasons for this; (2) the consent is given in written form either before a notary or with notarial certification of the document on which the heir has placed his consent by way of signature; and (3) the reasons and duration of the period for accepting the inheritance having lapsed are immaterial.

If a judicial decision is rendered to recognize the rights of an heir whose period for acceptance has lapsed, the principal consequence is possible redistribution of the property among all the heirs and the need to determine the respective share of each, or to the complete exclusion of certain heirs from the estate. If certificates of the right to inherit were issued, they would be deemed by the court to be invalid and entries made in the State registers for immoveable property might be annulled. In the event of conciliation amongst the heirs with regard to redistribution, the certificates of the right to inherit previously issued by a notary would be annulled and new certificates issued; the last would be the basis for re-registrations of immoveable property, for example, in a State register.

Inheritance foundations. By definition an inheritance foundation is a sole heir. Any other perception would undercut the very conception of the foundation. The foundation is formed solely on the basis of estate property which the foundation manages after the inheritance is opened in execution of the last will of the testator. Failure to accept the inheritance is inconceivable, which would be contrary to the will of the testator.

Other objective factors might result in the foundation not qualifying as an heir: invalidity of the will, or impossibility of founding the foundation. But this would not be an exercise of choice by the heir-foundation. As one commentator observed, the inheritance foundation is not an ordinary heir,, "but rather a means of consolidation, management, and distribution of property assets *mortis causa*".[11]

Inheritance transmission. The transmission of an inheritance is defined in Russian legal doctrine as the transfer in aggregate of two powers: the power to accept an inheritance and the power to refuse to accept an inheritance.[12] The Civil Code provides (Article 1156) that if an heir called to inherit by will or by operation of law dies after the opening of an inheritance without having succeeded in accepting that inheritance within the established period of limitation, the right to accept the inheritance passed to his heirs by operation of law, and if all the inherited property was bequeathed by will, to the decedent's heirs by will.

Four criteria therefore must be satisfied for inheritance transmission to operate: (1) an inheritance is opened after the death of a certain person; (2) there is a successor determined by law or by will to the estate of the decedent who has the right to inherit a share of the decedent's property – assuming he has not been deprived of the right to inherit and is not an unworthy heir; (3) the deceased heir, sometimes called in Russian the transmittent, dies after the opening of the estate without having succeeded in accepting it; (4) the right to inherit property directed by behest of the legislator to the transmittent passed to

11 Rents, in note 1 above, p. 262.

12 Abramenkov and Chugunov, note 3 above, p. 337.

his legal heirs or, if he left all his property by will, to his heirs by will, sometimes in Russian referred to as the transmittees.

It follows that the heirs of the transmittent upon the transmittent's death acquire by right of inheritance in two blocks of property: in the property of the transmittent himself, and in the property of the inheritor of the transmittent who did not leave a living successor. The decision whether to accept each of these transmissions lies with the transmittees themselves. Article 1156 is misleading when it provides that the right to accept the inheritance passed by way of transmission, for in fact the right to inherit as a whole passes by transmission, including the right to refuse to accept. It has been aptly observed that inheritance transmission is "singular transitory succession in the law of inheritance".[13]

A transmittee exercises the rights to inherit on the general grounds within the periods of limitation established by the Civil Code, subject to the proviso that if the period after the death of the transmittent for accepting the inheritance is less than three months, that period is extended to three months. If the period of limitation lapsed for justifiable reasons, a court may reinstate the period pursuant to Article 1155 of the Civil Code. The conciliation procedure for accepting an inheritance is not applicable in this situation. The right to an obligatory share in an inheritance, being a purely personal right, does not pass by way of inheritance transmission (Article 1156[3], Civil Code).

The innovations introduced by Article 1156 are, on the whole, regarded as an improvement by Russian commentators of the previously existing approach.[14]

REFUSAL OF INHERITANCE

The right to refuse to accept an inheritance, also characterized as the renunciation or right to renounce an inheritance, is

[13] V. A. Belov, Гражданское право [Civil Law] (2d ed.; 2012), I, p. 483.

[14] See S. A. Smirnov, in Petrov, note 1 above, pp. 291-292, who calls these innovations a "radical change" in the treatment of inheritance transmission and a "purification" of transmission from "historical delusions".

regarded as an integral element of the right of inheritance and known to all contemporary legal orders. Under Russian law only State or other public formations are forced heirs obliged to accept escheat property and an inheritance foundation and have no right of refusal (Articles 1116 and 1151, Civil Code).

The Digest of Laws of the Russian Empire recognized the pure or simple refusal (Article 1255), but not the directed refusal; however, assignment of the right to inherit was acceptable and frequently encountered, especially on the territories of the Poltava and Chernihiv provinces. Acceptance of the inheritance occurred from the moment of notarial certification of the assignment agreement; creditors of the estate might file demands against either the heir or the acquirer of the inheritance.

The 1922 RSFSR Civil Code (Article 433) permitted only the simple refusal and prohibited (Article 422) individuals outside the family of the deceased from receiving an inheritance. That prohibition was weakened in 1945 and removed from the 1964 RSFSR Civil Code; the latter permitted the redistribution of inheritance property among those called to inherit but resisted refusal to the benefit of outsiders.[15]

Concept and means of refusal of inheritance. The refusal of an inheritance has been described in doctrinal writings as a "strictly formal unilateral transaction by means of which an heir called to succeed after a deceased person renounced the property, or share thereof, due to him".[16] The decision whether to be an heir or not is consistent with the approach of the Civil Code (Article

[15] See the Decree of the Plenum of the Supreme Court of the USSR, 10 April 1957, No. 2, "On Judicial Practice with Regard to Cases on Inheritance", and before it, the Decree of the Plenum of the Supreme Court of the USSR, 20 June 1947, which prohibited refusal to the benefit of other heirs. For the view that only a simple refusal was permitted, see R. O. Khalfina, Право наследования в СССР [Right of Inheritance in the USSR] (1951), p. 58. Serebrovskii agreed with not allowing refusal, but alluded to the possibility of assigning an inheritance participatory share to another heir. See V. I. Serebrovskii, Очерки советского наследственного права [Survey of Soviet Inheritance Law] (1953), pp. 180-181, cited in Petrov, note 1 above, p. 298.

[16] Abramenkov and Chugunov, note 3 above, p. 339.

1) that civil rights and duties are acquired by the volition of and in the interest of the subject of civil law concerned and should, just as other civil rights and duties, be determined freely and without coercion of any kind whatsoever. The Civil Code provides (Article 1157) that the refusal of an inheritance should be taken within the same period of limitations for the acceptance of an inheritance. Until acceptance or refusal is determined by the relevant individuals or institutions concerned, the process of succession remains incomplete.

An heir who has accepted an inheritance has the right to change his mind if this decision is taken within the applicable period of limitations. This will normally arise in situations when the heir formally states his position before a notary or other competent official. If the heir relies upon actions of acceptance or rejection of an inheritance, these may be confirmed by a court, in which event the court may decide that the actions of the heir are tantamount to refusal (Article 1157(2), Civil Code). It is also possible that the heir will allow the period for acceptance to lapse but nonetheless the court deems him to have accepted and will not accept the arguments that the lapse was intended; the Civil Code does not expressly address this situation, which is regarded by some Russian jurists as an unfortunate and unjust omission.

The Civil Code imposes a number of requirements for the refusal of an inheritance: (1) a formal statement must be filed at the place of opening an inheritance with the competent official empowered to issue a certificate of the right to inherit; if the statement is not handed over personally by the heir, the signature thereof must be attested by analogy with the rules for acceptance of an inheritance. If the refusal is made via a representative of the refusing heir, the representative must produce a respective power of attorney expressly authorizing him to refuse the estate on behalf of the heir concerned (Article 1159); (2) a refusal may not be accompanied by conditions or reservations (Article 1158); (3) a refusal duly formalized and being in essence a valid transaction expressing the true and freely expressed intention of the heir may not be subsequently changed or revoked (Article 1157); (4) an heir may not refuse part of the property within the framework of a grounds of inheriting or ground for accepting an inheritance under which the heir accepted the inheritance. However, if property is due to an heir under several grounds of inheriting or grounds for acceptance of an inheritance, the heir has the right to refuse to accept under several or all these grounds (Article 1158); (5) a refusal of an inheritance by a minor or by a person limited in or lacking dispositive legal capacity is permitted only with the prior consent of trusteeship and guardianship agencies (Article 1157); (6) a testamentary legacy may be refused, but not with reservations or conditions or to the benefit of other persons (Article 1160); (7) refusal of escheat property is not permitted (Article 1157).

Types of refusal of inheritance. The Civil Code (Article 1157[1]) provides that an heir has the right to refuse an inheritance to the benefit of other persons (directed refusal) or without indicating the persons to whose benefit the heir is refusing the inheritance (pure or simple refusal).

The addressees of a directed refusal may be any persons from among heirs by will or by operation of law of any priority, irrespective of being called to inherit, who are not deprived of inheritance, including those called to inherit by right of representation or by way of inheritance transmission (Article 1158(1), Civil Code). In effect, the heir is not transferring property due to him under the estate, but assigning the right of inheritance as the aggregate of powers to accept or to refuse the inheritance. Russian legal doctrine is deeply divided as to the extent to which an heir may consummate a directed refusal.[17]

The present version of Article 1158, as amended 15 February 2016, consolidated what has been called the "liberal" approach to the refusal of an inheritance. The "conservative" variant held that a directed refusal was allowed only to the benefit of heirs called to inherit – an approach found in the Civil Code of the

[17] For the various approaches and theories, see Abramenkov and Chugunov, note 3 above, pp. 344-345.

Ukrainian SSR (Article 553). The "liberal" variant permitted a directed refusal to the benefit of any heir by operation of law or by will, irrespective of being called to inherit – the approach provided in the 1964 RSFSR Civil Code (Article 550). The difference would mean, for example, in Russia when inheriting by operation of law a son of the decedent could refuse an inheritance to the benefit of his uncle, whereas in Ukraine this would not have been allowed.

Although the Civil Code of the Russian Federation (Article 1158) seemed to embody the liberal variant, the Plenum of the Supreme Court of the Russian Federation construed the Article by proceeding from the conservative variant in its Decree of 29 May 2012, whereas prior to that Decree, notaries had understood Article 1158 in its liberal understanding. After the adoption of the said Decree, Russian courts ceased to recognize the liberal variant. In a suit brought to the Constitutional Court of the Russian Federation, the said Court by a Decree of 23 December 2013 held that the construction of Article 1158(1) was unconstitutional to the extent that it departed from the liberal variant. This led to the 2016 amendment of Article 1158 and the addition of the clause "irrespective of being called to inherit".[18]

In the interests of restoring full consistency to the legislative treatment of the directed refusal of an inheritance, one of the following approaches has been suggested. Either reject in principle the directed refusal and keep the right to accept an inheritance out of circulability, or reintroduce the conservative variant of the directed refusal, or keep the liberal modell but allow a refusal to the benefit of anyone; or reject the directed refusal and permit circulation of the right to accept an inheritance

[18] For details, see Petrov, in Petrov, note 1 above, pp. 301-302. According to Petrov, the occasion for the Plenum of the Supreme Court addressing this issue in its Decree of 29 May 2012 was the Commentary to the Civil Code of the Russian Federation, Part 3, published in 2010, in which K. B. Iaroshenko drew attention to the contradictions which led to combining the liberal approach and new groups of heirs – an example of Russian doctrinal critique leading to a change of Russian judicial practice, consequential judicial review at the constitutional level, and an amendment of the Civil Code.

limited only by the expressed or implied prohibition of the decedent.[19]

A directed refusal is not permitted: (1) to the benefit of persons who are not heirs by operation of law or by will; (2) to the benefit of persons deprived of inheritance; (3) to the benefit of persons who are unworthy heirs; (4) of property to be inherited by will if all the property the testator bequeathed to heirs designated by him; (5) of the right to an obligatory share in the estate; (6) if the heir is subdesignated as an heir (Article 1158, Civil Code).

When an heir refuses to accept an inheritance, that decision is irrevocable and differs from a simple failure to accept in due time. In the latter instance, a court may be requested to restore the lapsed period. The irrevocability of refusal is intended to protect the interests of third persons, especially other heirs and creditors of the decedent. Although a refusal may not be retracted, it may be contested in a judicial proceeding, usually for a defect of will.

INCREMENTS IN SHARES OF INHERITANCE

Increments in the participatory shares of an estate (*jus aderescendi*) occur as a legal consequence of the non-participation of an heir in legal succession after the death of a person because the heir has refused to accept the inheritance, or there has been a pure or simple refusal of an inheritance, or the heir has been deemed to be unworthy, or a will has been found to be invalid (Article 1161, Civil Code). In all these instances the part of the inheritance which would have been due to those heirs who have fallen away, or disappeared, passes to the heirs by operation of law in proportion to the inheritance shares due to each of them.

The 1922 RSFSR Civil Code rejected this principle and provided that participatory shares of heirs not called to inherit went to the State (Article 433). The rule on increments in shares was added in 1945 and included in the 1964 RSFSR Civil

[19] Petrov, in Petrov, note 1 above, p. 302.

Code (Article 551). The possibility of opening an inheritance simultaneously on two grounds raised the issue of how the increment should be distributed. Both civil codes resolved the issue in favor of heirs by operation of law except for the situation when all the property was bequeathed to several designated heirs. Successive call to inherit was unknown to Soviet inheritance law. The Civil Code of the Russian Federation followed its 1964 predecessor with some elaboration, working from the doctrinal positions of the Soviet period.[20]

The rules on increments operate to redistribute the share of an heir called to inherit but for one reason or another does not become the owner of the property due to him. These rules concern the acquisition of inheritance property and not the grounds of inheriting. This means that increments are not to be understood as a transfer of the right to inherit (such transfer being possible only in the case of a directed refusal to inherit or of inheritance transmission), but rather a redistribution of the participatory shares of the actual heirs, such redistribution not being by decision or consent of those heirs but a behest of the legislator who offers no alternative.

Increments to participatory shares in an inheritance are possible when the following conditions are simultaneously present: (1) there are several heirs called to inherit by will or by operation of law; (2) one of the heirs called falls away on the grounds specified in the Civil Code of the Russian Federation; (3) there are heirs who accepted the inheritance on a particular ground.

The grounds for an heir to disappear or fall away are: (1) failure to accept the inheritance; (2) pure refusal of an heir of the inheritance; (3) removal of the person from inheriting on the basis of unworthiness (Article 1117, Civil Code); (4) invalidity of the will in the part which gave rise to the right of the heir who disappeared to inherit. The last ground is criticized in Russian doctrinal writings for the infelicitous formulation thereof. Unworthy heirs have no right to inherit and thus

[20] Petrov, in Petrov, note 1 above, p. 308.

should not be regarded as having been called to inherit and have no participatory share in the inheritance. The same would apply to a will invalid in part, for if the will is invalid, it gives no right to a participatory share in the inheritance. In the view of jurists who take this view, the rule concerning increments to shares should not operate.

The Civil Code (Article 1161) addresses two situations in which the rules concerning increments of inheritance shares are applied. The first is when property passes only by operation of law or simultaneously by operation of law and by will. In this case the share of the heir who fell away is distributed among the heirs by operation of law in proportion to their shares. These shares will be equal in this example: when four heirs are called to inherit by operation of law and one of them has fallen away, the property would be distributed among the remaining three heirs as follows – the initial share of each heir was one-fourth of the estate; after one heir falls away, his one-fourth share is divided amongst the remaining heirs, increasing each share by one-twelfth, so that each of the three remaining heirs receives four-twelfths, or one-third, of the estate.

The second situation is when all the estate property was bequeathed to several heirs, and the share of the heir who fell away is distributed among the remaining heirs in proportion to their shares as determined in the will unless the testator established a different procedure for such distribution. An example: the testator left his property to three heirs – one-sixth, two-sixths (one-third), and three-sixths (one-half). If the heir to whom one-third fell away, the calculation would be as follows: first, determine by how much the share of the heir who fell away exceeds the share of the second heir, in this case three-sixths over one-sixth equals three. Thus, the heir who had the right to a three-sixth share should receive an incremental share three times greater than the heir who fell away: $4x = 1/3$, $x = 1/12$, which would mean that a 1/12 share should be added to the 1/6 share and 3/12 should be added to the heir who has a one-half share. The outcome will be that one heir will receive 3/12 (1/4) and the other 9/12 (3/4) shares respectively.[21]

The question arises as to what should occur if the will does not concern all the property in the estate, but only part thereof, and bequeaths specific articles to specific persons, of whom one falls away. How the specific property to be distributed among the remaining heirs raises conundrums. By way of example: the decedent leaves his motor vehicle to two relatives, and the rest of his property is inherited by operation of law. One relative falls away from the inheritance. Under Article 1161, the right of ownership in the motor vehicle would be distributed among the heirs by operation of law, although logically one might assume the share in the motor vehicle should go to the heir designated to receive that vehicle.[22]

FORMALIZATION OF RIGHT TO INHERIT

In prerevolutionary Russian law the competence to certify the right to inherit was vested in the courts (Article 1408, Statute of Civil Procedure). The heirs wishing to have evidence of inheritance rights would apply to the Russian court for confirmation. If there was a will, however, this was submitted to the court for confirmation. Failure to present the will to the court within the period of limitation meant that the will lost force unless the court restored the period.

The 1922 RSFSR Civil Code initially introduced judicial competence over the confirmation of inheritance rights, transferring these powers to a notary in 1928 (Article 435).

The right to inherit is among the absolute legal forms, as described in Russian legal doctrine, which requires that it be brought to the notice of all other persons. In Russian law the means of making inheritance a matter of public notice and advising the public at large that a particular individual has become an heir to the property of another natural person is

[21] The examples are given in Abramenkov and Chugunov, note 3 above, p. 348.

[22] The example is discussed by Chepig, note 3 above, p. 215.

the certificate of the right to inherit (Article 1162, Civil Code; Articles 36, 70-73, Fundamental Principles of Legislation on the Notariat). The certificate is confirmation of the acquisition of rights to property by way of inheriting, but does not itself give rise to those rights; the heir becomes the owner of things inherited, the subject of exclusive rights, and a party to obligations, and the like from the moment of opening the inheritance, on condition of accepting the inheritance. When an heir applies to a notary to receive a certificate of the right to inherit,[23] the heir is expressing a wish to publicly affirm the rights belonging to him to the inheritance due to him. The heir has a right to receive a certificate of the right to inherit, but not a duty to do so.

The realities of life, however, dictate that in a number of situations, an heir has no alternative to applying for a certificate of the right to inherit if he wishes to acquire or take possession of the inheritance property. This would be so if immoveable property subject to State registration is acquired by inheritance, for without the relevant certificate, it will be exceedingly difficult to register the change of ownership to the property.[24] Moreover, under the Civil Code (Article 1232), a certificate of the right to inherit is a basis for the State registration of rights to the results of intellectual activity and means of individualization. Such a certificate is essential for heirs to receive funds in bank accounts of the deceased.[25] The registration or re-registration of a weapon received by inheritance requires the submission of documents confirming that the weapon passed by way of

[23] With the adoption of the Consular Statute of the Russian Federation on 5 July 2010 (Article 39), Russian consular officials abroad lost the right to issue certificates of the right to inherit. Only a notary may issue such a certificate.

[24] Article 14, Federal Law "On the State Registration of an Immoveable", of 13 July 2015, No. 218-ФЗ, as amended.

[25] Point 14(a), Rules for the Conclusion of Testamentary Dispositions of Rights to Monetary Means in Banks, confirmed by Decree of the Government of the Russian Federation, 27 May 2002, No. 351. СЗ РФ (2002), no. 22, item 2097

inheritance.[26] A certificate of the right to inherit is the basis for making changes in the registers of owners of securities.[27]

The realities of life can also arise with respect to the place of accepting an inheritance. In one case a decedent had a permanent place of residence in Moscow but worked and had a temporary dwelling in Moscow Region. After his death, none of the heirs applied to the notarial office for a certificate of the right to inherit at the place where he temporarily resided, and the notarial office in Moscow Region upon receiving information of the decedent's death from his place of work, issued a certificate for the right to inherit to the State. The heirs, having accepted the estate in a timely manner in the City of Moscow, ultimately had to file suit in court to have the certificate of the right to inherit issued to the State declared invalid.[28]

An applicant for a certificate of the right to inherit must submit to the notary evidence of his status as an heir in the form of documents confirming the fact of death of the decedent, the time and place of opening the inheritance, the fact of marriage and/or being otherwise related to the decedent, the fact of being dependent upon the decedent and, if there is a will, a copy of the will; the rights of the decedent to particular property, such as certificates of the right of ownership to an immoveable, contracts for the acquisition of property, savings books, and so on. If an heir by operation of law cannot submit evidence of family or other relations with the deceased, he may nonetheless be included on the certificate of the right to inherit with the consent of other heirs who have such evidence and have accepted the inheritance (Article 72, Fundamental Principles of Legislation on the Notariat).

[26] Point 29, Rules for Turnover of Civilian and Employment Weapon and Ammunition Therefor on the Territory of the Russian Federation, confirmed by Decree of the Government of the Russian Federation, 21 July 1998, No. 814. СЗ РФ (1998), no. 32, item 3878, as amended.

[27] Article 8, Federal Law "On the Securities Market", of 22 April 1996. СЗ РФ (1996), no. 17, item 1918, as amended; transl. in W. E. Butler, *Russian Company and Commercial Legislation* (2003), pp. 642-647.

[28] The example is reported in S. P. Grishaev, Наследственное право [Inheritance Law] (2014), pp. 27-28.

There are several types of certificate to inherit. A certificate may be issued to all heirs who are called to inherit on a single ground (general, or joint, certificate), or may be issued to each heir individually (individual certificate), or may encompass all inheritance property as a whole (general certificate) or be issued for parts of the inheritance property (special certificate), depending upon the particular circumstances (Article 1162(1), Civil Code). If property is discovered after the certificate(s) are issued which was not included on them, an additional certificate may be issued. If the notary issues a certificate to a minor or to a person who lacks or is limited in dispositive legal capacity, the notary informs the trusteeship and guardianship agencies thereof. Public formations which acquire property by escheat also are issued a certificate of the right to inherit, although strictly speaking they are not heirs, but posthumous successors to the property.

Unless the Civil Code provides otherwise (Article 1163), a certificate of the right to inherit may be issued at any time after six months elapse from the moment when the inheritance opened. The exceptions arise when a special period for the acceptance of an inheritance operates, as, for example, when an heir has refused to accept an inheritance, or when there is reliable information that all the heirs have been identified and have made application for a certificate.

The issuance of a certificate of the right to inherit may be suspended by decision of a court if objective and temporarily insurmountable obstacles arise for the formalization of inheritance rights until these obstacles disappear, and also if there is a conceived but unborn child (Article 1163, Civil Code). To ensure the effective operation of the suspension, an attested copy of the judicial act should be submitted to the notary; the suspension operates from the moment of rendering until it is vacated by the court.[29] The suspension is binding on the notary and others irrespective of the reasons why the court rendered it.

[29] Before a suspension enters into force, the issuance of a certificate of the right to inherit may be postponed if there is information of any kind indicating that security measures are underway (notification by an heir, website of the court, and

Whether and when an heir chooses to obtain a right of the certificate to inherit, or actually receives it, has no bearing on the validity and effectiveness of the obligations of an heir.[30]

With respect to order or inscribed documentary securities which form part of an estate, a certificate of the right to inherit is no longer issued. Under Article 146(8), as amended, from 1 October 2013, rights are transferred to the said securities in the event of inheritance by a notation made by the notary on the security itself; this has the force of an endorsement or transfer from the preceding holder of the security.

so on).

[30] By way of illustration, more than six months after an inheritance was opened, a creditor was not prohibited from filing suit to levy execution against a debtor who had accepted the inheritance property but had not received a certificate of the right to inherit or registered his rights of ownership to the property. Ruling of the Supreme Court of the Russian Federation, 24 April 2013, No. 18-B12-9 (available on Consultant Plus).

Chapter 7

Protection and Management of Estate Property

The Civil Code of the Russian Federation requires (Article 1171), in the interests of the decedent, heirs, recipients of a testamentary legacy, and other interested persons (which may include creditors of the decedent), that the executor of a will or a notary at the place of opening an inheritance should take measures for the protection of the estate. The protection of inheritance property continues until the heirs have accepted the inheritance; if the inheritance is not accepted, until the period for acceptance expires.

GENERAL PROVISIONS

The individuals on whom the duty to protect inheritance property is placed either by legislation or by the will of the decedent include the notary, the executor of a will (Articles 1134 and 1135, Civil Code), officials of an agency of local self-government or of trusteeship and guardianship agency, and a consular official of the Russian Federation. These persons take measures for the protection of inheritance property at the place of opening the inheritance in accordance with Article 1115 of the Civil Code. The notary will act upon the application of one or several heirs or any of the other aforementioned persons. When an executor has been designated by a will, the notary will take measures to protect an inheritance by agreement with the executor. The executor may take measures independently or at the request of any of the heirs.

The notary will determine the period necessary for the protection of the inheritance property, being guided by the nature and value of the property and the time needed for heirs to enter into possession of the property. If the executor takes measures to protect inheritance property, these measures will continue for the period necessary to execute the will of the decedent. The notary at the place of opening the inheritance is obliged to notify the heirs in advance that measures to protect the inheritance property are being terminated.

DUTIES OF PERSONS RESPONSIBLE FOR ORGANIZING PROTECTION OF ESTATE PROPERTY

One of the principal duties of the notary is to determine precisely which property is part of the estate. To this end the notary may request banks, other credit organizations, and other juridical persons to communicate to the notary all available information concerning property belonging to the decedent. The information obtained may be disclosed to the executor and to the heirs by the notary. If the notary divulges this information to persons who do not have a right to receive it, the notary is professionally and personally liable to compensate damage caused as a consequence of such divulgence.

If the inheritance property is located in several places, the notary at the place of opening the inheritance should send through justice agencies a binding assignment to the notary where the property is situated to protect the inheritance property. However, if the notary at the place where the inheritance is opened knows which notary or local official should take measures to protect inheritance property, the assignment may be sent directly to them without going through justice agencies.

The transition to a market economy in Russia has considerably broadened the kinds of property that may pass by inheritance. Such property may include securities, participatory shares in the charter or contributed capital of economic societies and partnerships, exclusive rights, and the like which cannot or should not be removed from commercial turnover lest the interests of the heirs be prejudiced. The Civil Code Article 1173) establishes the duty of a notary when such property is involved to conclude an agreement on trust management with an appropriate trustee manager. If an executor has been appointed by a will, the executor will found the trust management. Contracts of trust management are regulated by Chapter 53 of the Civil

Code. They have little in common with the Anglo-American concept of trust and do not engage fiduciary duties on the part of the trustee manager. Depending upon the property which is the subject of trust management, the general regime applies, which may mean that certain trust management contracts are required to undergo State registration of the contract.

INVENTORY OF ESTATE PROPERTY

One of the principal methods used by a notary to protect inheritance property is to draw up an inventory of such property. The inventory is compiled in the presence of two witnesses who must satisfy the requirements set out in Article 1124 of the Civil Code. In particular, such witnesses may not be the notary or other person who attested the will; a person who is a beneficiary of the will or who received a testamentary legacy, or the spouse, parents, or children of such person, natural persons who are illiterate, or lack or are limited in dispositive legal capacity, persons with physical defects which clearly do not allow them to understand what is happening, or persons who do not have a sufficient command of the language in which the will was drawn up. When the inventory is being compiled, the executor of the will, heirs, and, when necessary, trusteeship and guardianship agency officials, creditors, or representatives of tax agencies may be present.[1]

Russian commentaries report that in notarial practice there is a view which holds that if there is information that one of the heirs has accepted the inheritance and possesses property which is part of the inheritance, an inventory may not be done upon the application of another heir, especially if the heir who

[1] In fact, creditors and representatives of tax agencies are not mentioned in the Civil Code (Article 1172) as being eligible to be present during an inventorying of estate property. The Methods Recommendations are broader in this respect and arguably are not consistent with the Civil Code. The formulation of the Civil Code, in turn, is regarded as too narrow and may lead to an "impingement of the rights of creditors of the decedent, which in practice may lead to abuses on the part of heirs". See E. A. Makarova, in T.E. Abova, M. M. Boguslavskii, and A. G. Svetlanov (eds.), Комментарий к Гражданскому кодексу Российской Федерации, части третьей [Commentary to Civil Code of the Russian Federation, Part Three] (2004), p. 253.

has accepted the inheritance is opposed to this. In this event the heir who is apprehensive of the loss of the property which is part of the inheritance must initiate a suit in court to determine the composition of the inheritance and request the court to take security measures.[2]

When preparing an inventory, a notary will act pursuant to the "Letter of the Federal Chamber of Notaries of 26 July 2013, "On Taking Measures by a Notary for the Protection of Inheritance Property".[3] An inventory must contain or specify: the full name of the notary performing the inventory and the date and number of the order of the justice agency appointing the notary to office, and the notarial district or name of the State notarial office; the date of receipt of the communication concerning inheritance property or assignment to take measures to protect inheritance property; the date of performing the inventory and information concerning the persons participating in the inventory; the full name of the decedent and last permanent place of residence thereof, time of death and location of property being inventoried; whether the premise was sealed before the arrival of the notary and by whom and whether the seal was disturbed; a detailed description of each article of inheritance property being inventoried.

Each page of the inventory must record the number of objects described thereon, and the last page must indicate the total number of articles or things inventoried. The inventory must include all property, including personal things, of the decedent. Statements of natural or juridical persons that individual things belong to them should be entered on the inventory and the persons concerned must be explained their right to bring suit in court to exclude such property from the inventory.

[2] E. A. Ostanina, in E. Iu. Petrov (ed.), Наследственное право: постатейный комментарий к статьям 1110-1185, 1224 Гражданского кодекса Российской Федерации [Inheritance Law: Article-by-Article Commentary to Articles 1110-1185, and 1224 of the Civil Code of the Russian Federation] (2018), p. 362.

[3] Available on Consultant Plus.

If the performance of the inventory is interrupted by lunch break, end of the work day, and so on or lasts for several days, the notary seals the premise each time. The inventory must contain an entry for each interruption and recommencement of work on the inventory, specifying the reasons and times and the state of the seal on the premise. At the end of the inventory the person is indicated who will be responsible for custody of the property; such person must be cautioned of criminal responsibility for failure to perform his duties properly.

The inventory is drawn up in not less than three examples, each signed by the notary, the witnesses, and the interested persons who took part.

If it is not possible to take measures to protect the inheritance property, for example, because the heirs or other persons who resided with the decedent object to the inventory, or do not present property to be inventoried, or property has been removed, and so on, the notary draws up an act to this effect and informs the interested persons and, when necessary, the empowered agency of State power or local self-government. The notary will advise the interested persons, if the property was removed, of their right to bring suit in court to demand and obtain the property missing from the estate. If the notary discovers when inventorying the property any items of historical, scientific, artistic, or other cultural value, the notary notifies the respective agencies of State power or local self-government. Weapons, daggers, ammunition, and explosives owned by the decedent are inventoried separately and transferred to the custody of the internal affairs agencies.[4]

The executor of a will, heirs, or trusteeship and guardianship agencies may, when estate property is being inventoried, request the notary to have a valuation of the property undertaken. The Civil Code permits the parties to agree a valuation amongst themselves. If, however, they cannot come to an agreement, the valuation will be undertaken by a professional independent

[4] See Article 20, Federal Law "On Weapons", of 13 December 1996, as amended. СЗ РФ (1996), no. 51, item 5681.

valuer or appraiser at the expense of the person who requested the valuation with subsequent distribution of these expenses among the heirs in proportion to the value of the inheritance received by each heir. If no one requests a valuation of the inheritance property, the notary who is preparing the inventory need not place a value by each article or thing inventoried.

If a professional valuation is required, this would be undertaken in accordance with the Federal Law on Valuation Activity in the Russian Federation of 29 July 1998, as amended.[5] Such valuation does not have tax implications, as it would likely have in the West, but there are other concerns. The appraised property may well be transferred while the inheritance process is being completed to someone's custody for safekeeping under a Contract of Keeping to which the inventory is attached. The party or person agreeing to keep the property in safekeeping would be liable for the property in the event of its loss in the amount of the appraised value on the inventory.

Monetary means, including money, which are part of the inheritance property are deposited with the notary. Currency valuables, precious metals and stones, articles made from them, and securities not requiring management services are placed in a bank under a contract of keeping, which is retained by the notary.

Food products pass to heirs unless they are perishable, in which case they are destroyed and the notary draws up an act concerning their destruction. Domestic livestock are passed to heirs or other persons in custody; if there are no heirs and no one else can be found to keep them, they are transferred to procurement organizations.

State awards specified by Russian legislation do not constitute part of an estate and pass after the death of the recipient to other persons in the procedure established by legislation to other persons, usually family members, pursuant to the Statute on State Awards of the Russian Federation,

[5] СЗ РФ (1998), no. 31, item 3813, as amended.

confirmed by Edict of the President of the Russian Federation, 7 September 2010, as amended.[6]

The Civil Code provides that the maximum amounts of remuneration under a contract of keeping or a contract of trust management of inheritance property are established by the Government of the Russian Federation (Article 1171[6]). The Government has determined that such remuneration may not exceed 3% of the appraisal value of the inheritance property.[7] If heirs act in the capacity of custodian or trustee manager, they are not remunerated for this service. Necessary expenses, however, are reimbursed to custodians, trustee managers, or heirs for keeping and/or managing the inheritance property.

MANAGEMENT OF ESTATE PROPERTY

The protection and management of estate property are closely intertwined when the estate property is of such a nature that merely holding the property in custody is not sufficient to protect the interests of the decedent, the heirs, the executor, or creditors and other interested persons. The notary will take measures for the management of property at the request of one or several heirs, the executor of the decedent's will, an agency of local self-government, a trusteeship and guardianship agency, or others who have an interest in the preservation of the inheritance property. If an executor has been designated, the notary will take measures for the management of estate property by agreement with the executor.

The executor likewise may take measures for the management of estate property at his own initiative or at the request of one or several heirs. Measures of property management, just as measures of property protection, are in place until the inheritance is accepted or the period for acceptance has lapsed. In most respects the procedures relating to the management of

6 СЗ РФ (2010), no. 37, item 4643, as amended.

7 Decree No. 350, 27 May 2002. СЗ РФ (2002), no. 22, item 2096.

estate property parallel those set out above with respect to the protection of estate property.

Most commonly the management of estate property is engaged by the presence in the estate of property such as an enterprise, property complexes, individual immoveables, or participatory share in the charter or contributed capital of an economic partnership or society, securities, or exclusive rights, or the like. Here a contract of keeping will not be satisfactory. The notary is most likely to have recourse to a contract of trust management under Chapter 53 of the Civil Code of the Russian Federation. In this event the notary will act as the founder of trust management (Article 1026, Civil Code) and enter into a contract of trust management (Article 1173, Civil Code).

Pursuant to the contract of trust management, the founder (in this case, the notary) transfers to the trustee manager for a determined period property in trust management, and the trustee manager is obliged to manage this property in the interests of the founder or beneficiary specified by the founder (Article 1012, Civil Code). Ownership does not pass to the trustee manager. The trustee manager has the right to conclude with respect to the property under management and in accordance with the contract of trust management any legal or actual actions in the interests of the beneficiary. However, before concluding a contract of trust management of inheritance property, a valuation must be undertaken by an independent valuer of the property being transferred to trust management. The trustee manager enters into transactions in his own name, indicating in so doing that he is acting as a trustee manager.

The trustee manager may be an individual entrepreneur or a commercial organization (except for a unitary enterprise). In the case of inheritance by will, if an executor has been appointed in the will the executor is considered to be a trustee manager from the moment he consents to be executor of the will. A State agency or agency of local self-government may not be a trustee manager. The trustee manager may not be a beneficiary under the contract of trust management. Such contracts must be in written form and, insofar as they involved immoveable property, are subject to State registration.

The trustee manager is liable for the failure to exercise due care over the property held in trust management and to compensate losses caused by failure to perform his duties properly or for the loss of or damage to property held in trust management.

Chapter 8

Division of Inheritance and Expenses among Heirs

The Russian Civil Code recognizes the concept of "necessary expenses" which are connected with the execution of a will, including remuneration to the executor if the will has so provided for this, and those incurred by reason of the imminent death of the decedent, funeral, burial, protection and management of inheritance property, and the like. These are compensated or reimbursed from the value of the estate (Article 1174). Demands for such compensation may be presented to the heirs who have accepted the inheritance or, before acceptance thereof, to the executor of the will or against the inheritance property. These expenses enjoy priority over debts of creditors of the decedent and are paid within the limits of the value of the estate.

Within these categories of expenses, those incurred in connection with the last illness, burial, and funeral of the decedent are first paid, followed by expenses for the protection and management of the inheritance property, and last by the expenses connected with execution of the will.

Any monetary assets of the decedent may be used to cover the expenses of the funeral, including in bank accounts and deposit accounts. The banks are obliged upon the decree of a notary to provide funds from these accounts to the individual specified in the decree for the payment of funeral and burial expenses. An heir specified in the decedent's will or in a testamentary disposition lodged with the bank or credit institution has the right at any time before six months elapse since the opening of the inheritance to withdraw monies necessary for the funeral and burial. However, a limit is imposed by legislation: such monies issued to the heir concerned or to the person specified in the notary's decree may not exceed one hundred minimum amounts of payment for labor established by law on the day of recourse to receive such monies.

Reimbursement of expenses is made on the basis of uncontested written evidence of the expenditures made (cashier receipts, court decisions which have entered into force, written certification of medical institutions, and the like). Witness testimony is not acceptable. Expenses are paid upon the application in writing of the interested person. No State duty or tariff is imposed for the issuance by a notary of an instruction to release monies from the estate for these purposes.

Expenses for the last illness of the decedent are compensated by a notary if they are confirmed by documentation; in the absence of documents, the notary will advise the debtors to seek judicial confirmation of the expenses. Insofar as these expenses involved the provision of care, the rates used are the average earnings of the person who bore these expenses.

The aforesaid expenses payable from the estate are recovered from cash in the estate; in the absence of cash resources, from bank deposits of the decedent; and in the absence of deposits or their insufficiency, from the realization of moveable property not subject to State registration. A notary is not empowered by Russian legislation to issue an instruction to dispose of moveable property subject to State registration or immoveable property for the purpose of meeting expenses of the estate.

After the expenses above are dealt with, the heirs who have accepted the inheritance are liable for debts of the decedent (Article 1175, Civil Code) jointly and severally (Article 323, Civil Code) within the limits of the value of the inheritance property which passed to each heir. An heir who has accepted an inheritance by way of inheritance transmission is liable for debts of the original decedent, but not for debts of the decedent from whom he received the right to inherit by way of transmission.

Creditors may submit their demands for repayment of debts of the decedent within the periods of limitation established for the respective demands by the Civil Code. These periods of limitation are not subject to interruption, suspension, or restoration.

DIVISION OF COMMON PROPERTY AMONG HEIRS

When inheritance property enters into the possession of several heirs by operation of law and/or will (unless specific objects are bequeathed to a certain person), from the day of the opening of the inheritance such property falls under the regime of the "common property of heirs". This would likewise be true if a particular object is bequeathed to several persons, including part by will or part by operation of law.

The 1922 RSFSR Civil Code and the 1964 RSFSR civil codes did not contain special rules relating to the inheritance of property by several persons. Doctrine and practice proceeded from the fact that "heirs become co-owners of inherited things, co-creditors of debtors of the decedent, and co-debtors for debts …".[1]

The Civil Code (Article 1164) speaks more precisely of the "common ownership of heirs". Article 1164 is an innovation in Russian civil law; prior to its introduction matters of this nature in practice were addressed through the general civil law provisions on common ownership. The provision is understood to refer to common participatory share ownership of heirs; common joint ownership cannot arise by way of inheritance. The formulation of Article 1164 does not indicate whether it applies to all rights to property or only to things. The majority of Russian commentators suggest that the sense of the Civil Code supports the broader interpretation.[2]

An example of the operation of common participatory ownership of heirs would be as follows: a will provides that

[1] Petrov and E. V. Kozhevina, in E. Iu. Petrov (ed.), Наследственное право: постатейный комментарий к статьям 1110-1185, 1224 Гражданского кодекса Российской Федерации [Inheritance Law: Article-by-Article Commentary to Articles 1110-1185, and 1224 of the Civil Code of the Russian Federation] (2018), pp. 327-328.

[2] See M. V. Teliukina, in T. E. Abova, M. M. Boguslavskii, and A. G. Svetlanov (eds.), Комментарий к Гражданскому кодексу Российской Федерации, части третьей [Commentary to Civil Code of the Russian Federation, Part Three] (2004), p. 235.

all property passes to a husband and a brother, and a motor vehicle to the sons. The sons would have common participatory share ownership in the vehicle, and the husband and brother, the same such ownership in all the remaining property. The Civil Code makes no distinction between those who may be common participatory share owners; natural persons who be owners equally with public formations if, for example, a will left property to the State and to a certain natural person.

In general, the regime of common participatory share ownership in inheritance property is regulated by Chapter 16 of the Civil Code, subject to certain exceptions established by the Civil Code. Heirs who inherit property in common participatory share ownership may modify the regime of this property by agreement amongst themselves. Most commonly they redivide the property. If, for example, three heirs of the first priority became the owners of a motor vehicle, a bank deposit, and a collection of antiques, under the general rule each heir has a one-third participatory share in this property. They may then conclude an agreement under which one heir acquires the motor vehicle, another the bank deposit, and the third takes the antiques. The regime of common participatory share ownership would thereupon terminate and each would become the sole owner of the divided property which he chose. Such an agreement would need to comply with the general rules concerning the form of transactions and contracts (Article 1165, Civil Code), including the written form and the possibility of notarial certification.

If there is immoveable property in the estate, an agreement to divide the ownership interests could be concluded only after the heirs obtained a certificate of the right to inherit this immoveable. However, if the State registration of the property was completed before the agreement to divide ownership was concluded, the agreement will serve as the basis for registering the ownership interests of the heirs. In this event it can happen that the share in the inheritance recorded in the certificate to inherit differs from the division of property contained in the agreement; the Civil Code expressly provides (Article 1165[3]) that this discrepancy should not serve as grounds for refusing to register the rights to immoveable property received as a result of dividing the inheritance.

Doctrinal commentary suggests that the principle of common ownership of tangible property might also be applied by analogy to intangible property, such as a bank deposit or intellectual property. Such assets would be distributed among the heirs in proportion to their participatory shares unless they agreed otherwise.

The procedure for concluding an agreement to divide property which passed by inheritance and the division itself have a number of distinctive features. First, an estate may not be divided if there is a child conceived during the life of the decedent but not born when the inheritance opened (Article 1166, Civil Code). If the child is born alive, he takes part in the division of the inheritance through his legal representative; otherwise, the inheritance will be divided amongst the existing heirs. As for minors or persons lacking or limited in dispositive legal capacity, they may participate in the division of property which has passed by inheritance through their legal representatives, trustees, or guardians, observing the requirements of Article 37 of the Civil Code that establish how a ward may dispose of property.

Second, when property is distributed amongst heirs some of them are granted preferential rights to certain elements of the estate property in order to preserve stable and extended relations that existed at the moment the inheritance was opened with regard to the possession and use of property or to protect the rights and interested of socially undefended persons (Articles 1168-1169, 1178-1179, Civil Code):

Indivisible things. Several rules operates with respect to such property. If the heir and the decedent were co-owners of an indivisible thing, the heir has the right to receive the participatory share in the right of ownership to this thing ahead of other heirs who were not owners of this thing with the deceased owner irrespective of whether they used this thing. Moreover, if there are no co-owners of an indivisible thing among the heirs but one of them used this thing on a legal basis jointly with the decedent, this heir has a preferential right to receive this thing as part of his participatory share in the inheritance. When there is a dwelling house or apartment and the like in the estate that cannot be divided in kind, a preferential right to this premise as part of his participatory share in the estate is enjoyed by that heir who resided in this premise on the day of opening of the inheritance and has no other housing.

Ordinary household articles. Heirs who resided jointly with the decedent on the day of opening the inheritance have a preferential right to these articles (Article 1169, Civil Code).[3] If several heirs satisfy this criterion, these articles may be distributed among them in proportion to their shares in the inheritance. Antiques and jewellery and the like are not considered to fall into this category. Precisely which articles do fall into this category is resolved by taking into account their consumer qualities or local customs. If an heir receives an incommensurate size of the estate under this rule, compensation may be due to the other heirs (Article 1170, Civil Code). The period for exercising these preferential rights is three years from the day of opening the inheritance (Article 1164, Civil Code);

Property complexes comprising enterprise or farmer economy. An heir who is a registered individual entrepreneur or a commercial organization which is an heir by will has a preferential right to receive an enterprise as part of his or its share in an estate. If there are no heirs or they do not take advantage of their preferential right, the enterprise as a whole enters the common participatory

[3] This rule operates even if there is a will and the ordinary household articles were not bequeathed. In practice the inheritance of these ordinary household articles is often the source of disputes. Whether the provision needed to be set out in an individual article of the Civil Code has been criticized. See O. N. Sadikov, Комментарий к Гражданскому кодексу Российской Федерации [Commentary to the Civil Code of the Russian Federation] (2010), I, p. 99. Article 1169 imposes no requirement of permanent or temporary residence or any minimum duration of time. Decisive is the fact of residing with the decedent on the day of opening the inheritance. See V. I. Archinova, Законодательство, регулирующее наследственные отношения[Legislation Regulating Inheritance Relations] (Vladikavkaz, 2005), p. 14.

share ownership of the heirs commensurate with their shares in the estate unless the heirs who accepted the inheritance have agreed otherwise. There is no legislative definition of "property complex", which sometimes leads to an enterprise itself being regarded as a property complex, or to a "complex thing" being regarded as a property complex. The intangible elements of an enterprise, such as business reputation, although part of the valuation of an enterprise passing by inheritance, are not addressed by the Civil Code as to whether they can be inherited separately from the enterprise itself.[4]

With regard to property comprising a farmer economy, the Civil Code (Article 1179) provides a preferential right to heirs who want to continue to engage in farming. If none of the heirs wishes to do so, or if the economy terminates upon the death of the decedent, the property comprising the farmer economy is subject to division on the general grounds, taking into account the provisions of the Civil Code regulating the division of land plots.

Third, responsibility for debts of the decedent means in Article 1175 of the Civil Code not only monetary obligations in the narrow sense of the word, but also duties of the heirs who have accepted the inheritance to perform tasks arising out of the opening of the inheritance. Heirs who have accepted an inheritance are liable for the debts of the decedent jointly and severally within the limits of the value of the inheritance property which has passed to them.

STATE DUTY

The Russian Federation imposes State duty for the performance of a number of services connected with inheritance matters. Sometimes these are flat charges; in other instances, they are a percentage of the value of the transaction. Although they are incorporated within the Tax Code of the Russian Federation

[4] See E. A. Khodyreva, Предприятие как объект наследственного правопреемства [The Enterprise as an Object of Inheritance Succession] (2013), p. 187.

(and during the Soviet era were addressed in a separate law), they are widely regarded in Russian legal doctrine as a "fee" or a "charge" rather than a tax, although they are undoubtedly intended as a source of revenue for the State. The legislative provisions are complex and are ameliorated by numerous exemptions.

For the issuance of a certificate of the right to inherit to children, spouse, parents, and natural brothers and sisters of the decedent,[5] State duty is payable in the amount of 1.3% of the value of the property, but not more than 100,000 rubles (Article 333.24(22), Tax Code).[6] For other heirs the State duty is 1.6% of the value of the property, but not more than one million rubles. For unsealing and reading out the contents of a closed will, State duty of 300 rubles is payable.

A special procedure applies for calculating State duty when a certificate of the right to inherit a means of transport is issued. The value of the vehicle is determined by forensic expert institutions of justice agencies or by organizations involved in the technical servicing and sale of means of transport. The valuation documents are appended to the documents held by the State notarial office. If the owner of the means of transport disagrees with the valuation, he may seek an independent valuation and protest the original valuation in a judicial proceeding. The notary will use the valuation as the basis for calculating the State duty to be paid.

The issuance of a certificate of the right to inherit for securities (bonds, bills of exchange, cheques, deposit and savings certificates, bearer bank savings books, bills of lading, stocks, and so on) is subject to State duty calculated at the market value, but not lower than the par value.

Certain estate property is excluded when determining the amount of State duty payable for the issuance of a certificate

[5] Neither the Civil Code nor the Family Code distinguish between natural and half brothers and sisters; why the Tax Code should have done so is inexplicable.

[6] In 2024 the exchange rate of the ruble fluctuated at about 90 to 100 rubles to the United States dollar.

of the right to inherit: dwelling houses and apartments if the heirs lived jointly with the decedent on the day of death thereof and continues to reside in this house or apartment after the death of the decedent; the property of persons who perished when performing their State or social duties or in the course of rescuing human life, protecting State property and legal order, or the property of individuals subjected to political repression; bank deposits; insurance proceeds under contracts of personal and property insurance; certain amounts of payment for labor, author's rights, and author's remuneration provided for by Russian intellectual property legislation.

When there are several heirs, whether by operation of law, will, or entitlement to an obligatory share, the duty is calculated on the share of the inheritance due to each heir. Detailed provisions exist for calculating duty when special certificates of the right to inherit are issued, or additional certificates, or amended certificates, including in some cases the possibilities of refunds or set-off.

Private notaries recover a notarial tariff for the issuance of a certificate of the right to inherit in the same amounts as the State duty provided for analogous actions in a State notarial office.

TAXATION OF INHERITANCE

There is no taxation of inheritance in the Russian Federation in the strict meaning of that term. The Tax Code of the Russian Federation provides in Article 217(18), as amended 1 July 2005, that the following types of revenues are not subject to taxation or are exempt from taxation: "revenues in monetary form or in kind received from natural persons by way of inheritance, except for remuneration paid to heirs (or legal successors) of the authors of works of science, literature, art, and also discoveries, inventions, and industrial designs". There is no tax on an estate as such, which has no separate existence or identity in Russian law.

Heirs incur certain taxation obligations from the moment an inheritance is opened. Land plots, for example, servicing dwelling houses, non-dwelling structures, and installations, are subject to land tax; the heirs to such plots or structures are responsible for the land tax from the moment of the death of the decedent or, if the decedent is declared by a court to be deceased, from the moment when the decision of the court so declaring enters into force.

Chapter 9

Defense of Inheritance Rights

In general, collegial actions or decisions and the actions or decisions of a single person, or a failure thereof to act, may be appealed to a Russian court if these violated the rights and freedoms of a natural person, created obstacles to a citizen exercising his rights and freedoms, or illegally placed a duty on a citizen or the individual was brought to responsibility illegally.[1]

RECOURSE TO RUSSIAN COURTS

With particular reference to inheritance matters, citizens have a right to appeal to a court an action incorrectly performed by a notary or a refusal of a notary to perform such an action. The application would be filed in the court at the location of the notary or official empowered to perform notarial actions. Only an interested person may appeal against the actions of a notary or officials performing notarial duties. For these purposes an interested person may be natural or juridical persons with respect to whom a notarial action was performed or to whom performance of such action was refused. The Procuracy also may initiate such an action on behalf of a natural person, as may any other person whose rights and interests were or might be adversely affected by a notarial action by filing a suit for this purpose.

By all accounts the number of inheritance matters that come before Russian courts is substantial. Courts in the City of Moscow from the entry into force of Part Three of the Civil Code through 2011 inclusive considered inheritance cases on the following questions: 43% were suits to deem certificates of the right to inherit to be invalid and recognize the right of ownership in an estate; 28% were applications to establish the fact of acceptance

[1] See Chapter 25, Code of Civil Procedure of the Russian Federation; transl. in W. E. Butler, *Russian Civil and Arbitrazh Procedure* (2012), pp. 98-100.

of an inheritance; 13% were application to extend or restore the period for accepting an inheritance; 10% of the suits were to deem a will to be invalid; 2% concerning deeming an heir to be unworthy and remove him from inheriting; 1.5% concerned the division of an estate; 0.6% sought the awarding of an obligatory share; and 0.1% sought to deem valid a will drawn up during an extraordinary situation.[2]

The right of an individual to appeal to a Russian court against notarial actions or a refusal to perform them is regarded in Russian legal doctrine as one of the major guarantees for the protection of personal and property rights. An appeal is considered by the court with the participation of the applicant, the notary or other official who performed or failed to perform the notarial action, and other interested persons; the failure of the notary or other official to appear in the court proceeding is not an obstacle to consideration of the case. A court decision which satisfies an application concerning the performance, or refusal to perform, a notarial action repeals the notarial action performed or requires that such action be performed.

State and private notaries are subject to administrative responsibility for failing or refusing to provide services to applicants or for abuse of powers pursuant to the Code of the Russian Federation on Administrative Violations.

EVIDENCE IN INHERITANCE CASES

When appealing a notarial action or failure to act to a court, the plaintiff needs to attach to the petition to sue notarially certified genuine documents, such as the will or other written evidence, including a certificate of the right to inherit, certificate of the

[2] Iu. F. Bespalov and A. Iu. Bespalova, *Дела о наследовании: некоторые спорные вопросы правоприменения* [Cases concerning Inheritance: Certain Controversial Questions of Law-Application] (2013), p. 3. For firsthand accounts of pre-judicial consideration of inheritance matters and the quality of an advokat's role in advising his clients, see Kathryn Hendley, *Everyday Law in Russia* (2017), pp. 200-201, 203-204. For Russian citizens wrestling with a hypothetical case and discussing whether to avail themselves of judicial recourse, see Kathryn Hendley, "To Go to Court or Not? The Evolution of Disputes in Russia", in Marina Kurkchiyan and Agnieszka Kubal (eds.), *A Sociology of Justice in Russia* (2018), pp. 40-67.

right of ownership to a participatory share in common property of spouses, and so on. If a notary has issued a decree refusing to perform a notarial action, the petitioner should append to the court appeal those documents which the applicant considers to be relevant. These need to be notarially certified or attested, together with the notary's decree refusing to perform the relevant actions.

Chapter 10

Private International Law Aspects of Inheritance

The increased mobility of the world's population in and of itself has enhanced the importance of private international law rules regulating the law applicable to inheritance. Millions of Russians and their relations live outside the Russian Federation and routinely move back and forth throughout the countries of the world.[1] Marriages between Russian citizens and foreigners are more common than previously. In the instance of Russia, the group of persons who may be called to inherit has been significantly enlarged in the post-Soviet era. So too have the market reforms in Russia expanded the range and scope of property and property rights that may be passed by inheritance, including elements of such property or property rights located outside Russia or rights arising from relations with foreign financial institutions and insurance companies. Inheritance matters with a foreign element have become routine phenomena for Russian courts and notaries.

LAW APPLICABLE TO INHERITANCE

Russian legal doctrine often prefers the Latin expression *lex successionis* to describe the law to which inheritance relations juridically connected with several national legal systems gravitates by its nature and which regulates those relations in essence.[2] Less abstractly, the *lex successionis* is "the law of a country subject to application to the entire aggregate of

[1] As of 1 July 2020 it was estimated that 10,838,386 Russians classified as international migrants lived outside Russia. These numbers will have significantly increased by reason of the Russian-Ukrainian conflict from 2022. See figures collected by Statista (available online). Other estimates include ca. three million ethnic Russians in Kazakhstan as of 2024; 3,100,000 in the United States; and 73,000 in the United Kingdom in 2020.

[2] See M. S. Abramenkov and P. V. Chugunov, Наследственное право [Inheritance Law] (2013), p. 401.

inheritance relations complicated by a foreign element".[3] There is no definition in Russian legislation of a "foreign element"; the term is used in Article 1186(1) of the Civil Code:

> The law subject to application to civil-law relations with the participation of foreign citizens or foreign juridical persons or civil-law relations complicated by another foreign element, including in instances when the object of civil rights is situated abroad, shall be determined on the basis of international treaties of the Russian Federation, present Code, other laws (Article 3[2]), and customs recognized in the Russian Federation.

Pursuant to the Federal Law "On the Legal Status of Foreign Citizens in the Russian Federation" of 25 July 2002, as amended, a foreign citizen is a natural person who is not a citizen of the Russian Federation and who has evidence indicating that such person is a citizen or subject of a foreign State. A close analysis of this provision suggests there are two types of foreign elements: what in Russian legal doctrine are the subject and object of legal relations. The subjects of law would include foreign citizens, foreign juridical persons, and legal entities which are not juridical persons. The objects of rights would include things and other objects situated outside the limits of the Russian Federation. It would seem that natural stateless persons also satisfy the criteria of a foreign element. Soviet and post-Soviet doctrinal writings suggest another type of foreign element: a legal fact, examples of which would include a transaction (such as a will), a delict, and the like.[4]

The *lex successionis* in Russia addresses general questions of inheritance and contains special rules relating to individual

[3] See M. B. Kasenova, in T. E. Abova, M. M. Boguslavskii, and A. G. Svetlanov (eds.), Комментарий к Гражданскому кодексу Российской Федерации, части третьей [Commentary to Civil Code of the Russian Federation, Part Three] (2004), p. 452.

[4] Among these writers are L. A. Lunts, N. I. Marysheva, and O. N. Sadikov, Международное частное право [International Private Law] (1984), pp. 5-6; M. M. Boguslavskii, Международное частное право [International Private Law] (2005), pp. 18-19; I. V. Getman-Pavlova, Международное частное право [International Private Law] (2005), pp. 17-19.

types of property such as immoveables, bank deposits, securities, exclusive rights, rights of demand, and others. Of the numerous diverse legal relations that arise in inheritance matters and are addressed individually by the Russian legislator, the most significant is the moment of opening an inheritance, which is also the moment by which the property of a decedent passes to other persons.

The law applicable to relations with regard to inheriting is determined under Part 3 of the Civil Code of the Russian Federation (Article 1224). Part 3 entered into force on 1 March 2002. The basic point of departure is that "relations with regard to inheriting shall be determined according to the law of the country where the decedent had his last place of residence ..." (Article 1224(1), Civil Code). On its face this formulation diverges from the 1991 Fundamental Principles of Civil Legislation of the USSR and Republics (Article 169), which contained the formulation "last *permanent* place of residence" (emphasis added), and from the Model Civil Code for Countries of the CIS (Article 1233), which referred to the "permanent place of residence", omitting the word "last".

Russian legal doctrine disposes of the divergences by making reference to a distinction between the "place of residence" of a natural person (Article 20, Civil Code) and the "place of sojourn" of a natural person (Article 27, 1993 Constitution of Russian Federation). Pursuant to Article 20, the "place of residence" is the place "where a citizen permanently or primarily resides", and in the instance of minors is the place of residence of their legal representatives. "Permanent" and "primarily" assumes that a citizen is always present in a certain place, although for intervals of time he may be absent from that place.[5]

If a natural person had a last place of residence on the territory of the Russian Federation, the *lex successionis* is determined by Russian law because the very concept[6] of last

[5] Note 3 above, p. 253.

[6] Article 1187 of the Civil Code of Russia provides that "When determining the law subject to application, the interpretation of legal concepts shall be effectuated

place of residence is subject to Russian law. If a Russian citizen had a last place of residence in the United Kingdom, on the other hand, the question of the applicable law to the estate would be decided by Russian law as to whether the decedent had at the moment of death a place of residence in Russia in the meaning of a "permanent place of residence", to which the answer in this example would be negative and the *lex successionis* would be the law of the United Kingdom.

As the Russian commentators observe, although there is nothing new in principle in the formulation of Article 1224(1) of the Civil Code, the element of "normative correlation" is an innovation in Russian inheritance law.[7] The *lex successionis* determines, pursuant to Articles 1115 and 1195 of the Civil Code, the place of opening the inheritance. If the decedent's last place of residence is unknown or is outside the Russian Federation, the criteria for determining the place of opening the inheritance are set out in Article 1115. The place of residence of a foreigner is determined on the basis of the foreigner's "personal law" (Article 1195, Civil Code). It should be added that, with regard to foreigners, whether they are deemed to have a "place of residence" in Russia is far from straight forward and is subject to the Federal Law on the Legal Status of Foreign Citizens in the Russian Federation[8] as implemented by subordinate legislation.[9]

Under the general rule of interpretation set out in the Civil Code (Article 1187), the concept "place of residence" will be interpreted in accordance with Russian law. Therefore, the Russian official, usually a notary, or agency competent to regulate the inheriting of moveable things and other property not categorized as immoveable must determine in which State

in accordance with Russian law unless provided otherwise by a law".

[7] See Kasenova, note 3 above, p. 454.

[8] СЗ РФ (2002), no. 30, item 3032, as amended; transl. in W. E. Butler, *Russian Foreign Relations and Investment Law* (2006), pp. 407-442.

[9] For the concepts of temporary sojourn, temporary residing, and permanent residing, and the attendant visa regimes, see Butler, ibid., Chapter 5.

the decedent permanently or primarily resided at the moment of opening the inheritance. This means not merely that the decedent sojourned in a particular place, but was there for a rather long time and on a legal basis. Under the Federal Law on the Legal Status of Foreigners, foreign citizens are deemed to be permanently residing on the territory of the Russian Federation if they had a residence permit. The legislator attaches no significance as to whether the person intended or not to acquire a domicile in a particular country. Moreover, the legal order regulating relations with regard to inheriting is not necessarily the same as the personal law of the decedent, although these may coincide as, for example, when the decedent permanently resides on the territory of the State of which he is a citizen.

Issues involving "place of residence" are encountered with frequently in Russian notarial practice. The following example has been discussed in Russian doctrinal writings:

> Russian citizen "R", formerly an Aeroflot crew members, moved in 1997 to Canada to work under contract and there married a Canadian citizen, "L". The couple settled in Montreal and lived there until "R" passed away from a heart attack in February 2003. The estate consisted of money in bank accounts in Canada and Russia, a motor vehicle loaned under a power of attorney to the decedent's daughter of his first marriage, and various moveables. The daughter of the deceased applied to the Russian notary for a certificate of the right to inherit, and this required that the place of residence of the deceased be ascertained. On one hand, if the concept "place of residence" in Article 20 of the Civil Code is identical to the same concept in Article 1224(1) of the Civil Code, the place of residence would be the place where the deceased was registered. In this event the *lex successionis* would be Russian law. On the other hand, if one took into account other facts when determining where the decedent lived, these would include: the decedent married a Canadian citizen and settled in Canada on a legal basis; the spouses arranged

> their existence there (employment, choice of schools for children, opening accounts in Canadian banks, and others). These circumstances might suggest that the decedent had a closer link with the legal order of his actual, but not legal, residence and that Canadian law should be the *lex successionis*.[10]

Makovskii[11] and Marysheva[12] have suggested that the need to determine the primary place of residence of the decedent arises when he resided in several countries. In their view the notary or judge should give preference to the country with which the decedent had the closest stable links, and these may become manifest from where he resided with his family or had a permanent dwelling or job, and the like.

Russian legislation, legal doctrine, and judicial practice contains no precise legal criteria for determining the permanent or primary place of residence, especially when a foreign element is involved. An evaluation of the totality of circumstances is not required, but the Russian court is required to justify its determination. Other doctrinal sources suggest that all relevant facts be considered, among them: (1) the presence of the decedent's family members (in particular, spouse or partner and any dependents) at the place of residence; (2) the duration and regularity of the deceased's presence at the place of residence and the conditions and reasons for that presence; (3) the predominant use of a particular dwelling for residence and/or the incurring of expenses for its maintenance; (4) legal status permitting residence in the country of the place of residence and its nature (permanent or temporary; renewable or non-

[10] See I. G. Medvedev, Международное частное право и нотариальная деятельность [Private International Law and Notarial Activity] (2d ed.; 2005), pp. 113-114.

[11] A. L. Makovskii, in A.L. Makovskii and E. A. Sukhanov (eds.), Комментарий к части третьей Гражданского кодекса Российской Федерации [Commentary to Part Three of the Civil Code of the Russian Federation] (2003), p. 487.

[12] N. I. Marysheva, in N. I. Marysheva and K. B. Iaroshenko (eds.) Комментарий к Гражданскому кодексу Российской Федерации, части третьей (постатейный) [Commentary to the Civil Code of the Russian Federation, Part Three (Article-by-Article)] (2004), p. 566.

renewable); (5) tax residence status at the place of residence; (6) the existence of voting rights at the place of residence; (7) the location of the deceased's property at the place of residence; (8) other evidence indicating that the deceased intended to live at the place of residence only temporarily and return to another permanent place of residence.[13]

When determining the limits of operation of the *lex successionis*, legal relations relating to inheriting should be distinguished from questions which are the prerequisite for the right to inherit. The right to inherit is a derivative of the right of ownership: only things, property rights, or rights of demand which may be in the ownership of natural persons may be inherited. Russian legislation determines what is a moveable thing or an immoveable thing (Articles 130-132, Civil Code); Articles 1205 to 1207 of the Civil Code make provision for the first time as to the law applicable to rights to a thing. These distinctions of a general nature extend to inheritance because the very distinction is central to deciding which law is applicable to the inheritance of the thing or the rights thereto. Immoveable property is inherited according to the law of the country where it is located; moveable property, pursuant to the law where the decedent has his last place of residence.

> *Example.* As a result of a marital dispute "M", a citizen of Russia permanently resident with his family in Geneva, was murdered. The court in the Canton of Geneva upon the application of the son (who was of legal age) of the deceased designated an inventory to be made of the decedent's property and the notary in the same Canton to determine who the heirs of "M" were. Simultaneously, "P" applied to a notary in Moscow to accept the inheritance of "M" and sought a certificate of the right to inherit by operation of law in the interests of her minor son who was, according to the birth certificate,

[13] I. G. Rents, in E. Iu. Petrov (ed.), Наследственное право: постатейный комментарий к статьям 1110-1185, 1224 Гражданского кодекса Российской Федерации [Inheritance Law: Article-by-Article Commentary to Articles 1110-1185, and 1224 of the Civil Code of the Russian Federation] (2018), pp. 445-446.

> the illegitimate son of the decedent and herself. She indicated that the decedent owned an apartment in Moscow and a house in Geneva and bank deposits in Russia and Switzerland. Under Article 1224(1) of the Russian Civil Code, the law of the Russian Federation would apply with respect to the Moscow apartment and the law of the Canton of Geneva to the bank deposits and house in Geneva.[14]

Russian law not only classifies immoveable and moveable property, but likewise determines the content of such property rights and any limitations on them. Land plots, for example, may be alienated or pass from one person to another to the extent that the turnover of land plots is permitted by legislation pursuant to the constitutional principle that foreign citizens and stateless persons enjoy rights and bear duties in the Russian Federation equally with citizens of the Russian Federation except for instances established by a federal law or international treaty (Article 62(3), 1993 Russian Constitution). There are, accordingly, lands that may not be in private ownership of natural or juridical persons at all and lands that may be in the ownership of Russian natural persons, but not foreigners or stateless persons (Article 15(3), Land Code).[15] However, foreign citizens and stateless persons do have the right to acquire in ownership buildings, structures, and installations, including the land plots beneath them, and may accordingly bequeath or inherit these plots.

Specific limitations on the ownership by foreigners of land plots and therefore the right to bequeath or inherit them include land plots in border territories or other specially established territories of the Russian Federation (Article 15, Land Code); land plots granted for personal subsidiary husbandry or the construction of dachas, gardening, or individual construction; lands of agricultural designation or a participatory share in the right of common ownership of such agricultural lands (other

[14] Cited in Medvedev, note 10 above, p. 106.

[15] СЗ РФ (2001), no. 44, item 4147, as amended.

than by right of lease). If the acceptance of an inheritance leads to a violation of these rules, the heir is obliged to alienate the land or respective participatory share therein.[16]

Pursuant to changes introduced by legislation of 8 August 2024, the charter of a personal foundation created under Russian law may provide for the application of foreign law to relations with the participation of the personal foundation, founder of this foundation, beneficiary of this foundation, and also persons who are members of organs of this foundation if these are relations with the participation of foreign citizens or foreign juridical persons or relations complicated by another foreign element.

REGULATION OF CONFLICTS OF LAW

Article 1224 contains in the present Civil Code of the Russian Federation a number of innovations with respect to conflicts of law. Exceptions are provided from the general rule concerning the determination of the status of inheriting in accordance with the law of the last place of residence of the decedent. First, the inheritance of an immoveable is made subject to the law of the place where the immoveable is located (*lex rei sitae*). Second, if the immoveable is entered in a State register of the Russian Federation, the law of inheritance is subject to Russian law. Certain objects under Russian law are equated to immoveables: aircraft, ships, and space objects are the principal examples (Article 130, Civil Code).

As noted above, a will is regarded in Russian legal doctrine and civil legislation as a unilateral transaction (Article 1118, Civil Code) which creates rights and duties from the moment of opening of an inheritance. The validity of such a transaction is addressed by Article 1224(2) of the Civil Code. The capacity

[16] A treaty between the Republic Belarus and Russian Federation on Equal Rights of Citizens, concluded 25 December 1998, provides that the citizens of the two countries enjoy an equal right to the acquisition, possession, use, and disposition of property on the territory of the Contracting Parties (Articles 3 and 6). For citizens of Belarus and Russia this Treaty effectively removes limitations on the right to inherit on one another's territory.

of a person to draw up or revoke a will, including with respect to immoveable property, and the form of a will or the act of revocation of a will are determined by the law of the country where the testator had a place of residence at the moment of drawing up such will or act.[17] If, however, the will satisfies the requirements of the place of drawing up the will or act of revocation or the requirements of Russian law, the will or revocation thereof may not be deemed invalid as a consequence of the failure to comply with the form. This formulation sets out three alternatives of compliance with respect to form: (1) the law of the country where the testator had a place of residence at the moment of drawing up the will; (2) the law of the place of drawing up the will; (3) the requirements of Russian law.

> *Example.* "S", a citizen of Israel, died in a Moscow apartment. He had drawn up a will in Israel, where he periodically lived, according to the simple written form with the participation of a lawyer in Israel and lodged the will for safekeeping in an Israeli bank. This will was deemed to be formally valid in Russia because, first, the will satisfied the requirements of the place where the testator lived at the moment of drawing up the will and, second, the will met the requirements in force at the place where the will was drawn up.[18]

Russian law attaches no legal significance to what the estate comprises for the purpose of determining the dispositive legal capacity of a testator and the formal validity of a testamentary disposition or act revoking such.

The Russian Federation is not a party to any of the general international treaties, which are not numerous, regulating inheritance relations. The principal regional treaties in which

[17] The Russian legislator opted after lengthy doctrinal discussions for place of residence rather than citizenship, although the criterion of citizenship had its proponents. See, for example, E. A. Vasil'ev and A. S. Komarov, Гражданское и торговое право зарубежных государств [Civil and Trade Law of Foreign States] (2010), I, p. 423.

[18] Medvedev, note 10 above, p. 135.

the Russian Federation participates[19] are the Minsk Convention on Mutual Legal Assistance with Regard to Civil, Family, and Criminal Cases, concluded 22 January 1993, in the version of the Protocol of 28 March 1997, and the Kishinev (Chisinau) Convention on Legal Assistance and Legal Relations in Civil, Family, and Criminal Matters of 7 October 2002. A number of bilateral treaties of the Russian Federation on legal assistance or consular relations address inheritance matters (China, Greece, Sweden, United Kingdom, and others).

The Minsk and Kishinev conventions and the great majority of bilateral legal assistance treaties proceed from certain general principles, including the principle of national regime. They distinguish between moveable and immoveable property and consolidate the *lex successionis* by providing that the distinction between moveable and immoveable property is determined by the legislation of that country on whose territory the property is situated. The legislation of the country where an immoveable is located determines the procedure for inheriting.

As for movable property, the approach differs. In some treaties the inheriting of moveable property is regulated by the legislation of that country of which the decedent was a citizen at the moment of death (for example, the Treaty on Legal Assistance between Poland and the Russian Federation of 16 September 1996). In others, by the legislation of the country on whose territory the decedent had a last permanent place of residence (for example, Treaty between Egypt and Russia of 23 September 1997; Treaty between Iran and Russia, of 5 March 1996).

The treaties contain conflicts norms resolving issues arising out of escheat property. Escheat immoveable property passes to the State on whose territory the immoveable is situated. Escheat moveable property is inherited in accordance with the law of

[19] The Kishinev Convention on Legal Assistance and Legal Relations in Civil, Family, and Criminal Matters of 7 October 2002 entered into force for the Russian Federation on 28 June 2023.

the State of which the decedent was a citizen at the moment of death.

The dispositive legal capacity to make or revoke a will and the form of a will are resolved variously by the treaties: either by legislation of the country of citizenship of the decedent, or by legislation of the place of drawing up or revoking the will. The Minsk Convention takes a different approach (Article 47): testamentary dispositive legal capacity to draw up or revoke a will and the form of the will are determined by the law of the country where the testator had a place of residence at the moment of drawing up the will or revocation; however, these cannot be deemed to be invalid as a consequence of the failure to comply with the form if the form satisfies the requirements of the law of the place where it was drawn up.

> *Example.* A notary in Moscow Region refused to issue a certificate of the right to inherit to Elena Pugast, resident of Estonia, for a participatory share in an apartment in suburban Moscow which belonged to Liubov Timofeevna Pugast, who died in May 2009. The death certificate issued in Estonia contained only the forename and surname of the decedent: Liubov Pugast. The notary doubted that Liubov Pugast and Liubov Timofeevna Pugast were the same person. Elena Pugast appealed to a Russian court, which reviewed the documents submitted to the notary and found that the notary acted illegally in refusing to issue the certificate. Article 44 of the Minsk Convention provided that citizens of States parties might inherit on equal conditions and to the same extent. Although in Russia the full name of a natural person consists of the forename, patronymic, and surname (Article 19), in Estonia the patronymic is not used. The personal law of Pugast was Estonian law under the Russian Civil Code (Article 1195). The notary was ordered to issue the certificate.[20]

[20] Summarized from the account in E.A. Kirillova, Основания наследования в гражданском праве Российской Федерации [Grounds of Inheritance in the Civil Law of the Russian Federation] (2012), p. 16.

The treaties regulate the procedure for proceedings in inheritance matters. With regard to moveable property, the institutions of that country on whose territory the decedent had a place of residence at the moment of death are competent to carry on the proceedings. With regard to immoveable property, the institutions of that country on whose territory this property is situated are competent to do so.

This approach extends to the procedure for accepting an inheritance, as noted in Russian judicial practice:

> By an appellate ruling of the Judicial Division for Civil Cases of the Moscow City Court of 4 March 2014, a lower court decision was affirmed in which the claimant sued a Moscow notary to deem invalid a certificate on the right to inherit. The decedent actually resided in Ukraine but was not registered for residence there. By operation of law the decedent left an estate including a land plot, dwelling house, and sundry moveables in Russia. The Moscow notary issued a certificate of the right to inherit to the claimant that also listed other heirs for a bank deposit in a Moscow bank. The claimant in the meantime applied to an Odessa notary in Ukraine for a certificate of the right to inherit the land plot, dwelling house, and Russian bank deposit. The court of first instance refused to recognize the Ukrainian certificate relating to the bank deposit, noting that the claimant had taken no actions in Russia to accept the inheritance by applying to a notary in the area where the bank was located within the six-month period of limitations, whereas the other heir had done so. Because the decedent at the moment of death was not registered anywhere and lived outside the Russian Federation, the place of opening the inheritance is the location of his movable property on the territory of the Russian Federation.[21]

[21] Appellate Ruling of Moscow City Court, 4 March 2014, Case No. 33-6458/2014, summarized from Iu. F. Bespalov, A. Iu. Kasatkina, and Z. V. Kameneva, Наследование: спорные вопросы правоприменения [Inheritance: Disputed

As the commentators noted, in order to accept an inheritance situated on the territory of the Russian Federation, actions must be performed which testify to the acceptance of the inheritance as provided by Russian legislation. Performing analogous actions on the territory of a foreign State with respect to the inheritance on the territory of the foreign State do not simultaneously accept the inheritance in Russia.[1]

The treaties make provision for measures to be taken to protect estate property.

Questions of Law-Application] (2d ed.; 2023), pp. 229-232.

1 Ibid., p. 232.

Chapter 11

Inheritance of Business Assets

Depending on the organizational-legal form of the entrepreneurial or business asset created or registered in the Russian Federation, various issues of inheritance may arise. We address below some of those commonly encountered.[1]

ENTREPRENEURIAL STRUCTURES AND INHERITANCE IMPLICATIONS

Business assets may take various forms. Among them are material assets (moveable and immoveable property), financial assets (money in cash or deposits in Russian and foreign currency, bills of exchange, debtor indebtedness, financial investments, and the like), or intangibles (results of intellectual activity and other examples of intellectual ownership). These in turn may generate certain obligations arising out of contracts, transactions, budgetary contributions (pensions, other obligatory payments), or those engaged as a result of causing harm. Whether these pass by way of inheritance usually depends upon their legal regime, first and foremost the organizational-legal form in which the respective business is organized. As a rule, either stocks or the rights connected with participation in economic partnerships or societies, production cooperatives, or peasant economies comprise what is inherited rather than individual objects. This follows from the specific features of the legal status of the juridical persons concerned as reflected in the Civil Code of the Russian Federation and the constitutive documents of those juridical persons.

Article 1176 of the Civil Code provides that within the composition of an inheritance of a participant of a full partnership or full partner in a limited partnership, participant of a society

[1] This chapter is especially indebted to T. A. Batrova, Наследование бизнес-активов: учебное пособие [Inheritance of Business-Assets: Instructional Manual] (2023).

with limited or additional responsibility, and member of a production cooperative is the participatory share (or share) of this participant (or member) in the contributed (or charter) capital (or property) of the respective partnership, society, or cooperative. If in accordance with that Code, other laws, or constitutive documents of an economic partnership or society or production cooperative the consent of the other members of the partnership or society or members of a cooperative is required for entry of an heir into the economic partnership or production cooperative or transfer of a participatory share to an heir in the charter capital of an economic society and such consent is refused to the heir, the said heir has the right to receive from the economic partnership or society or production cooperative the actual value of the inherited participatory share (or share) or part of the property corresponding to it in the procedure provided for by the Civil Code applicable to the said instance, other laws, or constitutive documents of the respective juridical person.

In practice, these observations are most relevant to full partnerships, limited responsibility societies (OOO), and production cooperatives. With respect to full partnerships, there is a legislative presumption of receiving the consent of the other participants (Article 78(2), Civil Code). That presumption reflects the personal trust nature of the relations of the full partners and the need for personal participation in the affairs of the partnership.

The matter is decided differently with respect to the OOO and the production cooperative. Under Article 93(6) of the Civil Code, the participatory share in the charter capital of the OOO passes to the heirs of citizens who are participants of the OOO unless provided otherwise by the charter of the OOO (reiterated in Article 21(8), 1998 Federal Law on the OOO). The Constitutional Court of the Russian Federation noted that this arrangement took into account the legal nature of the OOO as an organization based on the "economic self-determination of citizens and self-regulation". An OOO is permitted to provide additional guarantees in its charter of its property rights", in particular by a "prohibition against the alienation of a participatory share or part thereof to persons who are not participants of the society or to indicate the necessity to obtain consent for such alienation". If such consent is required and refused, the heir concerned has the right to receive the actual value of the participatory share or part thereof from the society. The Court considered that this regulation was essential to ensure a "reasonable balance of the economic interests of individual participants" of the OOO and the society as a whole.[2]

So too in a production cooperative: in the event a member of the cooperative passes away, the heirs thereof may be admitted as members of the cooperative unless provided otherwise by the charter of the cooperative (Article 106^5(4), Civil Code; Article 7(3), 1996 Federal Law "On Production Cooperatives").[3] The general rationale is the same as for the OOO above.

In both instances, however, Russian legislation on the OOO and production cooperative leaves the question of the passing of the right of heirs to participate in the management of the OOO or production cooperative to the respective entity. The Federal Law on the OOO (Article 11) requires that the charter of the OOO must be adopted unanimously, which means that the heir must consent to subsequent limitations on the rights of his heirs to participate in the affairs of the OOO.

If equity interests may pass to heirs within the juridical persons addressed above, what of debt obligations of the decedent? Depending on Russian legislation and charter provisions, subsidiary responsibility for debt obligations may arise for heirs in full partnerships or kommandit partnerships, and in instances provided by the charter, within production cooperatives. Responsibility for such obligations is limited to

2 Ruling of the Constitutional Court of the Russian Federation, 3 July 2014, No. 1564-O. Available on Consultant+.

3 C3 PΦ (1996), no. 20, item 231, as amended. Also see Article 16(7), 1995 Federal Law "On Agricultural Cooperative Societies". C3 PΦ (1995), no. 50, item 4870, as amended.

the value of the property which otherwise would have passed to the heir.

In the case of an individual entrepreneur who dies, the Russian courts have been inclined to the view that duties pass to an heir which arose under contracts to be performed by the entrepreneurial activity of the entrepreneur. It would follow that heirs who accepted an inheritance are obliged to pay for a good delivered by the deceased individual entrepreneur pursuant to Article 1178 of the Civil Code. Obligations is understood in the context to extend not only to those known at the moment the inheritance is opened, but also to those of the decedent not terminated at the moment of his death. There consequently may be a risk of subsidiary responsibility for heirs in recovery of a debt is pursued by creditors of the decedent.

Subsidiary Responsibility. In Russian judicial practice the question has arisen as to whether the debt of a decedent which arose as a result of his subsidiary responsibility by reason of the bankruptcy of a juridical person under his control is part of the decedent's estate. Some courts have answered this question in the affirmative. Otherwise, they note, the possibility might occur of the heirs receiving property acquired by the decedent from the creditors by illegal means, such property in effect enjoying immunity against the claims of creditors, which would be unjust.[4] Situations arise when bankruptcy proceedings may be commenced with regard to a citizen after the death thereof or declaration of the death thereof.

Corporative Rights. Rights and duties inextricably connected with the person of the decedent are not part of an estate. Corporative rights which a decedent had may be conditioned, as noted above, by the requirement of obtaining consent to the transfer to the heirs of a participatory share in the charter capital of a juridical person, although there is support for the proposition that, pursuant to Article 1176 of the Civil Code,

[4] Ruling of the Judicial Division for Economic Disputes, Supreme Court of the Russian Federation, 16 December 2019, No. 305-ЭС19-15056, re: Case No. A04-7886-/2016. Available on Consultant +.

there pass "to heirs of participants of private commercial organizations not only property rights, but also corporative rights of participation in such juridical persons".[5] The status of a decedent as a bankrupt likewise is connected with the person of a decedent, subject to the above observations concerning suits relating to the rights to a thing that passed to heirs.

The rights of spouses to a participatory share of the deceased spouse in the charter capital of an economic society as part of jointly acquired property during marriage and the procedures and conditions for the acquisition of such rights are resolved in accordance with corporative legislation. The widow of a participatory shareholder in an OOO in which that participatory share was in common ownership did not simultaneously become, when being issued a certificate of the right of inheritance, a participant in the OOO irrespective of the consent of the other participants of the OOO. The major shareholder of the OOO refused such consent and was within his rights to do so under the charter of the OOO.[6]

PROTECTION AND MANAGEMENT OF ESTATE ASSETS

Business assets which comprise part of an estate frequently require immediate steps to ensure their preservation in the interests of heirs. The responsibility for taking such measures will fall, as a rule, upon the executor of the will or upon the notary at the place where the inheritance is opened. The executor undertakes measures at own initiative within a period necessary to execute the will by virtue of the duties placed on him or her by the decedent or at the demand of one or several heirs. The notary will undertake measures to protect and manage the inheritance upon the application of one or several heirs, or the executor the will, or upon the request of an agency of local self-government, trusteeship and guardianship council,

[5] L. A. Gros', «О наследовании корпоративных прав» [On the Inheritance of Corporative Rights], Цивилист [Civilist], no. 3 (2006). Available on Consultant+.

[6] Decree of Tenth Arbitrazh Appellate Court, 20 November 2018, Case No. A41-59549/2017. Available on Consultant+.

or other persons acting in the interests of preserving inheritance property.

Under Article 1171(4) of the Civil Code, a notary is granted the right to resolve the issue of taking measures to protect inheritance property, having regard to the character and value of the estate. The notary undertaking such measures must be convinced that the property concerned is part of the inheritance; that is, belonged to the decedent (Article 1112, Civil Code). There are several sources which the notary may rely upon to form this opinion:

(1) documents of agencies of State power of the Russian Federation or subjects of the Russian Federation; such as judicial acts, agencies of local self-government, competent agencies and officials; foreign States, or notaries, including in electronic form;

(2) State registers and federal information resources;

(3) the unified information system of a notary;

(4) the statements of persons who have applied to the notary for notarial actions to be undertaken and other persons involved in the undertaking of notarial actions;

(5) documents and information emanating from natural and juridical persons, including information resources.

Depending on what the estate property comprises, the notary will request a bank, other credit organization, or other juridical person about the existence or presence of property belonging to the decedent; these institutions, in turn, are required to provide such information. The notary will send through the territorial agency of the Ministry of Justice of the Russian Federation or to a notary or official an assignment to protect and/or manage inheritance property which is not located at the place where the inheritance is opened. The notary will compile an inventory of inheritance property in the presence of two witnesses (also present may be the executor of the will, heirs, and, when appropriate, representatives of trusteeship and guardianship agencies). The notary will place on deposit in his or her own public deposit account cash money discovered during the inventory. Currency valuables, precious metals and stones, manufactures thereof, and securities not requiring management are passed under contract to a bank for safekeeping. The territorial police are notified if a weapon is discovered during the inventory. Other property identified during the inventory is transferred to an heir under contract or to another person, at the discretion of the notary. If necessary, trust management is arranged.[7]

When an executor has been designated by a will, the notary undertakes the measures above by arrangement with the executor. Protective measures are taken by the notary within a period which the notary designates and necessary for the heirs to take possession of the estate property, having regard to its nature and value. When Russian legislation determines that notarial actions may be taken by an official of an agency of local self-government or by a consular official of the Russian Federation, those individuals may undertake measures to protect and manage estate property.

The inventory of inheritance property is a key document. Documents discovered when compiling the inventory which are not part of an estate and are not included on the inventory may nonetheless be passed to a bank for safekeeping (Article 921, Civil Code). If such documents confirm facts and information necessary for the issuance of a certificate on the right to an inheritance, it is recommended that they be provisionally appended to the file of the inheritance for subsequent transfer to heirs with copes thereof being retained in the inheritance file.[8]

[7] These procedures are set out in the Methods Recommendations for the Formalization on Inheritance Rights, confirmed by Decision of the Board of the Federal Chamber of Notaries, 25 March 2019, Protocol 03/19. Available on Consultant+.

[8] On the essential documents necessary to issue a certificate on the right to an inheritance, see the 1993 Fundamental Principles of Legislation on the Notariat, as amended, and the Reglament of the Performance by Notaries of Notarial Actions Establishing the Amount of Information Necessary for a Notary to Perform Notarial Actions and Means for the Fixing Thereof, confirmed by Order of the Ministry of Justice of the Russian Federation, 30 August 2017, No. 156. Available on Consultant+.

The inventory of inheritance property is drawn up in one copy, signed by the notary, witnesses, and persons present, and attached to the inheritance file. If persons who have the right to be present refuse to sign the inventory, that fact is reflected thereon.

Inheritance property not requiring management is transferred by the notary under a contract for keeping to any one of the heirs, and if this is not possible, to another person at the discretion of the notary. When inheritance occurs by will in which an executor is designated, the executor arranges the keeping of the inheritance property himself or by concluding a contract of keeping with one or several heirs or, at his discretion, another person. If not only protection, but also management, is required, the notary arranges trust management.

TRUST MANAGEMENT OF INHERITANCE PROPERTY

Frequently business assets require management as well as protection. The exception is under inheritance by will in which the decedent appoints an executor, who is deemed to be a trustee manager of the inheritance property from the moment he or she consents to be the executor of the will.

Russian legislation does not link the establishment of trust management with the instructions of a decedent. It suffices if an heir notifies a notary of the acceptance of an inheritance whose very nature requires respective actions by the notary, although in practice instances are encountered of heirs requesting a notary to organize trust management of the inheritance property. Likewise, notarial and judicial practice on occasion have allowed a notary to refuse to establish trust management if it is ascertained that the true purpose of requesting trust management is not concern for the property but a wish to use the property for personal advantage. A Russian court, for example, having determined that a particular heir put himself forward to protect a motor vehicle and trailer not in the interests of heirs of the first priority but to use the vehicle and trailer for personal purposes, held that the decree of the notary to refuse to perform a notarial action was justified on this occasion.[9]

With respect to securities elicited with preparing an inventory of inheritance property and requiring management, or when heirs apply for trust management to be established over stocks or participatory shares in the charter or contributed capital of a corporate juridical person, shares, leased immoveables, and the like, the notary will establish trust management. Such trust management does not require the consent of the juridical persons whose equity interests are being made to such trust management. One Russian court pointed out:

> Legal norms do not link the transfer of the participatory share of a decedent in the charter capital of an OOO to the heirs thereof and the possibility of the conclusion of a contract of trust management of inheritance property with the consent of the participants of the OOO. The contract of trust management of inheritance property is concluded for the purposes of the preservation thereof for the period of acceptance by the heirs of the inheritance, the transfer of the participatory share in the charter capital of the society from the deceased participant to his heirs not being dependent on the presence or absence of a contract of trust management of the inheritance property, from which it follows that the conclusion of such contract does not signify the transfer of the participatory share in the charter capital to his heirs, and consequently, the consent of the participants of the OOO to the transfer of the participatory share in the charter capital in the event of the conclusion of a contract of trust management of inheritance property is not required.[10]

9 Ruling of Leningrad Regional Court, 27 June 2013, No. 33-2356/2013. Available on Consultant+.

10 Decision of Elisovskii District Court, Kamchatka Territory, 12 July 2019; cited in Batrova, note 1 above, p. 31.

This outcome may leave the participants of the OOO in a difficult position. One course of action available to them is to request the notary or executor of the will to appoint a trustee manager, or to request an arbitrazh court to appoint an external manager of the society (Article 57, Civil Code), or to seek the exclusion of the heir as a participant of the OOO (Article 10, Federal Law on the OOO).[11]

What consequences follow if the heir or other persons do not request in good time the undertaking of measures to manage inheritance property or the executor of a will or the notary fail to promptly undertake the necessary measures? One Russian court has ruled that the OOO has the right to take "necessary actions without the participation of such trustee manager unless other circumstances prevent continuation of the activity of the society".[12]

The lawfulness of establishing trust management is under some doubt if the charter of an OOO prohibits the transfer of a participatory share to heirs of a deceased participant without the consent of the OOO participants to such transfer or a refusal to give such consent, which is grounds for the transfer of a participatory share to the society itself. The Methods Recommendations concerning the inheritance of participatory shares in the charter capital of an OOO, confirmed in 2010, note that when the consent of participants in an OOO to the transfer of the participatory shares of a deceased member is required, such consent must be received before trust management is established, which means before confirmation of the possibility to confirm that the participatory share is part of an estate.

Judicial practice takes the view that establishing trust management is possible under these circumstances, but draws attention to the limited powers of the trustee manager. Instances are known of courts determining that decisions of

[11] Decree of the Presidium of the Supreme Arbitrazh Court of the Russian Federation, 27 March 2012, No. 12653/31. Available on Consultant+.

[12] Decree of the Arbitrazh Court of the Eastern Siberian District, 3 May 2017, No. Ф02-1611/2916.

an extraordinary meeting of an OOO were invalid because the trustee manager was the sole participant and he lacked corporative rights and duties, the heirs had none yet, and merely possessed a property right to have the participatory shares bought in by the society.[13]

Valuation of Property. Pursuant to Article 1173 of the Civil Code, before the conclusion of a contract of trust management of inheritance property an evaluation must be conducted by an independent valuer of that part of the property which is transferred on trust management. Given that in order to formalize inheritance rights to such assets a report must be submitted on their market value by the heirs simultaneously with other documents, it may be used also to establish trust management.

The contract to undertake a valuation must contain: the purpose for undertaking it; the description of the items to be valued; the type of value to be determined, which will be market value; the remuneration for conducting the valuation; the date of determining the value of the items, which will be the date of opening the inheritance; information concerning the valuer, including his compliance with the requirements of independence, insurance of civil liability, membership in valuer organization(s), and reference to the Federal Standard Valuation (FSO) which is subject to application, among others.

The requirements for valuing stocks, shares in share funds, production cooperatives, participatory shares in charter (or contributed) capital, and a property complex of an organization or part thereof as solitary property of a going concern are set out in FSO "Valuation of Business" (FSO No. 8), confirmed by Order of the Ministry of Economic Development of Russia of 1 June 2015, No. 326. Pursuant to this document, in addition to general information required by FSO No. 1, "General Concepts

[13] Ruling of the Supreme Court of the Russian Federation, 18 October 2019, No. 303-ЭС19-17609. Available on Consultant+.

of Valuation, Approaches and Requirements for Conducting a Valuation",[14] the following data is essential:

(1) data concerning the object of valuation, in particular: when valuing stocks – quantity, category (or type), number and date of State registration of stock issue; when valuing participatory shares in charter (or contributed) capital of an organization – amount of participatory shares to be valued; when valuing shares in a share fund of a production cooperative – amount of shares to be valued, quantity of shares; when valuing the property complex of an organization – description of composition thereof;

(2) full and abbreviated firm name of organization (including organizational-legal form), stocks, shares in share fund, participatory shares in charter (or contributed) capital whose property complex is being valued, location thereof, basic State registration number.

Of three approaches utilized when valuing, the revenue approach is most widely used. Whatver approach is used, the valuer must be given copies of the charter of the enterprise, death certificate of the owner, balance sheets of the organization for the last three to five years or in the absence thereof, tax declarations; and other standard materials. The ultimate product is a Report on the Valuation of a Business, submitted either in paper form or electronically.

Typically, a valuation report will contain information characterizing the activity of the going concern relating to the creation and development of the business; conditions in which the business is functioning; information about the goods, product, services, and/or work produced or offered, results of business activity for a representative period on the basis of which a conclusion can be drawn about the most probable character of future indicators of business activity; financial information and forecasts of likely business performance. The prospects for the

[14] Confirmed by Order of the Ministry of Economic Development of Russia, 20 May 2015, No. 297.

branch of activity in which the organization operates will be considered, including relevant market information.

As for securities, the report will contain information about the structure of the charter (or contributed) capital or share fund of the going concern (par value, number of placed and voting common or voting and non-voting preferred stocks) and similar data on other types of going concerns which are not joint-stock societies; dividend history, and other profit distributions. Documents which do not conform to the requirements of the FSO are not recognized as a report on valuation and therefore not regarded as a basis for concluding a trust management of property contract.

Under Article 1015 of the Civil Code, an individual entrepreneur or commercial organization, except for a unitary enterprise, may be a trustee manager, When the trust management of property is undertaken on the grounds provided for by a law, as in the case of an inheritance, the trustee manager may be a citizen who is not an entrepreneur or a noncommercial organization, except an institution. Property is not subject to transfer in trust management to a State agency or agency of local self-government.

The trustee manager may not be a beneficiary under the contract of trust management of property. Reading this requirement literally and given that a beneficiary under a trust management contract for inheritance property is not designated, a proposed heir may act in this capacity if appointed with the consent of other heirs known at the moment of appointment, and if there are objections, on the basis of a court decision. However, judicial resistance to this state of affairs is known:

> The entry of an heir as a trustee manager may lead to a conflict of interests of the managing heir, on one side, with the other heirs – on the other, inasmuch as the managing heir acquires with respect to the inheritance property powers which the other heirs may not possess. Moreover, trust management is founded before the entry of an heir into possession of the inheritance property.

> However, the property transferred on trust management is considered to be encumbered to the benefit of the trustee manager, and the heirs cannot possess, use, or dispose of such property without the consent of the trustee manager. Thus, the heir, in acting as the trustee manager of the inheritance property, is endowed with the right to use and dispose of the inheritance property before entering into the inheritance, which does not conform to the provisions of inheritance law.[15]

The situation with respect to a testamentary legacy is clear, for the recipient of a testamentary legacy is designated as a beneficiary under Article 1137 of the Civil Code and is therefore excluded from acting as a trustee manager.

The Civil Code allows inheritance property to be transferred to several trustee managers, each of whom has powers to manage the inheritance property unless the trust management contract or the will provides that the trustee managers exercise their powers jointly. Presumably if acting jointly they would form a common position in taking decisions with regard to property management. This would seem to follow from the legislative consolidation of a notarial duty to dissolve the trust management contract if disagreements arise between the trustee managers with regard to the exercise of their rights and duties, demand the submission of reports by them, and appoint a new trustee manager(s).

The question of heirs agreeing to candidacies for the position of trustee manager deserves special attention. It is presumed that such consent is essential given that the trustee manager is acting in the interests of the heirs. It can be more complicated if the trustee manager is acting in the interests of a minor. Russian legislation (Article 37, Civil Code) does not specifically indicate that the consent of a trusteeship or guardianship agency must be obtained to the appointment of a trustee manager acting for a minor. Judicial practice requires that the consent of the legal

[15] Decision of Tuapse City Court, Krasnodar Territory, 4 July 2019, No. 2-539/2019. Available on Consultant+.

representative of the minor be obtained before the conclusion of a contract with a trustee manager which specifies that the minor is the beneficiary. If the alienation of inheritance property is not involved and there is no remuneration to the trustee manager, the courts are usually content with the consent of legal representative being sufficient.[16]

The rights and duties of a trustee manager are determined by the Civil Code (Article 1020). The trustee manager exercises within the limits provided for by a law and the contract of trust management of property the powers of the owner with respect to property transferred in trust management. The disposition of immovable property the trustee manager effectuates in the instances provided for by the contract of trust management, which means that immoveables must be disposed of only in the instances provided by a trust management contract.

Corporate rights are intangibles ("non-property" rights) are not inherited but pass to heirs together with the property comprising a participatory share in the capital of the juridical person unless provided otherwise in the charter of the said juridical person. Judicial and notarial practice proceed from the fact that the establishment of trust management enables the uncertainty of the constituent participants in the juridical person to be eliminated and secures a balance between the interests of the heirs of the deceased participant and the ability of the juridical person to continue to operate. However, Russian courts have taken different positions with regard to the extent of the powers of the trustee manager.

The majority of Russian courts have been of the view that Russian legislation imposes no limitations of the corporate decisions which a trustee manager may take, including the appointment or dismissal of the general director, without whom a juridical person cannot operate (Article 53, Civil Code). The operative premise is that insofar as the composition of participants in the juridical person is indeterminate because

[16] Decision of the Frunze District Court, City of Saratov, No. 2-260/2017, cited in Batrova, note 1 above, p. 39.

the inheritance issue has not been resolved and the participants cannot take part in voting, the corporate rights are exercised by the trustee manager, who bears personal responsibility established by law for the decisions taken. It follows, in this view, that until State registration of the information concerning the transfer of the participatory share in the charter capital by way of inheritance, the management of those participatory shares, including voting at general meetings, may be exercised by the trustee manager acting in the interests of the heirs.[17]

Notarial practice takes an analogous approach, where it is considered to formally separate the property rights of a participant of a juridical person with limited responsibility for the concomitant corporate rights would violate the integrity of the participatory share in the charter capital as an "autonomous subject of civil rights".[18]

The alternative approach takes a strict view of the powers which a trustee manager possesses. The trustee manager should confine his or her activities solely to the protection of the inheritance property and is not authorized to take corporate decisions, especially as these may prove to be harmful to the interests of the heir.

There are problems with both approaches which arise from the interval of time between the opening of an inheritance and the culmination of title vesting in an heir to corporate equity interests. On one hand, the "protection" function placed on a trustee manager with respect to intangibles is not realistically confined to physical protection, but neither does placing additional powers on a trustee manager by contract solve the problem because the heir is merely in expectation of receiving

[17] Decree of the Thirteenth Arbitrazh Appellate Cassational Court, 23 October 2013, re: No. A56-21035/2013; Decision of the Dzerzhinskii District Court, City of Volgograd, 16 June 2015, No. 2-4752/2015, cited in Batrova, p. 40.

[18] «Обобщение вопросов, возникающих в нотариальной практике при применении отдельных норм Федерального закона «Об обществах с ограниченной ответственностью» [Generalization of Questions Arising in Notarial Practice when Applying Individual Norms of the Federal Law "On Limited Responsibility Societies"], Нотариальный вестник [Notarial Herald] (2010), p. 47.

the inheritance and may not actually do so. If the trustee manager is authorized to exercise corporate powers in the interim in expectation of the inheritance vesting, those powers are, in principle, dealing with speculative matters. Neither approach seems, moreover, to take full account of the interests of the corporate vehicle, which may be harmed by ill-advised decisions taken by a trustee manager or by the absence of clarity or certainty about the interests of the corporate vehicle itself, which may need prompt and informed decision-making. The Russian legislator continues to find challenging the proper balance to be achieved not only between the interests of the heirs vis-à-vis other equity stakeholders, but also the responsibility that all stakeholders bear by law to the corporate vehicle, which includes actions or failures to act that may paralyze the operations of the juridical person.

Conflicts of interest can occur if a participant in a corporate vehicle is also chosen as a trustee manager, at least with respect to deciding controversial issues. One relevant case entailed an individual acting as the sole participant in an OOO and also acting as the trustee manager on behalf of two heirs to a participatory share in the same corporate vehicle. The decision which he adopted acting in both capacities prejudiced the corporate rights of the heirs and would have alienated property of the corporate vehicle against the wishes of the heirs. The court regarded this as a conflict of interests and abuse of right.[19]

Under Article 1020(2) of the Civil Code, the rights acquired by the trustee manager as a result of actions relating to the trust management of property are included in the property transferred in trust management. The duties which arise as a result of such actions of the trustee manager are performed at the expense of this property. In order to defend the rights to property in trust management the trustee manager has the right to demand any elimination of a violation of his rights (Articles 301, 302, 304, and 305, Civil Code). The trustee manager is required to submit

[19] Decree of Federal Arbitrazh Court of the Northwestern District, 17 May 2013, re: No. A56-24767/2011.

to the founder of the management and beneficiary a report concerning his activity within the periods and in the procedure established by the contract of trust management of property.

NEGOTIATION OF TRUST MANAGEMENT CONTRACT

A trust management contract must be concluded in written form. If such contract involved business assets in the form of immoveables or an enterprise as a property complex, the contract needs to be concluded in the contract form used for the sale of an immoveable. Immoveable property transferred to trust management must undergo State registration in the same procedure as the transfer of rights of ownership to such property. Failure to comply will mean that the contract is invalid.

Federal legislation providing that trust management of immoveable property is subject to State registration mentions trust management in passing as a form of the limitation of rights to and encumbrance on such property. This means that any rights to immoveable property connected with its disposition on conditions of trust management must be registered on the basis of documents determining those legal relations. In describing the object of trust management, the notary or executor of the will must indicate in detail the distinctive features. In the case of a participatory share in the charter capital of a corporate vehicle: the size thereof in the form of percentage or fraction, par value (if applicable), full name of the juridical person; basic State registration number, tax identification number, State registration number under which the charter is registered, address, and market valuation of the participatory share to be inherited.

Article 1016 of the Civil Code contains the material conditions of a trust management contract. Among these are the name of the juridical person or the name of the citizen in whose interests the management of the property are to be effectuated (the founder of the management or the beneficiary). Except for instances of a testamentary legacy, this requirement is almost impossible to satisfy and in judicial practice recognized as inadvisable: the heirs who have accepted the inheritance may repeatedly change during the operation of the contract.

Another material condition is the amount and form of remuneration to be paid to the trustee manager if the contract provides for such payment. Russian courts take the view that the absence of such a provision for remuneration does not mean the contract was "not concluded" because the applicable Government decree determines a maximum fee of 3% of the valuation of the inheritance property. The parties are left to decide. If remuneration is to be paid, whether the remuneration should be in kind from the revenues of the corporate vehicle or in money.[20]

INHERITANCE OF RIGHTS TO RESULTS OF INTELLECTUAL ACTIVITY

Some of what falls into this category would be classified as intellectual property by most western lawyers, but the Russian phrase is broader and includes:

(1) the results of intellectual activity in literature, the arts, science, computer software, databases, performances, and phonograms;

(2) such results in the scientific-technical fields: inventions, utility models, industrial designs, selection achievements; topologies of integral microcircuits; and production secrets or know-how;

(3) such creations or "means of individualization" as: trademarks and service marks and commercial designations.

These are all addressed in Part Four of the Civil Code. Insofar as some may belong solely to juridical persons, they are

[20] See the Decree of the Government of the Russian Federation of 27 May 2002, No. 350, "On Confirmation of the Maximum Amount of Remuneration Under a Contract of Keeping of Inheritance Property and Contract of Trust Management of Inheritance Property". СЗ РФ (2002), no. 22, item 2096, as amended.

excluded from the possibility of inheritance. This would include firm names and exclusive rights to television or broadcasting transmissions. Insofar as they figure in inheritance relations, they do so as part of the inheritance of an enterprise or property complex and may be part of the inheritance of a participatory share in the charter capital of a juridical person.

The situation would be otherwise for an individual entrepreneur, for in that instance the results of intellectual activity may be a business asset. In the case of a name of the place of origin of a good duly certified loses force upon the death of an individual entrepreneur who holds such a certificate. Similar difficulties arise in connection with the exclusive right to a production secret or know-how, for insofar as this commercial secret may pass by inheritance, this requires the divulgence of information which may result in the know-how ceasing to be confidential.[21] Domain names pose a similar issue, which in Russia are not objects of intellectual rights. The precise legal regime under which they exist and operate is indeterminate, and Russian legislation does not address the possibility of their being registered to multiple persons or regard domain names as an autonomous means of individualization.

Batrova observes that in matters of inheritance, the dual nature of intellectual rights should be taken into account: intellectual rights include a "property character" and may also be personal non-property rights (right of authorship, right to name, right to inviolability of a work, right to publication, and others) and other rights (right of pursuit, right of access, right to remuneration, and others). Article 1112 of the Civil Code provides that "personal non-property rights and other nonmaterial benefits shall not be within the composition of an inheritance". These means, in effect, that "only exclusive rights

[21] For a discussion of some complexities, see O. V. Ruzakova, «Вопросы наследования интеллектуальных прав» [Questions of the Inheritance of Intellectual Rights], in Iu. V. Gongalo, et al. (eds.), Актуальные вопросы наследственного права [Topical Questions of Inheritance Law] (2016).

whose content is predetermined by the specific nature of the result of intellectual activity" may be inherited.[22]

When rights to intellectual activity are capable of being inherited, they are subject to temporal and territorial constraints. Temporal because they are usually protected, if duly registered when necessary, for a fixed period, subject to any renewals and extensions. Once those have expired or been exhausted, they in effect disappear. Territorial because they are recognized and protected, if duly registered, only within the territory of the State where registered. This is especially true of patents and means of individualization.

As for personal non-property rights, some are linked inextricably with the person of the deceased and not capable of inheritance, such as the right of authorship, the right to a name, or the right of access to a work. Others are not exclusive but nonetheless accompany the inheritance of property of the decedent: for example, the right of pursuit (Article 1293, Civil Code), which is inalienable but passes heirs until it expires. Patent rights are generally inheritable, as are rights granted under license.

As for a married couple, an exclusive right to a result of intellectual activity created by one spouse is not their common property (Article 256, Civil Code) and is inherited as the property of the author of t hat result and is not part of the spousal share of the marital property. If, however, the said exclusive right was acquired at the expense of common revenues of the spouses under a contract concerning the alienation of such right, the said result is their common property unless provided otherwise by the contract and is inherited pursuant to Article 1150 of the Civil Code protecting the right of the surviving spouse to part of the property acquired during marriage with the decedent and is in their joint ownership.

[22] Batrova, note 1 above, p. 95.

CIVIL CODE OF THE RUSSIAN FEDERATION

PART ONE

...

Article 123[20-1]. Creation of Inheritance Foundation, Conditions of Management Thereof, and Liquidation Thereof [added by Federal Law of 29 July 2017, No. 259-ФЗ; lost force by Federal Law of 1 July 2021, No. 287-ФЗ. СЗ РФ (2017), no. 31(I), item 4808; (2021), no. 27(1), item 5115]

Article 123[20-2]. Management of Inheritance Foundation [added by Federal Law of 29 July 2017, No. 259-ФЗ; lost force by Federal Law of 1 July 2021, No. 287-ФЗ. СЗ РФ (2017), no. 31(I), item 4808; (2021), no. 27(1), item 5115]

Article 123[20-3]. Rights of Beneficiaries of Inheritance Foundation [added by Federal Law of 29 July 2017, No. 259-ФЗ; lost force by Federal Law of 1 July 2021, No. 287-ФЗ. СЗ РФ (2017), no. 31(I), item 4808; (2021), no. 27(1), item 5115]

1[1]. Personal Foundations

[added by Federal Law of 1 July 2021, No. 287-ФЗ. СЗ РФ (2021), no. 27(I), item 5115]

Article 123[20-4]. Basic Provisions on Personal Foundation [added by Federal Law of 1 July 2021, No. 287-ФЗ. СЗ РФ (2021), no. 27(I), item 5115]

1. A unitary noncommercial effectuating the management of property transferred thereto by a citizen for a determined period or in perpetuity after his death by a notary or property inherited from this citizen, and also other property in accordance with management conditions confirmed by him, shall be deemed to be a personal foundation [as amended by

Federal Law of 8 August 2024, No. 237-ФЗ. СЗ РФ 2024), no. 33(I), item 4393].

2. A personal foundation may be created by a notary after the death of a citizen in accordance with his will (inheritance foundation). The provisions of the present Code concerning personal foundations shall apply to inheritance foundations unless established otherwise by the present Code or arises from the peculiarities of the legal status of inheritance foundations.

The founder of a personal foundation shall have the right to provide in the charter of a personal foundation created during his lifetime that after his death such personal foundation shall continue its activity in accordance with the charter confirmed by the founder and the management conditions, such personal foundation may not be liquidated after the death of the founder thereof by decision of the organs thereof.

3. A citizen who has created a personal foundation during his lifetime or provided in his will for the creation of an inheritance foundation shall be deemed to be the founder of the personal foundation.

The replacement of the founder of a personal foundation shall not be permitted. When creating personal foundations, the co-founding by several persons shall not be permitted except for instances when spouses transferring common property to the personal foundation are the founders of the personal foundation (Article 256).

4. The property of a personal foundation shall belong to the personal foundation by right of ownership. The founder of a personal foundation shall not have the rights to property of a foundation created by it [as amended by Federal Law of 8 August 2024, No. 237-ФЗ. СЗ РФ 2024), no. 33(I), item 4393].

The value of property to be transferred to a personal foundation (except for an inheritance foundation) by the founder thereof when creating a personal foundation may not be less than one hundred million rubles, the value of this property being determined on the basis of a valuation of its market value.

5. A personal foundation shall have the right to engage in entrepreneurial activity corresponding to the purposes determined by the charter of the personal foundation and necessary for the achievement of those purposes. In order to effectuate entrepreneurial activity a personal foundation shall have the right to create economic societies or to participate in them.

6. The founder of a personal foundation shall bear subsidiary responsibility for obligations of this personal foundation in the event of the insufficiency of its property, and the personal foundation, except for an inheritance foundation, shall bear subsidiary responsibility with its property for obligations of the founder of a personal foundation during three years from the day of creation thereof. In exceptional instances, if creditors of the personal foundation or founder of a personal foundation for justifiable reasons do not have the possibility to turn with demands against the founder of a personal foundation or personal foundation within the said period, this period may be extended by a court, but by not more than five years from the day of creation of the personal foundation.

7. The decision of a founder of a personal foundation concerning the founding of the personal foundation is subject to notarial certification. A will whose conditions provide for the creation of an inheritance foundation must include in itself the decision of the testator concerning the founding of the inheritance foundation, charter of the foundation, and also the management conditions of the inheritance foundation. Such will shall be subject to notarial certification.

8. The constitutive document of a personal foundation shall be the charter thereof.

The founder of a personal foundation shall have the right to confirm the management conditions of a personal foundation and other internal documents of the personal foundation binding upon all organs of the personal foundation.

The charter of a personal foundation and management conditions of a personal foundation shall be subject to notarial certification.

Unless established otherwise by the present Code or charter of a personal foundation, information concerning the contents of management conditions of a personal foundation and content of other internal documents of a personal foundation shall not be subject to divulgence and shall be confidential.

Unless provided otherwise by the charter of a personal foundation, the management conditions of a personal foundation and other internal documents of a personal foundation may, during the lifetime of the founder of the foundation be changed by him. After the death of the founder of a personal foundation, the charter of the personal foundation, management conditions of the personal foundation, and other internal documents of the personal foundation confirmed by the founder during his lifetime may not be changed, except for changes on the basis of the decision of a court upon the demand of any organ of the personal foundation in instances when the management of such foundation on the former conditions has become impossible under circumstances whose arising was when such foundation was created would never have been assumed [as amended by Federal Law of 8 August 2024, No. 237-ФЗ].

The charter of an inheritance foundation and management conditions of an inheritance foundation may not be changed after the creation of the inheritance foundation, except for changes on the basis of the decision of a court upon the demand of any organ of the inheritance foundation in instances when the management of the inheritance foundation on the former conditions has become impossible under circumstances whose arising when such foundation was created would never have been assumed, and also in the event it will established that the beneficiary of the inheritance foundation is an unworthy heir (Article 1117) only this circumstance was not known at the moment of creation of the inheritance foundation.

9. The name of the personal foundation must include the words "personal foundation". The name of an inheritance foundation must include the words "inheritance foundation".

10. The reorganization of a personal foundation (except for an inheritance foundation) shall be permitted in the form of merger, accession, division, or separation on condition that as a result of such reorganization a personal foundation(s) created by the same founder are formed. The transformation of a personal foundation into a socially-useful foundation by decision of the founder also shall be permitted during the lnifetime of the founder of a personal foundation.

The reorganization of a personal foundation after the death of the founder thereof shall not be permitted except for transformation of the personal foundation into a socially-useful foundation in the instances provided by the management conditions of the personal foundation and Article 12320-5(6) of the present Code.

11. The liquidation of a personal foundation shall be effectuated by decision of a court:

(1) in the procedure and on the grounds provided for by Article 61(3), points (1)-(4), of the present Code, and also upon the suit of the empowered State agency in the event of the effectuation by by personal foundation of activity specified in legislation of the Russian Federation on foreign agents [as amended by Federal Law of 8 August 2024, No. 237-ФЗ. СЗ РФ 2024), no. 33(I), item 4393];

(2) upon the demand of the one-person executive organ of the personal foundation in connection with the ensuing of the period before the expiry of which the personal foundation was created;

(3) upon the demand of the one-person executive organ of the personal foundation in connection with the ensuing of circumstances specified in the management conditions of the personal foundation;

(4) upon the demand of the beneficiary of the personal foundation in the event of the impossibility of forming the organs of the personal foundation (absence of quorum in collegial organs, absence of one-person executive organ);

(5) upon the demand of a one-person executive organ of a personal foundation in connection with the impossibility of an extension for three years unless another period is provided by the charter of the personal foundation to fulfill the conditions provided by the founder of the personal foundation in accordance with which the beneficiaries of the personal foundation are subject to determination.

Property remaining after the liquidation of the personal foundation shall be subject to transfer to beneficiaries of the personal foundation commensurate to the volume of their rights to receive property or revenue from the activity of the personal foundation unless the management conditions of the personal foundation have provided other rules for the distribution of the remaining property, including the transfer thereof to persons who are not beneficiaries. In the absence of the possibility to determine the persons to whom the property remaining after the liquidation of the personal foundation is subject to transfer, such property shall be subject to transfer to the ownership of the founder(s) of the personal foundation, and if at this moment the marriage between the founders who transferred common property to the foundation is dissolved – to the common participatory share ownership of the founders, whose participatory share ownership in the property transferred to them shall be deemed to be equal unless established otherwise by an agreement between them or by decision of a court. In the absence of the possibility to determine the persons to whom transfer of the property remaining after liquidation of the inheritance foundation is subject, such property shall be subject to transfer in accordance with the decision of a court to the ownership of the Russian Federation [as amended by Federal Law of 8 August 2024, No. 237-ФЗ. СЗ РФ 2024), no. 33(I), item 4393].

12. A report on the use of property of a personal foundation shall not be subject to publication, except for instances provided by the management conditions of the personal foundation.

Article 123[20-5]. Conditions of Management of Personal Foundation [added by Federal Law of 1 July 2021, No. 287-ФЗ. СЗ РФ (2021), no. 27(I), item 5115]

1. The management conditions of a personal foundation may include in themselves provisions concerning the transfer to determined persons (beneficiaries of the personal foundation) or to individual categories of persons from an indeterminate group of persons (hereinafter – individual categories of persons) of all the property of the personal foundation or part thereof, including when circumstances ensue relatijve to which whether they will ensue or not is unknown.

2. It may be provided by the management conditions of a personal foundation that the beneficiaries of the personal foundation or individual categories of persons to whom the transfer of the property of the personal foundation is subject shall be determined by the organs of the personal foundation in accordance with the management conditions of the personal foundation.

3. The procedure for the transfer to beneficiaries of the personal foundation or to individual categories of persons of the entire property of the personal foundation or part thereof, including revenues from the activity of the personal foundation, must be determined by the management conditions of the personal foundation by means of an indication of the type and dimension of the property to be transferred or procedure for determining the type and dimension of the property, including property right (for example, rights to use of property, rights to payment for work, services to be rendered by third persons to beneficiaries of the personal foundation or individual categories of persons), period or periodicity of the transfer of property, and also to circumstances in the event of the ensuing of which such transfer is effectuated.

4. Any participants of relations regulated by civil legislation may be beneficiaries of a personal foundation, except for commercial juridical persons. The founder of a personal foundation may not be a beneficiary of a personal foundation unless provided otherwise by the charter of this foundation.

5. A beneficiary of a personal foundation shall have the right to demand from the personal foundation, and the beneficiary of an inheritance foundation shall have the right to demand from the notary or inheritance foundation to familiarize them with that upart of the management conditions of the personal foundation which contains the procedure for the determination and appointment of the organs of the personal foundation, provisions concerning the transfer to this beneficiary of all or part of the property of the personal foundation, and also a description of the circumstances in the event of the ensuing of which such transfer is effectuated.

6. No later than six months from the day of death of a citizen who has founded a personal foundation during lifetime, if the management conditions of this foundation after the death of the founder provide solely provisions concerning the transfer of all the property of the personal foundation to individual categjories of persons from an indeterminate group of persons, such foundation shall be subject to transformation into a socially-useful foundation (Article 12317), the charter of the personal foundation, the management conditions of the personal foundation, and other internal documents of the personal foundation confirmed by the founder thereof not being subject to change, and information concerning the new name of this foundation and concerning the change of its organizational-legal form shall be reflected in the unified State register of juridical persons.`

Article 123$^{20-6}$. Rights of Beneficiary of Personal Foundation [added by Federal Law of 1 July 2021, No. 287-ФЗ. СЗ РФ (2021), no. 27(I), item 5115]

1. A beneficiary of a personal foundation shall have the right to receive property in accordance with the management

conditions of the personal foundation, and also other rights provided by the present Code.

The rights of a beneficiary of a personal foundation may not pass to other persons, including in the event of universal legal succession, except for instances of the transformation of the beneficiary – juridical person, unless the management conditions of the personal foundation provide for the termination of the rights of such beneficiary in the event of its transformation. Execution may not be levied against the rights of the beneficiary of a personal foundation, including the beneficiary of an inheritance foundation, for obligations of such beneficiary. Transactions concluded with a violation of these rules shall be void.

2. The rights of a citizen-beneficiary of an inheritance foundation shall not pass by way of inheritance. The rights of a beneficiary-juridical person of an inheritance foundation shall terminate in the event of the reorganization of the beneficiary-juridical person, except for an instance of transformation, unless the management conditions of the inheritance foundation provided for the termination of the rights of such beneficiary in the event of its transformation.

After the death of a citizen-beneficiary or liquidation of a beneficiary-juridical person, and also in the event of a renunciation declared to an inheritance foundation in notarial form of the beneficiary of an inheritance foundation of the right to receive property, the new beneficiaries of the inheritance foundation shall be determined in accordance with the management conditions of the inheritance foundation, in particular, they may be determined by way of sub-designation.

3. In instances provided by the charter of the inheritance foundation, a beneficiary shall have the right to request and to receive from a personal foundation information concerning the activity of the personal foundation.

4. A beneficiary of a personal foundation shall have the right to demand the conducting of an audit of the activity of the personal foundation by an auditor selected by him. In the event

of the conducting of such an audit, the services of the auditor shall be paid for at the expense of the beneficiary of the personal foundation upon whose demand it is conducted. The expenses of the beneficiary of the personal foundation for payment of the services of the auditor may be compensated to him by decision of the trusteeship council at the expense of the means of such foundation.

5. In the event of a violation of the management conditions by a personal foundation which entail the arising of losses for a beneficiary of the personal foundation, the last shall have the right to demand the compensation thereof if this right is provided for by the charter of the personal foundation.

6. A beneficiary shall not be liable for obligations of the personal foundation, and the personal foundation shall not be liable for obligations of the beneficiary.

Article 123^{20-7}. Management of Personal Foundation [added by Federal Law of 1 July 2021, No. 287-ФЗ. СЗ РФ (2021), no. 27(I), item 5115]

1. During the lifetime of the founder of a personal foundation, the composition of organs, the functions thereof, and the persons within the composition of the organs of this foundation shall be determined in accordance with the charter and management conditions of the personal foundation [as amended by Federal Law of 8 August 2024, No. 237-ФЗ. СЗ РФ 2024), no. 33(I), item 4393].

After the death of the citizen who founded the personal foundation during his lifetime, the organs of the personal foundation shall be formed and changed in accordance with the charter and management conditions of this personal foundation , the persons entering the composition of the organs of the personal foundation or having the right to enter the compositin of the organs of this foundation, and also the beneficiaries of this foundation, shall have the right to demand the forming and changing of the organs of the personal foundation in accordance with the charter thereof and management conditions of the foundation. The procedure may be provided by the charter of the personal foundation and management conditions of the personal foundation for determining the members of the collegial organs of the personal foundation and the persons effectuating the powers of the one-person executive organ of the personal foundation in the event of their withdrawal, including provision for the sub-designation of the said persons from a determined list.

2. Any natural person or juridical person designated in accordance with the charter of the personal foundation, except for the founder of the personal foundation, may act as the one-person executive organ of a personal foundation or member of the collegial organ of a personal foundation.

A beneficiary of an inheritance foundation may not act as a one-person executive organ of an inheritance foundation or member of a collegial organ of an inheritance foundation.

3. In instances provided by the charter of a personal foundation, a high collegial organ and trusteeship council shall be created therein, in the composition of which may be a beneficiary or the founder of the personal foundation.

The creation also may be provided by the charter of a personal foundation of a supervisory organ of the personal foundation, the powers of which shall consist in the effectuation of supervision over the activity of organs of the personal foundation, in agreeing the performance by the personal foundation of legally significant actions determined in the charter, and/or in the adoption of decisions concerning the termination before time of the powers of the one-person executive organ of the personal foundation who violated his duty to act in good faith or reasonably in the interests of the personal foundation and/or beneficiaries thereof, and concerning the designation temporary one-person executive organ of a personal foundation.

4. The procedure for the payment and amount of remuneration to the person effectuating the powers of a one-person executive organ of a personal foundation, members of the trusteeship council of a personal foundation, or members

of other organs of a personal foundation, and also the person effectuating the functions of the supervisory council of a personal foundation, may be provided by the management conditions of the personal foundation, for the performance of their duties.

5. The necessity to receive consent of the high collegial organ of a personal foundation, supervisory organ of the personal foundation, or other organ of the personal foundation for the conclusion by the personal foundation of transactions specified in the charter may be provided by the charter of the personal foundation.

6. An audit of the activity of a personal foundation shall be conducted on the grounds provided by the management conditions of the personal foundation, and also upon the demand of a beneficiary of the personal foundation, in the procedure provided by Article 12320-6(4) of the present Code.

7. If within a year from the day of the necessity arising for forming the organs of an inheritance foundation or organs a personal foundation created during the lifetime of the founder and continuing its activity after his death such organs are not formed (absence of quorum in collegial organs, absence of one-person executive organ), such organs shall be subject to liquidation upon the demand of the beneficiaries of such foundations or empowered State agency. Until the expiry of the said period, the organs (f they exist) of an inheritance foundation or personal foundation created during the lifetime of the founder and continuing their activity after his death shall continue to effectuate the activity of this inheritance foundation or of this personal foundation in accordance with the management conditions of such foundations.

Article 123$^{20-8.}$ Creation of Inheritance Foundation and Management Thereof [added by Federal Law of 1 July 2021, No. 287-ФЗ. СЗ РФ (2021), no. 27(I), item 5115]

1. After the death of a citizen who has provided in his will for the creation of an inheritance foundation, such inheritance foundation shall be subject to creation upon the application

sent to the empowered State agency by the notary keeping the inheritance file, appending to the application drawn up during6 the life of the said citizen the decision thereof concerning the founding of the inheritance foundation and the charter of the foundation confirmed by this citizen and after the creation thereof shall be called to inherit under the will in the procedure provided by Section V of the present Code.

The inheritance foundation may be created on the basis of the decision of a court upon the demand of the executor or beneficiary of the inheritance foundation in the event of the failure of the notary to perform the duties with regard to the creation of the inheritance foundation.

The notary keeping the inheritance file shall be obliged to send to the empowered State agency the application concerning State registration of the inheritance foundation no later than three work days from the day of opening the inheritance file after the death of the citizen who provided in his will for the creation of the inheritance foundation. The inheritance foundation shall not be subject to registration upon the expiry of one year from the day of opening the inheritance.

The actions of a notary with regard to the creation of an inheritance foundation may be contested by beneficiaries of the inheritance foundation, executor, or heirs if dispositions of the decedent contained in the will or decisions concerning the founding of the inheritance foundation relative to the creation of the inheritance foundation or conditions of the management thereof have been violated by the notary

2. When creating an inheritance foundation, the notary who has received an application from the inheritance foundation concerning the acceptance of the inheritance shall be obliged to issue to such foundation a certificate of the right to inherit within the period specified in the decision on founding the inheritance but no later than than the period provided for by Article 1154 of the present Code. In the event of the failure of the notary to perform the said duties, the inheritance foundation shall have the right to appeal the failure of the notary to act.

3. Before the sending by the notary of the application on State registration of the inheritance foundation specified in point 1, paragraph three, of the present Article to the empowered State agency, the notary shall propose to the persons specified in the decision on founding the inheritance foundation or the persons who might be determined in the procedure established by the decision on founding the inheritance foundation to become a member of the organs of the inheritance foundation. In the event of the consent of the said persons to become a member of organs of the inheritance foundation, the notary shall send information concerning them to the empowered State agency.

In the event of the refusal of a person specified in the decision on founding the inheritance foundation to become a member of the organs of the inheritance foundation and impossibility to form the organs of the inheritance foundation in accordance with the decision on founding the inheritance foundation, the notary shall not have the right to send the application on the creation of the inheritance foundation to the empowered State agency.

4. The replacement of members of collegial organs of an inheritance foundation and of a person exercising the powers of a one-person executive organ of an inheritance foundation shall be effectuated in the procedure provided by the charter of the inheritance foundation. The charter of an inheritance foundation may provide the procedure for determining the members of collegial organs of the inheritance foundation and person exercising the powers of a one-person executive organ of the inheritance foundation in the event of the withdrawal thereof, including providing for the sub-designation onf the said persons from a determined list.

5. The conditions for management of an inheritance foundation must include the provisions specified in Article 12320-5(1) and (3) of the present Code.

The conditions for the management of an inheritance foundation before the notary sends the application specified in point 1, paragraph three, of the present Article shall be brought to the information by him or her to persons who are members of organs of the inheritance foundation and may be divulged only to beneficiaries in accordance with Article 12320-5(5) of the present Code, and also in instances provided by a law to agencies of State power and agencies of local self-government.

6. A one-person executive organ of an inheritance foundation shall be obliged to keep the charter of the inheritance foundation and changes and additions made therein which have been registered in the established procedure, the decision on founding the inheritance foundation, documents confirming the right of the inheritance foundation to its property, document containing the conditions for management of the inheritance foundation, yearly reports, bookkeeping documents, documents of bookkeeping (or financial) reports, protocols of meetings of collegial organs of the inheritance foundation, reports of valuers, opinions of internal audit commission (or internal auditor) of the inheritance foundation, auditor of the inheritance foundation, State and municipal financial control agencies, judicial acts relating to disputes connected with the management of the inheritance foundation, and other documents provided by the present Code, charter of the inheritance foundation, and conditions of management of the inheritance foundation.

The charter of an inheritance foundation may provide for the keeping of documents specified in paragraph one of the present point with a notary according to the rules provided by legislation on the notariat.

...

PART THREE

[Excerpts][2]

SECTION VI. INHERITANCE LAW

Chapter 61. General Provisions on Inheritance

Article 1110. Inheriting

1. In the event of inheriting, the property of a deceased (inheritance, inheritance property) shall pass to other persons by way of universal legal succession, that is, in unchanged form as a single whole and at one and the same moment, unless it follows otherwise from the rules of the present Code.

2. Inheriting shall be regulated by the present Code and by other laws, and in the instances provided for by a law, by other legal acts.

Article 1111. Grounds of Inheritance

Inheriting shall be effectuated by will, by an inheritance contract, and by operation of law [as amended by Federal Law of 19 July 2018, No. 217-ФЗ. СЗ РФ (2018), no. 30, item 4552].

Inheriting by operation of law shall occur when and insofar as it is not changed by a will, and also in other instances established by the present Code.

Article 1112. Inheritance

Within the composition of an inheritance shall be the things and other property, including property rights and duties, which belonged to the decedent on the day of opening the inheritance.

Rights and duties shall not be within the composition of an inheritance which are inextricably connected with the person of the decedent, in particular, the right to alimony, the right to compensation of harm caused to the life or health of a citizen,

[2] Translation from W. E. Butler, *Civil Code of the Russian Federation* (2021).

and also rights and duties whose transfer by way of inheriting is not permitted by the present Code or by other laws.

Personal nonproperty rights and other nonmaterial benefits shall not be within the composition of an inheritance.

Article 1113. Opening of Inheritance

An inheritance shall open with the death of a citizen. The declaration by a court of a citizen to be deceased shall entail the same legal consequences as the death of the citizen.

Article 1114. Time of Opening of Inheritance

1. The time of opening an inheritance shall be the moment of death of the citizen. When declaring a citizen to be deceased, the day of opening an inheritance shall be the day of entry into legal force of the decision of the court concerning the declaring of the citizen to be deceased, and when in accordance with Article 45(3) of the present Code the day of death of a citizen is deemed to be the day of his supposed perishing, – the day and moment of death specified in the decision of the court [as amended by Federal Law of 30 March 2016, No. 79-ФЗ. СЗ РФ (2016), no. 14, item 1909].

2. Citizens deceased on the same day shall be considered for the purposes of inheritance legal succession to be deceased simultaneously and shall not inherit one after the other if it is impossible to establish the moment of death of each of such citizens. The heirs of each of them shall be called to inherit in so doing [as amended by Federal Law of 30 March 2016, No. 79-ФЗ. СЗ РФ (2016), no. 14, item 1909].

Article 1115. Place of Opening of Inheritance

The place of opening an inheritance shall be the last place of residence of the decedent (Article 20).

If the last place of residence of a decedent who possessed property on the territory of the Russian Federation is unknown or situated beyond the limits thereof, the place of opening an inheritance in the Russian Federation shall be deemed to be the location of such inheritance property. If such inheritance property is situated in various places, the place of opening the inheritance shall be the location of the immoveable property within its composition or of the most valuable part of the immoveable property, and in the absence of immoveable property – the location of moveable property or most valuable part thereof. The value of the property shall be determined by proceeding from its market value.

Article 1116. Persons Who May Be Called to Inherit

1. Citizens alive at the moment of opening an inheritance, as well as conceived during the life of the decedent and born alive after the opening of the inheritance, may be called to inherit [as amended by Federal Law of 30 March 2016, No. 79-ФЗ. СЗ РФ (2016), no. 14, item 1909].

Juridical persons specified therein and existing on the day of opening an inheritance also may be called to inherit by will, and an inheritance foundation founded in execution of the last will of the decedent expressed in a will [as amended by Federal Law of 29 July 2017, No. 259-ФЗ. СЗ РФ (2017), no. 31(I), item 4808].

2. The Russian Federation, subjects of the Russian Federation, municipal formations, foreign States, and international organizations may be called to inherit by will, and to inherit by operation of law – the Russian Federation, subjects of the Russian Federation, and municipal formations in accordance with Article 1151 of the present Code [as amended by Federal Law of 29 November 2007, No. 281-ФЗ. СЗ РФ (2007), no. 49, item 6042].

Article 1117. Unworthy Heirs

1. Citizens who by their intentional unlawful actions directed against the decedent, any of the heirs thereof, or against the effectuation of the last will of the decedent expressed in the will, facilitated or attempted to facilitate the calling of themselves or other persons to inherit, or facilitated or attempted to facilitate an increase of the participatory share of the inheritance due to them or to other persons, if these circumstances have been

confirmed in a judicial proceeding, shall not inherit either by operation of law or by will. However, citizens to whom the decedent after their loss of the right to inherit bequeathed property shall have the right to inherit this property.

Parents after children with respect to whom the parents were deprived of parental rights in a judicial proceeding and not restored in such rights on the day of opening the inheritance shall not inherit by operation of law.

2. Upon the demand of an interested person, a court shall remove from inheriting by law citizens who have maliciously avoided the fulfillment of duties placed on them by virtue of a law with regard to maintenance of the decedent.

3. A person who does not have the right to inherit or removed from inheriting on the basis of the present Article (unworthy heir) shall be obliged to return in accordance with the rules of Chapter 60 of the present Code all property unfoundedly received by him from the composition of the inheritance.

4. The rules of the present Article shall extend to heirs having the right to an obligatory participatory share in the inheritance.

5. The rules of the present Article respectively shall apply to a testamentary legacy (Article 1137). When the subject of a testamentary legacy was the fulfillment of determined work for an unworthy recipient of a testamentary legacy or rendering to him of a determined service, the last shall be obliged to compensate the heir who has performed the testamentary legacy for the value of work fulfilled for the unworthy recipient of the testamentary legacy or service rendered to him.

Chapter 62. Inheriting by Will

Article 1118. General Provisions

1. One may dispose of property in the event of death by means of concluding a will or concluding an inheritance contract. The rules of the present Code concerning a will shall apply to an inheritance contract unless arises otherwise from

the essence of the inheritance contract [as amended by Federal Law of 19 July 2018, No. 217-ФЗ. СЗ РФ (2018), no. 30, item 4552].

2. A will may be concluded by a citizen possessing at the moment of conclusion thereof dispositive legal capacity in full.

3. A will must be concluded personally. The conclusion of a will and the conclusion of an inheritance contract through a representative shall not be permitted [as amended by Federal Law of 19 July 2018, No. 217-ФЗ. СЗ РФ (2018), no. 30, item 4552].

4. A will may be concluded by one citizen, and also by citizens married to one another at the moment of concluding it (joint will of spouses). The rules of the present Code on a will shall apply to spouses who have concluded a joint will.

In a joint will of spouses they shall have the right at joint discretion to determine the following consequences of the death of each them, including which ensued simultaneously: bequeath the common property of spouses, and likewise the property of each of them to any persons; determine by any means the participatory share of heirs in the respective inheritance estate; determine the property within the inheritance estate of each spouse if the determination of property within the inheritance estate of each spouse does not violate the rights of third persons; deprive of inheritance one, several, or all heirs by operation of law without indicating the reasons for such deprivation; include in the joint will of spouses other testamentary dispositions, the possibility of the performance of which is provided by the present Code. The conditions of a joint will of spouses shall operate in the part not contrary to the rules of the present Code on the obligatory participatory share in the inheritance (including the obligatory participatory share in the inheritance, the right to which emerged after the drawing up of the joint will of spouses), and also prohibition of the inheriting by unworthy heirs (Article 1117).

A joint will of spouses shall lose force in the event of the dissolution of marriage or deeming the marriage to be invalid both before and after the death of one of the spouses.

In the event of the deeming of the expression of will of one of the spouses in the event of their concluding a joint will which does not correspond to the requirements of a law in the procedure provided by Article 1131(2), paragraph three, of the present Code, the norms of the present Code shall be subject to application to such will concerning contested or void transactions, depending on the grounds of invalidity of the expression of will of one of the spouses.

One of the spouses at any time, including after the death of the other spouse, shall have the right to conclude a subsequent will, and also to revoke the joint will of spouses.

If a notary certifies the subsequent will of one of the spouses, accepts a closed subsequent will of one of the spouses, or certifies the instruction of one of the spouses concerning revocation of the joint will of spouses during the life of both spouses, he shall be obliged to send to the other spouse in the procedure provides by legislation on the notariat and notarial activity a notification concerning the fact of concluding such subsequent wills or revocation of the joint will of spouses [as amended by Federal Law of 19 July 2018, No. 217-ФЗ. СЗ РФ (2018), no. 30, item 4552].

5. A will shall be a unilateral transaction which creates rights and duties after the opening of the inheritance.

6. The rights and duties provided by the inheritance contract shall arise after the opening of the inheritance, except for duties which by virtue of the inheritance contract may arise before the opening of the inheritance and have been placed on that party to the contract which may be called to inherit for the decedent (Article 1116). The rules of the present Code on a will, unless arises otherwise from the essence of the inheritance contract, shall apply to the decedent who concluded the inheritance contract [added by Federal Law of 19 July 2018, No. 217-ФЗ. СЗ РФ (2018), no. 30, item 4552].

Article 1119. Freedom of Will

1. A testator shall have the right at his discretion to bequeath property to any persons, by any means to determine the participatory shares of heirs in the inheritance, to deprive of an inheritance one, several, or all heirs by operation of law, without specifying the reasons for such deprivation, and in the instances provided by the present Code to include in the will other dispositions. A testator shall have the right to revoke or change a concluded will in accordance with the rules of Article 1130 of the present Code [as amended by Federal Law of 18 December 2006, No. 231-ФЗ. СЗ РФ (2006), no. 52(I), item 5497].

The freedom of will shall be limited by the rules concerning an obligatory participatory share in an inheritance (Article 1149).

2. A testator shall not be obliged to communicate to anyone the content, conclusion, change, or revocation of a will.

Article 1120. Right to Bequeath Any Property

A testator shall have the right to conclude a will containing a disposition concerning any property, including that which he may acquire in future.

A testator may dispose of his property or any part thereof, having drawn up one or several wills.

Article 1121. Designation and Subdesignation of Heir in Will

1. A testator may conclude a will to the benefit of one or several persons (Article 1116) both within and not within the group of heirs by operation of law.

2. A testator may specify in a will another heir (subdesignation of heir) if the heir designated by him in the will or an heir of the testator by operation of law dies before the opening of the inheritance, or simultaneously with the testator, or after the opening of the inheritance without succeeding to accept it, or does not accept the inheritance for other reasons or renounces

it, or will not have the right to inherit or will be removed from inheriting as unworthy.

Article 1122. Participatory Share of Heirs in Bequeathed Property

1. Property bequeathed to two or several heirs without specifying their participatory shares in the inheritance and without specifying which things or rights within the composition of the inheritance are intended for which of the heirs shall be considered to be bequeathed to the heirs in equal participatory shares.

2. A specification in the will of parts of an indivisible thing (Article 133) intended for each of the heirs in kind shall not entail the invalidity of the will. Such thing shall be considered to be bequeathed in equal participatory shares corresponding to the value of these parts. The procedure for the use by heirs of this indivisible thing shall be established in accordance with the parts of that thing intended for them in the will.

The participatory shares of the heirs and the procedure for use of such thing shall be specified with the consent of the heirs, in accordance with the present Article, in the certificate on the right to an inheritance with respect to an indivisible thing bequeathed by parts in kind. In the event of a dispute between the heirs, their participatory shares and the procedure for the use of an indivisible thing shall be determined by a court.

Article 1123. Secrecy of Will

A notary, other person certifying a will, interpreter, executor of a will, witnesses, spouse participating in the conclusion of a joint will of spouses, spouse present during the certification of the will of the other spouse, party to an inheritance contract, notaries having access to information contained in the unified information system of the notariat and persons processing data of the unified information system of the notariat, persons having access to information concerning the certification or revocation of a will to be sent by consular sections of diplomatic representations of the Russian Federation or consular institutions of the Russian Federation through a federal agency of executive power effectuating functions with regard to the working out and realization of State policy and normative-legal regulation in the sphere of international relations of the Russian Federation to a federal notarial chamber for the entry of such information in the register of notarial actions of the unified information system of the notariat,, and also a citizen signing a will or inheritance contract in place of the testator or decedent, shall not have the right before the opening of an inheritance to divulge information concerning the content of the will or inheritance contract, conclusion thereof, change, or revocation. A person who is not the executor of the will, notary, or other person certifying the will shall not have the right to divulge the said information after the opening of the inheritance also if divulgence of the said information would be contrary to Article 152^2 of the present Code [as amended by Federal Laws of 2 October 2012, No. 166-ФЗ, of 19 July 2018, No. 217-ФЗ, and of 24 July 2023, No. 362-ФЗ. СЗ РФ (2012), no. 41, item 5531; (2018), no. 30, item 4552; (2023), no. 31(III), item 5788].

In the event of a violation of the secrecy of a will, the testator shall have the right to demand contributory compensation of moral harm, and also to take advantage of other means of defense of civil rights provided for by the present Code.

The submission by a notary or other person certifying a will of information concerning the certification of the will or revocation of the will, submission by the notary of information concerning certification of an inheritance contract, and notification of renunciation by the decedent of the inheritance contract to the unified information system of the notariat in the procedure established by the Fundamental Principles of Legislation of the Russian Federation on the Notariat shall not be divulgence of a secret, and also sending notification concerning the fact of the conclusion after the joint will of spouses of a subsequent will of one of the spouses or revocation by one of the spouses of the joint will of spouses, or sending to the parties of an inheritance contract a copy of the notification concerning renunciation by the decedent of an inheritance contract [as amended by Federal Laws of 2 October 2012, No. 166-ФЗ, and of 19 July 2018, No.

217-ФЗ. СЗ РФ (2012), no. 41, item 5531; (2018), no. 30, item 4552].

A will of both spouses the notary shall have the right to certify in the presence of both spouses [added by Federal Law of 29 July 2017, No. 259-ФЗ. СЗ РФ (2017), no. 31(I), item 4808].

After the death of one of the spouses who drew up a joint will, the executor of the will and notary shall have the right to divulge in connection with the performance by them of their duties only information relating to the consequences of the death of this spouse [added by Federal Law of 19 July 2018, No. 217-ФЗ. СЗ РФ (2018), no. 30, item 4552].

Article 1124. General Rules Affecting Form and Procedure for Concluding Will

1. A will must be drawn up in written form and certified by a notary. Certification of a will by other persons shall be permitted in the instances provided for by Article 1125(7), Article 1127, and Article 1128(2) of the present Code.

The failure to comply with the rules established by the present Code concerning written form of a testament and certification thereof shall entail the invalidity of the will.

Drawing up a will in simple written form shall be permitted only by way of exception in the instances provided for by Article 1129 of the present Code.

The drawing up of a will with the use of electronic or other technical means (Article 160(1), paragraph two, of the present Code) shall not be permitted [paragraph added by Federal Law of 18 March 2019, No. 34-ФЗ. СЗ РФ (2019), no. 12, item 1224].

2. When in accordance with the rules of the present Code witnesses are present during the drawing up, signature, and certification of a will or when the will is transferred to a notary, there may not be such witnesses and may not sign the will in place of the testator:

the notary or other person certifying the will;

the person to whose benefit the will has been drawn up or a testamentary legacy has been made, the spouse of such person, his children, and parents;

citizens not possessing dispositive legal capacity in full;

illiterate persons;

citizens with physical defects which clearly do not enable them to be aware in full of the essence of what is happening;

persons not possessing in sufficient degree the language in which the will has been drawn up, except for instances when a closed will is drawn up;

spouse when concluding a joint will of spouses [added by Federal Law of 19 July 2018, No. 217-ФЗ. СЗ РФ (2018), no. 30, item 4552];

parties to an inheritance contract [added by Federal Law of 19 July 2018, No. 217-ФЗ. СЗ РФ (2018), no. 30, item 4552].

3. When in accordance with the rules of the present Code the presence of a witness is obligatory during the drawing up, signature, and certification of a will or when transferring it to a notary, the absence of a witness when performing the said actions shall entail the invalidity of the will, and the failure of the witness to conform to the requirements established by point 2 of the present Article may be grounds for deeming a will to be invalid.

4. On a will must be specified the place and date of certification thereof, except for the instance provided for by Article 1126 of the present Code.

5. The decision of the testator concerning the founding of an inheritance foundation, the charter of the foundation, and also the conditions for management of the foundation shall be an integral part of a will whose conditions provide for the creation of an inheritance foundation. Such will shall be drawn up in three examples, two of which must be kept with the notary which certified such will. All examples of the will shall be subject to notarial certification [added by Federal Law of 29

July 2017, No. 259-ФЗ, as amended by Federal Law of 23 May 2018, No. 120-ФЗ. СЗ РФ (2017), no. 31(I), item 4808; (2018), no. 22, item 3044].

In the procedure provided by legislation on the notariat and notarial activity, the notary conducting a notarial matter shall after the death of the testator be obliged to receive the electronic form of the decision concerning the founding of an inheritance foundation and the electronic form of the charter of the inheritance foundation and transfer them to the empowered State agency, and also request from the notary who kept the example of the will one example of the will and, upon the receipt thereof, transfer to the person fulfilling the functions of the one-person executive agency of the inheritance foundation, one example of the decision on founding the inheritance foundation, charter of the inheritance foundation, and conditions for management of the inheritance foundation. Upon the application of the beneficiary, the notary shall be obliged to transfer thereto a copy of the decision on founding the inheritance foundation together with copies of the charter of the inheritance foundation and conditions for management of the inheritance foundation [added by Federal Law of 29 July 2017, No. 259-ФЗ, as amended by Federal Law of 23 May 2018, No. 120-ФЗ. СЗ РФ (2017), no. 31(I), item 4808; (2018), no. 22, item 3044].

Article 1125. Notarially-Certified Will

1. A notarially-certified will must be written out by the testator or written down from his words by the notary, and a joint will of spouses must be transmitted to the notary by both spouses or written down from their words by the notary in the presence of both spouses. When writing out or writing down the will technical means (computer, typewriter, and others) may be used [as amended by Federal Law of 19 July 2018, No. 217-ФЗ. СЗ РФ (2018), no. 30, item 4552].

2. A will written down by a notary from the words of the testator must before signature thereof be read out in full by the testator in the presence of the notary, and a joint will of spouses

written by one of the spouses before the signature thereof must be read out in full by the other spouse in the presence of the notary. If the testator is not in a state personally to read out the will, the text thereof shall be read aloud for him by the notary, concerning which a respective notation shall be made on the will specifying the reasons for which the testator could not personally read out the will [as amended by Federal Law of 19 July 2018, No. 217-ФЗ. СЗ РФ (2018), no. 30, item 4552].

3. A will must be signed by the testator in his own hand.

If the testator by virtue of physical defects, grave illness, or illiteracy cannot sign the will in his own hand, at his request it may be signed by another citizen in the presence of the notary. The reasons for which the testator could not sign the will in his own hand must be specified on the will, as well as the surname, forename, and patronymic and place of residence of the citizen who signed the will at the request of the testator in accordance with a document certifying the identity of this citizen.

4. When drawing up and notarially-certifying a will, a witness may be present at the wish of the testator.

If a will is drawn up and certified in the present of a witness, it must be signed by him and on the will must be specified the surname, forename, patronymic, and place of residence of the witness in accordance with a document certifying his identity.

5. A notary shall be obliged to warn the witness, each of the spouses when certifying the joint will of spouses, spouse present during the certification of the will of the other spouse, and also a citizen signing the will in place of the testator, about the need to comply with secrecy of the will (Article 1123) [as amended by Federal Law of 19 July 2018, No. 217-ФЗ. СЗ РФ (2018), no. 30, item 4552].

5[1]. When certifying the joint will of spouses, a notary shall be obliged to effectuate the video-fixation of the procedure of concluding the joint will of spouses unless the spouses have objected to this [added by Federal Law of 19 July 2018, No. 217-ФЗ. СЗ РФ (2018), no. 30, item 4552].

6. When certifying a will, a notary shall be obliged to explain to the testator the content of Article 1149 of the present Code and to make a respective inscription about this on the will.

7. When the right to perform notarial actions has been granted by a law to officials of agencies of local self-government and to officials of consular institutions, a will may be certified in place of the notary by the respective official in compliance with the rules of the present Code concerning the form of the will, procedure for notarial certification thereof, and secrecy of the will [as amended by Federal Law No. 46-ФЗ, 25 February 2023. СЗ РФ (2023), no. 10, item 1569].

Article 1126. Closed Will

1. A testator shall have the right to conclude a will without providing in so doing to other persons, including a notary, the possibility to familiarize themselves with the content thereof (closed will).

2. A closed will must be written out in the own hand and signed by the testator. The failure to comply with these rules shall entail the invalidity of the will.

3. A closed will in a sealed envelope shall be transferred to a notary in the presence of two witnesses, who shall place on the envelope their signatures. The envelope signed by the witnesses shall be sealed in their presence by the notary in another envelope, on which the notary shall make an inscription containing information concerning the testator from whom the notary has accepted the closed will, place and date of acceptance thereof, surname, forename, and patronymic, and place of residence of each witness in accordance with a document certifying identity.

In accepting from the testator an envelope with a closed will the notary shall be obliged to explain to the testator the content of point 2 of the present Article and Article 1149 of the present Code and to make a respective inscription thereof on the second envelope, and also to issue to the testator a document confirming acceptance of the closed will.

4. Upon the presentation of a certificate concerning the death of the person who concluded a closed will, the notary not later than fifteen days from the day of submission of the certificate shall open the envelope with the will in the presence of not less than two witnesses and interested person who wished to be present from among the heirs by operation of law. After opening the envelope, the text of the will contained therein shall be read out at once by the notary, after which the notary shall draw up and together with the witnesses sign a protocol certifying the opening of the envelope with the will and containing the full text of the will. The original of the will shall be kept by the notary. A notarially-certified copy of the protocol shall be issued to the heirs.

5. Joint wills of spouses, inheritance contracts, and also wills containing a decision to found an inheritance foundation, may not be closed. Failure to comply with this requirement shall entail the nullity of the said wills and contracts [added by Federal Law of 29 July 2017, No. 259-ФЗ. СЗ РФ (2017), no. 31(I), item 4808; as amended by Federal Law of 19 July 2018, No. 217-ФЗ. СЗ РФ (2018), no. 30, item 4552].

Article 1127. Wills Equated to Notarially-Certified Wills

1. There shall be equated to notarially-certified wills:

(1) wills of citizens situated for care in hospitals, military hospitals, and other medical organizations under in-patient conditions or residing in in-patient organizations of social service, certified by chief doctors, their deputies for the medical section or duty doctors of those hospitals, military hospitals, and other in-patient medical organizations, and also heads of military hospitals, directors (or deputy directors thereof), of such organizations of social service [as amended by Federal Laws of 28 March 2017, No. 39-ФЗ, and of 3 April 2023, No. 101-ФЗ. СЗ РФ (2017), no. 14, item 1998; (2023), no. 14, item 2378];

(2) wills of citizens situated during voyages on vessels sailing under the State Flag of the Russian Federation certified by the masters of those vessels;

(3) wills of citizens on prospecting, arctic, Antarctic, or other similar expeditions certified by the heads of those expeditions, Russian Antarctic stations or seasonal field bases [as amended by Federal Law of 5 June 2012, No. 51-ФЗ. СЗ РФ (2012), no. 24, item 3068];

(4) wills of military servicemen, and in stationing centers for military units, formations, institutions, and military instructional institutions where there are no notaries, also the wills of civilian persons working in those units, formations, institutions, and military instructional institutions, members of their families, and members of the families of military servicemen, certified by the commanders (or heads) of the respective military units, formations, institutions, or military instructional institutions [as amended by Federal Law of 3 April 2023, No. 101-ФЗ. СЗ РФ (2023), no. 14, item 2378];

(5) wills of citizens in places of deprivation of freedom certified by the heads of places of deprivation of freedom.

2. A will equated to a notarially-certified will must be signed by the testator in the presence of the person certifying the will and a witness also signing the will.

The remainder of the rules of Articles 1124 and 1125 of the present Code respectively shall apply to such will.

3. A will certified in accordance with the present Article must be as soon as this is possible be sent by the person certifying the will through territorial agencies of the federal agency of executive power effectuating law-application functions and functions with regard to control and supervision in the sphere of the notariat to a notary at the place of residence of the testator. If the place of residence of the testator is known to the person certifying the will, the will shall be sent directly to the respective notary [as amended by Federal Law of 29 April 2008, No. 54-ФЗ. СЗ РФ (2008), no. 18, item 1939].

4. If in any of the instances provided for by point 1 of the present Article a citizen intending to conclude a will expresses the wish to invite a notary for this and there is a reasonable

possibility to fulfill this wish, the persons who have been granted the right to certify a will in accordance with the said point shall be obliged to take all measures to invite the notary to the testator.

5. A joint will of spouses and inheritance contract may not be certified in the procedure provided by the present Article [added by Federal Law of 19 July 2018, No. 217-ФЗ. СЗ РФ (2018), no. 30, item 4552].

Article 1128. Testamentary Dispositions of Rights to Monetary Means in Banks

1. The rights to monetary means deposited by a citizen as a contribution or in any other account of a citizen in a bank may at the discretion of the citizen be bequeathed either in the procedure provided for by Articles 1124-1127 of the present Code, or by means of the conclusion of a testamentary disposition in written form in that branch of the bank in which this account is situated. With respect to means in the account such testamentary disposition shall have the force of a notarially-certified will.

2. A testamentary disposition of rights to monetary means in a bank must be signed in the testator's own hand, specifying the date of drawing up thereof and certified by an employee of the bank having the right to accept for performance dispositions of a client with respect to means in his account. The procedure for concluding testamentary dispositions of monetary means in banks shall be determined by the Government of the Russian Federation.

3. Rights to monetary means with respect to which a testamentary disposition has been concluded in a bank shall be within the composition of the inheritance and shall be inherited on the general grounds in accordance with the rules of the present Code. These means shall be issued to heirs on the basis of a certificate on the right to an inheritance and in accordance with it, except for instances provided for by Article 1174(3) of the present Code.

4. The rules of the present Article respectively shall apply to other credit organizations which have been granted the right to attract monetary means of citizens as contributions or in other accounts.

Article 1129. Will in Extraordinary Circumstances

1. A citizen who is in a position clearly threatening his life and by virtue of extraordinary circumstances which have formed is deprived of the possibility to conclude a will in accordance with the rules of Articles 1124-1128 of the present Code may set out their last will with respect to their property in simple written form.

The setting out by a citizen of last will in simple written form shall be deemed to be his will if the testator in the presence of two witnesses in his own hand wrote out and signed a document, from the content of which it follows that it represents a will.

2. A will concluded in the circumstances specified in paragraph one of point 1 of the present Article shall lose force if the testator within a month after the termination of these circumstances does not take advantage of the possibility to conclude a will in another form provided for by Articles 1124-1128 of the present Code.

3. A will concluded in extraordinary circumstances in accordance with the present Article shall be subject to performance only on condition of confirmation by a court upon the demand of interested persons of the fact of the conclusion of the will in extraordinary circumstances. The said demand must be declared before the expiry of the period established for acceptance of the inheritance.

4. Joint wills of spouses, inheritance contracts, and also wills containing a decision on founding an inheritance foundation may not be concluded in extraordinary circumstances. The failure to comply with this requirement shall entail the nullity of the said wills and contracts [added by Federal Law of 19 July 2018, No. 217-ФЗ. СЗ РФ (2018), no. 30, item 4552].

Article 1130. Revocation and Change of Will

1. A testator shall have the right to revoke or change a will drawn up by him at any time after the conclusion thereof, without specifying in so doing the reasons for the revocation or change thereof.

In order to revoke or change a will the consent of no one shall be required, including persons designated as heirs in the will being revoked or changed.

2. A testator shall have the right by means of a new will to vacate the previous will as a whole or to change it by means of revocation or change of individual testamentary dispositions contained therein.

A subsequent will not containing direct instructions concerning revocation of a previous will or individual testamentary dispositions contained therein shall vacate this previous will wholly or in the part in which it is contrary to the subsequent will.

A will vacated wholly or partially by a subsequent will shall not be reinstated if the subsequent will is revoked by the testator wholly or in respective part.

3. In the event of the invalidity of a subsequent will, inheriting shall be effectuated in accordance with the previous will.

4. A will may be revoked also by means of an instruction concerning the revocation thereof. An instruction concerning the revocation of the will must be concluded in the work established by the present Code for the conclusion of the will. The rules of point 3 of the present Article shall apply respectively to an instruction concerning the revocation of a will.

5. A will concluded in extraordinary circumstances (Article 1129) may be revoked or changed only by a will.

6. A testamentary disposition in a bank (Article 1128) may be revoked or changed only by a testamentary disposition of the rights to monetary means in the respective bank.

Article 1131. Invalidity of Will

1. In the event of a violation of the provisions of the present Code entailing the invalidity of a will, depending upon the grounds of the invalidity, a will shall be invalid by virtue of being deemed to be such by a court (contestable will) or irrespective of deeming such (null will).

2. A will may be deemed by a court to be invalid upon the suit of the person whose rights or legal interests have been violated by this will.

The contesting of a will before the opening of an inheritance shall not be permitted.

The joint will of spouses may be contested upon the suit of any of the spouses during their life. After the death of one of the spouses, and also after the death of the surviving spouse, the joint will of spouses may be contested upon the suit of a person whose rights or legal interests have been violated by this will [paragraph added by Federal Law of 19 July 2018, No. 217-ФЗ. СЗ РФ (2018), no. 30, item 4552].

3. Slips of the pen and other insignificant violations of the procedure for drawing up thereof, signature, or certification, if it is established by a court that they do not influence the understanding of the expression of will of the testator, may not serve as grounds for invalidity of a will.

4. Both a will as a whole and individual testamentary dispositions contained therein may be invalid. The invalidity of individual dispositions contained in a will shall not affect the remaining part of the will if it can be supposed that it would have been included in the will also in the absence of the dispositions which are invalid.

5. The invalidity of a will shall not deprive persons specified therein as heirs or recipients of a legacy of the right to inherit by law or on the basis of another valid will.

Article 1132. Interpretation of Will

When a will is interpreted by a notary, executor of the will, or by a court the literal meaning of the words and expressions contained in the will shall be taken into account.

In the event of an ambiguity in the literal meaning of any provision of a will, it shall be established by means of contrasting this provision with other provisions and the meaning of the will as a whole. In so doing the fullest effectuation of the supposed will of the testator must be ensured.

Article 1133. Performance of Will

The performance of a will shall be effectuated by the heirs by will, except for instances when the performance thereof wholly or in determined part shall be effectuated by the executor of the will (Article 1134).

Article 1134. Executor of Will

1. A testator may assign performance of a will to an executor (executor of the will) specified by him in the will, irrespective of whether such person is an heir. A citizen or juridical person may be the executor of a will [as amended by Federal Law of 29 July 2017, No. 259-ФЗ. СЗ РФ (2017), no. 31(I), item 4808].

A testator shall have the right at any time to replace the executor of the will or to abolish the appointment of the executor of a will (Article 1130) [paragraph added by Federal Law of 29 July 2017, No. 259-ФЗ. СЗ РФ (2017), no. 31(I), item 4808]

The consent of the person to be an executor of the will shall be expressed in an inscription in his own hand on the will itself, or if a juridical person is appoint as the executor of the will – in an inscription in the own hand of the person who by virtue of a law has the right to act in the name of such juridical person without a power of attorney, or in a statement appended to the will, or in a statement given to a notary within a month from the day of opening the inheritance [as amended by Federal Law of 29 July 2017, No. 259-ФЗ. СЗ РФ (2017), no. 31(I), item 4808].

The consent of a person to be the executor of a will may be revoked at any moment before the opening of an inheritance by means of the executor of the will sending notification to the testator and to the notary who certified the will, and after the opening of the inheritance – by means of sending notification to the notary [as amended by Federal Law of 29 July 2017, No. 259-ФЗ. СЗ РФ (2017), no. 31(I), item 4808].

2. After the opening of an inheritance a court may free the executor of a will from his duties at the demand of the heirs, including an inheritance foundation, when there are circumstances testifying to the improper performance of his duties by the executor of the will or of a threat of a violation of interests of heirs protected by a law as a result of the actions (or failure to act) of the executor of the will [as amended by Federal Law of 29 July 2017, No. 259-ФЗ. СЗ РФ (2017), no. 31(I), item 4808].

Article 1135. Powers of Executor of Will

1. The powers of the executor of a will shall be based on the will by which he was designated executor and shall be certified by a certificate issued by a notary.

2. Unless provided otherwise in the will, the executor of a will must take measures necessary for performance of the will, including to:

(1) ensure the transfer to the heirs of inheritance property due to them in accordance with the will of the testator expressed in the will and a law;

(2) perform in the interests of heirs in his own name all necessary legal and other actions for the purposes of the protection of the inheritance and management thereof, or in the absence of the possibility to perform such actions, to apply to a notary to take measures for the protection of the inheritance [as amended by Federal Law of 29 July 2017, No. 259-ФЗ. СЗ РФ (2017), no. 31(I), item 4808];

(3) receive monetary means due to the testator and other property for transfer thereof to heirs, if this property is not subject to transfer to other persons (Article 1183[1]);

(4) perform a testamentary imposition or demand from heirs the performance of a testamentary legacy (Article 1137) or testamentary imposition (Article 1139).

2[1]. The testator may provide in a will for actions which the executor of the will is obliged to perform, and also actions from the performance of which he is obliged to refrain, including shall have the right to provide for the duty of the executor of the will to vote in the highest organs of corporations as specified in the will. In a will whose conditions provide for the creation of an inheritance foundation the testator may also indicate the powers of the executor of the will relating to the performance of factual and legal actions connected with the creation of the inheritance foundation [added by Federal Law of 29 July 2017, No. 259-ФЗ. СЗ РФ (2017), no. 31(I), item 4808].

3. The executor of a will shall have the right in his own name to conduct affairs connected with the performance of a will, including in a court and other State agencies and State institutions.

4. When performing actions relating to the protection of inheritance property and management thereof, the executor of a will shall act as a trustee manager (Article 1173). The executor of a will may transfer the effectuation of trust management to a third person unless this is prohibited by the will [added by Federal Law of 29 July 2017, No. 259-ФЗ. СЗ РФ (2017), no. 31(I), item 4808].

Article 1136. Compensation of Expenses Connected with Performance of Will

The executor of a will shall have the right to compensation at the expense of the inheritance of necessary expenses connected with performance of the will, and also to receipt remuneration above the expenses at the expense of the inheritance if this has been provided for by the will.

Article 1137. Testamentary Legacy

1. A testator shall have the right to place on one or several heirs by will or by operation of law the performance at the expense of the inheritance of any duty of a property character to the benefit of one or several persons (recipient of legacy),

who shall acquire the right to demand performance of the duty (testamentary legacy).

A testamentary legacy must be established in the will.

The content of a will may be exhausted by the testamentary legacy.

2. The subject of a testamentary legacy may be the transfer to the recipient of a legacy in ownership, in possession in another right to a thing, or for use things within the position of an inheritance, transfer to the recipient of the legacy of a property right within the composition of the inheritance, acquisition for the recipient of the legacy and transfer to him of other property, the fulfillment for him of determined work or the rendering to him of a determined service, or the effectuation to the benefit of the recipient of the legacy of period payments, and so on.

In particular, on a heir to whom a dwelling house, apartment, or other dwelling premise passes the testator may place the duty to provide to another person for the period of life of that person or for another period the right to use this premise or a determined part thereof.

In the event of subsequent transfer of the right of ownership to property within the composition of an inheritance to another person, the right of use of this property granted under testamentary legacy shall retain force.

3. To relations between the recipient of a legacy (creditor) and heir on whom the testamentary legacy has been placed (debtor) shall apply the provisions of the present Code on obligations, unless follows otherwise from the rules of the present Section and essence of the testamentary legacy.

4. The right to receive a testamentary legacy shall operate for three years from the day of opening the inheritance and shall not pass to other persons. However, the recipient of a legacy in a will may subdesignate another recipient of the legacy if the recipient of the legacy designated in the will dies before the opening of inheritance or simultaneously with the decedent, or refuses to accept the testamentary legacy, or does not take

advantage of his right to receive the testamentary legacy, or is deprived of the right to receive the testamentary legacy in accordance with the rules of Article 1117(5) of the present Code.

Article 1138. Performance of Testamentary Legacy

1. An heir on whom a testamentary legacy has been placed by a testator must perform it within the limits of the value of the inheritance which has passed to him, deducting the debts of the testator with regard to it.

If an heir on whom a testamentary legacy has been placed has the right to an obligatory participatory share in an inheritance, his duty to perform the legacy shall be limited to the value of the inheritance which has passed to him which exceeds the amount of his obligatory participatory share.

2. If a testamentary legacy has been placed on several heirs, such legacy shall encumber the right of each of them to the inheritance commensurately to the participatory share thereof in the inheritance insofar as not provided otherwise by the will.

3. If the recipient of a legacy is deceased before the opening of the inheritance or simultaneously with the testator, or refused to accept the testamentary legacy (Article 1160), or did not take advantage of his right to receive the testamentary legacy within three years from the day of opening of the inheritance, or was deprived of the right to receive the testamentary legacy in accordance with the rules of Article 1117 of the present Code, the heir obliged to perform the testamentary legacy shall be relieved from this duty, except for the instance when the recipient of the legacy has subdesignated another recipient of the legacy.

Article 1139. Testamentary Imposition

1. A testator may in a will place on one or several heirs by will or by operation of will the duty to perform any action of a property or nonproperty character directed toward the effectuation of a generally-useful purpose or the effectuation of another purpose not contrary to a law, including an action relating to the burial of the testator in accordance with his will

(testamentary imposition). Such duty may be placed on the executor of the will on condition of singling out in the will part of the inheritance property for performance of the testamentary imposition [as amended by Federal Law of 29 July 2017, No. 259-ФЗ. СЗ РФ (2017), no. 31(I), item 4808].

A testator shall have the right also to place on one or several heirs the duty to maintain household animals belonging to the testator, and also to effectuate necessary supervision and care over them.

2. To a testamentary imposition, the subject of which are actions of a property character, shall apply respectively the rules of Article 1138 of the present Code.

3. Interested persons, the executor of the will, and any of the heirs shall have the right to demand performance of a testamentary imposition in a judicial proceeding unless provided otherwise by the will.

Article 1140. Transfer to Other Heirs of Duty to Perform Testamentary Legacy or Testamentary Imposition

If as a consequence of circumstances provided for by the present Code the participatory share of an inheritance due to the heir on whom the duty to perform a testamentary legacy or testamentary imposition was placed passes to other heirs, the last, insofar as does not follow otherwise from the will or a law shall be obliged to perform such legacy or such imposition.

Article 1140^{1}. Inheritance Contract [added by Federal Law of 19 July 2018, No. 217-ФЗ. СЗ РФ (2018), no. 30, item 4552]

1. A decedent shall have the right to conclude with any of the persons who may be called to inherit (Article 1116) a contract whose conditions determine the group of heirs and procedure for the transfer of rights to property of the decedent after his death to parties to the contract surviving the decedent or to surviving third persons who may be called to inherit (inheritance contract). An inheritance contract also may contain a condition on the executor and place on persons participating in the inheritance contract who may be called to inherit the duty

to perform any actions of a property or non-property character not contrary to a law, including perform testamentary legacies or testamentary impositions.

The consequences provided by an inheritance contract may be placed in dependence on circumstances which have ensued by the day of opening the inheritance relating to which it was unknown when concluding the inheritance contract whether they would ensue or not ensue, including circumstances fully dependent on the will of one of the parties (Article 327[1]).

2. After the death of the decedent, heirs, executor, parties to the inheritance contract who survived the decedent, and surviving third persons, and also the notary who conducted the inheritance matter, may demand the performance of duties established by the inheritance contract during the period of performance by them of their duties relating to the protection of inheritance property and management of such property until the issuance of a certificate concerning the right to inherit.

3. In the event of the renunciation by a party to the inheritance contract of the inheritance, the inheritance contract shall retain force with respect to the rights and duties of other parties thereof if it is possible to suppose that it would have been concluded without the inclusion therein of rights and duties of the party who renounced the inheritance.

4. The rights and duties of a party to an inheritance contract arising from the inheritance contract shall be inalienable and non-transferable by other means.

5. An inheritance contract in which spouses participate, and also persons who may be called to inherit for each of the spouses (Article 1116), may determine the procedure for the transfer of rights to common property of the spouses or the property of each of them in the event of the death of each of them, including which ensued simultaneously, to the surviving spouse or to other persons; determine the property in the estate of each spouse if this does not violate the rights of third persons, and also may contain other dispositions of spouses, in particular a condition concerning the appointment of an executor or

executors acting in the event of the death of each of the spouses. In the event of the conclusion of such an inheritance contract, the rules on the decedent shall apply to the spouses.

An inheritance contract specified in paragraph one of the present point shall lose force in connection with the dissolution of marriage before the death of one of the spouses, and also in connection with the deeming of a marriage to be invalid.

An inheritance contract specified in paragraph one of the present point shall repeal the operation of a joint will of spouses concluded before the conclusion of this inheritance contract.

6. The conditions of an inheritance contract shall operate in the part not contrary to the rules of the present Code concerning an obligatory participatory share in the inheritance (including an obligatory participatory share in the inheritance, the right to which emerged after the conclusion of the inheritance contract), and also the prohibition of unworthy heirs to inherit (Article 1117). In the event provided by point 5, paragraph one, of the present Article, the conditions of an inheritance contract shall operate in the part not contrary to the rules of the present Code concerning an obligatory participatory share in the inheritance when there is one of the spouses having the right to an obligatory participatory share, and also the rules on the prohibition of unworthy heirs to inherit when there is one of the spouses who is an unworthy heir.

If the right to an obligatory share to an inheritance emerged after the conclusion of an inheritance contract, the obligations provided by the inheritance contract of the heir under the inheritance contract shall be reduced proportionally to the reduction of part of the inheritance due to him after satisfaction of the right to an obligatory participatory share in the inheritance.

7. An inheritance contract must be signed by each of the parties to an inheritance contract and shall be subject to notarial certification. In the event one of the party evades notarial certification of the inheritance contract, the provisions of Article 165 of the present Code shall not apply.

When certifying an inheritance contract, the notary shall be obliged to effectuate the video-fixation of the procedure of conclusion of the inheritance contract unless the parties to the inheritance contract have declared an objection to this.

8. A decedent shall have the right to conclude one or several inheritance contracts with one or several persons who may be called to inherit.

If one property of the decedent was the subject-matter of several inheritance contracts concluded with different persons, in the event of the acceptance by them of the inheritance that inheritance contract which was concluded earlier shall be subject to application.

9. A change of or dissolution of an inheritance contract shall be permitted only during the life of the parties to this contract by agreement of the parties thereto or on the basis of the decision of a court in connection with a material change of circumstances, including in connection with the possibility emerging of persons being called to inherit who have a right to an obligatory participatory share in the inheritance.

10. A decedent shall have the right to perform at any time a unilateral renunciation of an inheritance contract by means of notification of all the parties to the inheritance contract concerning such renunciation. Notification concerning renunciation of the inheritance contract by the decedent shall be subject to notarial certification. The notary who certified the notification concerning the renunciation of an inheritance contract by the decedent shall be obliged in the procedure provided by legislation on the notariat and notarial activity within three work days to send a copy of this notification to the other parties to the inheritance contract.

A decedent who has renounced an inheritance contract shall be obliged to compensate the other parties to the inheritance contract for losses which arose with them in connection with the performance of the inheritance contract at the moment of receiving a copy of the notification concerning the renunciation of the inheritance contract by the decedent.

Other parties to an inheritance contract shall have the right to perform a unilateral renunciation of the inheritance contract in the procedure provided by a law or the inheritance contract.

11. An inheritance contract may be contested during the life of the decedent upon the suit of a party to the inheritance contract, and after the opening of the inheritance upon the suit of a person whose rights or legal interests have been violated by this inheritance contract.

12. After the conclusion of an inheritance contract, the decedent shall have the right to conclude any transactions with respect to property belonging thereto and otherwise dispose of property belonging to him by his will and in his own interest, even if such disposition deprives a person who might be called to inherit of rights to property of the decedent. An agreement otherwise shall be void.

Chapter 63. Inheriting by Operation of Law

Article 1141. General Provisions

1. Heirs by operation of law shall be called to inherit by way of the priority provided for by Articles 1142-1145 and 1148 of the present Code.

The heirs of each subsequent priority shall inherit if there are no heirs of preceding priorities, that is, if the heirs of preceding priorities are lacking, or no one of them has the right to inherit, or they all have been removed from inheriting (Article 1117), or deprived of inheritance (Article 1119[1]), or none of them has accepted the inheritance, or they all have refused the inheritance.

2. The heirs of another priority shall inherit in equal participatory shares, except for heirs inheriting by right of representation (Article 1146).

Article 1142. Heirs of First Priority

1. Children, the spouse, and parents of the decedent shall be heirs of the first priority by operation of law.

2. Grandchildren of the decedent and descendants thereof shall inherit by right of representation.

Article 1143. Heirs of Second Priority

1. If there are no heirs of the first priority, the heirs of the second priority by operation of law shall be full or half brothers and sisters of the decedent, grandfather and grandmother thereof both on the side of the father and on the side of the mother.

2. Children of full and half brothers and sisters of the decedent (nephews and nieces of the decedent) shall inherit by right of representation.

Article 1144. Heirs of Third Priority

1. If there are no heirs of the first and second priorities, the heirs of the third priority by operation of law shall be full or half brothers and sisters of parents of the decedent (uncles and aunts of the decedent).

2. First cousins of the decedent shall inherit by right of representation.

Article 1145. Heirs of Subsequent Priorities

1. If there are no heirs of the first, second, or third priorities (Articles 1142-1144), relatives of the decedent of the third, fourth, and fifth degrees of kinship who are not relegated to heirs of the preceding priorities shall receive the right to inherit by operation of law.

The degree of kinship shall be determined by the date of births separating the relatives one from the other. The birth of the decedent himself shall not be within this number.

2. In accordance with point 1 of the present Article shall be called to inherit:

as heirs of the fourth priority, relatives of the third degree of kinship – great-grandfather and great-grandmother of the decedent;

as heirs of the fifth priority, relatives of the fourth degree of kinship – children of full cousins of the decedent (grandchildren once removed) and own brothers and sisters of his grandfather and grandmother (grandfathers and grandmothers once removed);

as heirs of the sixth priority, relatives of the fifth degree of kinship – children of grandchildren once removed of the decedent (great-grandchildren once removed), children of his brothers and sisters once removed (nephews and nieces once removed), and children of his grandfathers and grandmothers once removed (uncles and aunts once removed).

3. If there are no heirs of the preceding priorities, stepchildren, stepdaughters, step-father, and step-mother of the decedent shall be called to inherit as heirs of the seventh priority by operation of law.

Article 1146. Inheriting by Right of Representation

1. The participatory share of an heir by operation of law who has died before the opening of an inheritance or simultaneously with the decedent (Article 1114(2)) shall pass by right of representation to his respective descendants in the instances provided for by Article 1142(2), Article 1143(2), and Article 1144(2) of the present Code, and shall be divided between them equally [as amended by Federal Law of 30 March 2016, No. 79-ФЗ. СЗ РФ (2016), no. 14, item 1909].

2. Descendants of an heir by operation of law deprived by the decedent of inheritance (Article 1119[1]) shall not inherit by right of representation.

3. Descendants of an heir who dies before the opening of the inheritance or simultaneously with the decedent (Article 1114(2)) and who did not have the right to inherit in accordance with Article 1117(1) of the present Code shall not inherit by right of representation [as amended by Federal Law of 30 March 2016, No. 79-ФЗ. СЗ РФ (2016), no. 14, item 1909].

Article 1147. Inheriting by Adopted Persons

1. When inheriting by operation of law, an adopted person and his descendant, on one side, and the adoptive person and his relatives, on the other, shall be equated to relatives by origin (blood relatives).

2. An adopted person and his descendant shall not inherit by operation of law after the death of the parents of the adopted person and others of his relatives by origin, and the parents of the adopted person and others of his relatives by origin shall not inherit by operation of law after the death of the adopted person and his descendant, except for instances specified in point 3 of the present Article.

3. When in accordance with the Family Code of the Russian Federation an adopted person retains by decision of a court relations with one of the parents or other relatives by origin, an adopted person and his descendant shall inherit by operation of law after the death of these relatives, and the last shall inherit by operation of law after the death of the adopted person and his descendant.

Inheriting in accordance with the present point shall not exclude inheriting in accordance with point 1 of the present Article.

Article 1148. Inheriting by Dependents Not Having Labor Capacity of Decedent

1. Citizens relegated to heirs by operation of law specified in Articles 1143-1145 of the present Code who lack labor capacity on the day of opening the inheritance but are not within the group of heirs of that priority which is called to inherit shall inherit by operation of law together and equally with the heirs of that priority if not less than a year before the death of the decedent they were dependent on him, irrespective of whether they resided jointly with the decedent or not.

2. To heirs by operation of law shall be relegated citizens who are not within the group of heirs specified in Articles 1142-1145 of the present Code but on the day of opening the inheritance did not have labor capacity and not less than a

year before the death of the decedent were dependent on him and resided jointly with him. When there are other heirs by operation of law they shall inherit together and equally with heirs of that priority which is called upon to inherit.

3. In the absence of other heirs by operation of law dependents not having labor capacity of the decedent specified in point 2 of the present Article shall inherit autonomously as heirs of the eighth priority.

Article 1149. Right to Obligatory Participatory Share in Inheritance

1. Minors and children not having labor capacity of the decedent, the spouse and parents thereof not having labor capacity, and also dependents not having labor capacity of the decedent shall be subject to being called to inherit on the basic of Article 1148(1) and (2) of the present Code, and shall inherit irrespective of the content of the will not less than half of the participatory share which would have been due to each of them when inheriting by operation of law (obligatory participatory share), unless provided otherwise by the present Article [as amended by Federal Law of 29 July 2017, No. 259-ФЗ. СЗ РФ (2017), no. 31(I), item 4808].

2. The right to an obligatory participatory share in an inheritance shall be satisfied from the remaining unbequeathed part of inheritance property, even if this leads to a reduction of the rights of other heirs by operation of law to this part of the property, and in the event the unbequeathed part of the property is not sufficient to effectuate the right to an obligatory participatory share – from that part of the property which has been bequeathed.

3. To an obligatory participatory share shall be credited all that an heir having the right to such participatory share receives from the inheritance on any ground whatsoever, including the value of a testamentary legacy established to the benefit of such heir.

4. If effectuation of the right to an obligatory participatory share to an inheritance entails the impossibility to transfer to the heir by will property to which the heir having the right to an obligatory participatory share was not used during the life of the decedent and the heir by will used for habitation (dwelling house, apartment, other dwelling premise, dacha, and the like) or used as the principal source of receiving means for existence (implements of labor, creative studio, and the like), a court may, taking into account the property position of the heirs having the right to an obligatory participatory share, reduce the amount of the obligatory participatory share or refuse to award it.

5. An heir having the right to an obligatory participatory share and who is the beneficiary of an inheritance foundation shall lose the right to an obligatory participatory share. If such heir during the period established for acceptance of an inheritance declares to the notary conducting the inheritance matter the renunciation of all rights of the beneficiary of an inheritance foundation, he shall have the right to an obligatory participatory share in accordance with the present Article.

In the event an heir renounces the rights of a beneficiary of an inheritance foundation, a court may reduce the amount of the obligatory participatory share of this heir if the value of the property due to him as a result of the inheritance materially increased the amount of the means necessary for the maintenance of a citizen, taking into account the reasonable requirements and he has obligations on the date of opening the inheritance to third persons, and also the average amount of expenses and standard of living before the death of the decedent [added by Federal Law of 29 July 2017, No. 259-ФЗ. СЗ РФ (2017), no. 31(I), item 4808].

Article 1150. Rights of Spouse When Inheriting

The right to inherit belonging to a surviving spouse of the decedent by virtue of a will or law shall not diminish the right thereof to part of the property acquired during marriage with the decedent and being their joint ownership. The participatory share of the deceased spouse in this property determined in accordance with Article 256 of the present Code shall be within the composition of the inheritance and pass to heirs in accordance with the rules established by the present Code.

It may be provided otherwise by a joint will of spouses or inheritance contract [paragraph added by Federal Law of 19 July 2018, No. 217-ФЗ. СЗ РФ (2018), no. 30, item 4552].

Article 1151. Inheriting of Escheat Property

1. If heirs are lacking both by operation of law and by will, or none of the heirs has the right to inherit, or all heirs have been removed from inheriting (Article 1117), or none of the heirs had accepted the inheritance, or all the heirs have refused the inheritance and in so doing none of them has specified that he is refusing in favor of another heir (Article 1158), the property of the deceased shall be considered to be escheat.

2. The following escheat property situated on the respective territory shall pass by way of inheriting by operation of law to the ownership of a city or rural settlement or municipal district (with regard to inter-settlement territories) or municipal or city area [as amended by Federal Law of 14 April 2023, No. 121-ФЗ. СЗ РФ (2023), no. 16, item 2758]:

dwelling premise;

land plot, and also buildings, installations, and other objects of immoveable property located thereon;

participatory share in the right of common participatory share ownership on the objects of immoveable property specified in paragraphs two and three of the present point.

If the said objects are located in a subject of the Russian Federation – city of federal significance Moscow, St. Petersburg of Sevastopol, they shall pass to the ownership of this subject of the Russian Federation.

A dwelling premise specified in paragraph two of the present point shall be included in the respective housing fund of social use.

Other escheat property shall pass by way of inheriting by operation of law to the ownership of the Russian Federation [as amended by Federal Laws of 29 November 2007, No. 281-ФЗ, 23 July 2013, No. 223-ФЗ, and 3 July 2015, No. 333-ФЗ. СЗ РФ (2007), no. 49, item 6042; (2013), no. 30(I), item 4056; (2016), no. 27(II), item 4266].

3. The procedure for inheriting and recording of escheat property passing by way of inheriting by operation of law to the ownership of the Russian Federation, and also the procedure for the transfer thereof to the ownership of subjects of the Russian Federation or ownership of municipal formations, shall be determined by a law [as amended by Federal Law of 29 November 2007, No. 281-ФЗ. СЗ РФ (2007), no. 49, item 6042].

Chapter 64. Acquisition of Inheritance

Article 1152. Acceptance of Inheritance

1. In order to acquire an inheritance an heir must accept it.

In order to acquire escheat property (Article 1151) acceptance of an inheritance is not required.

2. Acceptance by an heir of part of the inheritance shall mean acceptance of the entire inheritance due to him, irrespective of what it consists of or where it was situated.

When calling an heir to inherit simultaneously on several grounds (by will and by operation of law, or by way of inheritance transmission and as a result of opening an inheritance, and the like), an heir may accept the inheritance due to him with regard to one of these grounds, several of them, or all grounds.

Acceptance of an inheritance on condition or with reservations shall not be permitted.

3. Acceptance of an inheritance by one or several heirs shall not mean acceptance of the inheritance by remaining heirs.

4. An accepted inheritance shall be deemed to belong to the heir from the day of opening the inheritance irrespective of the time of actual acceptance, and also irrespective of the moment

of State registration of the right of the heir to inherited property when such right is subject to State registration.

Article 1153. Means of Acceptance of Inheritance

1. The acceptance of an inheritance shall be effectuated by the filing at the place of opening the inheritance with a notary or official empowered in accordance with a law to issue a certificate on the right to an inheritance an application of the heir to accept the inheritance or application of an heir concerning the issuance of a certificate on the right to an inheritance.

If the application of the heir is transferred to the notary by another person or is sent by post, the signature of the heir on the application must be certified by a notary, official empowered to perform notarial actions (Article 1125[7]), or person empowered to certify a power of attorney in accordance with Article 1127 of the present Code [as amended by Federal Laws of 7 May 2013, No. 100-ФЗ, and of 3 April 2023, No. 101-ФЗ. СЗ РФ (2013), no. 19, item 2327; (2023), no. 14, item 2378].

The acceptance of an inheritance through a representative shall be possible if the power to accept an inheritance is specially provided for in the power of attorney. A power of attorney shall not be required for the acceptance of an inheritance by a legal representative.

2. It shall be deemed, so long as not proved otherwise, that an heir has accepted an inheritance if he has performed actions testifying to the actual acceptance of the inheritance, in particular if the heir:

entered into possession or management of inheritance property;

took measure with regard to preservation of inheritance property and defense thereof against infringements or claims of third persons;

made expenses at his own account for maintenance of inheritance property;

paid debts at his own account of the decedent or received monetary means from third persons due to the decedent.

3. The acceptance of an inheritance by an inheritance foundation shall be effectuated in the procedure provided by Article 123[20-8](2) of the present Code [added by Federal Law of 29 July 2017, No. 259-ФЗ, as amended by Federal Law of 1 July 2021, No. 287-ФЗ. СЗ РФ (2017), no. 31(I), item 4808; (2021), no. 27(I), item 5115].

Article 1154. Period for Acceptance of Inheritance

1. An inheritance may be accepted within six months from the day of opening the inheritance.

In the event of the opening of an inheritance on the day of the supposed perishing of a citizen (Article 1114[1]), the inheritance may be accepted within six months from the day of entry into legal force of the decision of the court declaring him to be deceased.

2. If the right to inherit arises for other persons as a consequence of a refusal by an heir of an inheritance or elimination of an heir on the grounds established by Article 1117 of the present Code, such persons may accept the inheritance within six months from the day the right to inherit arose with them.

3. Persons for whom the right to inherit arises only as a consequence of the failure of another heir to accept an inheritance may accept the inheritance within three months from the day of the end of the period specified in point 1 of the present Article.

Article 1155. Acceptance of Inheritance upon Expiry of Established Period

1. Upon the application of the heir who has allowed the period to lapse established for acceptance of an inheritance (Article 1154), a court may restore this period and deem the heir to have accepted the inheritance if the heir did not know and should not have known about the opening of the inheritance or allowed this period to lapse for other justifiable reasons and on condition that the heir who allowed the period to lapse established for acceptance of an inheritance had recourse to a court within six months after the reasons for the lapse of his period disappeared.

Upon deeming an heir to have acceptance an inheritance, the court shall determine the participatory share of all heirs in the inheritance property and, when necessary, determine the measures with regard to defense of the rights of the new heir to receive the participatory share of the inheritance due to him (point 3 of the present Article). Previously issued certificates on the right to an inheritance shall be deemed by the court to be invalid.

2. An inheritance may be accepted by an heir upon the expiry of the period established for the acceptance thereof without recourse to a court on condition of the consent in written form to this of all the remaining heirs who have accepted the inheritance. If such consent in written form is given by the heirs not in the presence of a notary, their signatures on documents concerning consent must be certified in the procedure specified in Article 1153(1), paragraph two, of the present Code. The consent of heirs shall be grounds for annulment by the notary of a previously issued certificate on the right to inheritance and the basis for the issuance of a new certificate.

If on the basis of a previously issued certificate State registration was effectuated of the rights to immoveable property, the decree of the notary concerning the annulment of the previously issued certificate and the new certificate shall be the basis for making respective changes in the entry on State registration.

3. An heir who has accepted an inheritance after the expiry of the established period in compliance with the rules of the present Article shall have the right to receive the inheritance due to him in accordance with the rules of Articles 1104, 1105, 1107, and 1108 of the present Code which, in the event specified in point 2 of the present Article, shall apply insofar as not provided otherwise in an agreement among the heirs concluded in written form.

Article 1156. Transfer of Right to Acceptance of Inheritance (Inheritance Transmission)

1. If an heir called to inherit by will or by operation of law dies after the opening of the inheritance without succeeding to accept it in the established period, the right to accept the inheritance due to him shall pass to his heirs by operation of law, and if all inheritance property was bequeathed – to his heirs by will (inheritance transmission). The right to accept an inheritance by way of inheritance transmission shall not be within the composition of the inheritance opened after the death of such heir.

2. The right to accept an inheritance belonging to a deceased heir may be effectuated by his heirs on the general grounds.

If the part of the period established for acceptance of an inheritance comprises less than three months after the death of an heir, it shall be extended up to three months.

Upon the expiry of the period established for acceptance of an inheritance the heirs of the deceased heir may be deemed by a court to have accepted the inheritance in accordance with Article 1155 of the present Code if the court finds the reasons for the lapse of this period by them to be justifiable.

3. The right of an heir to accept part of an inheritance as an obligatory participatory share (Article 1149) shall not pass to his heirs.

Article 1157. Right to Refuse Inheritance

1. An heir shall have the right to refuse an inheritance to the benefit of other persons (Article 1158) or without specifying the persons to whose benefit he is refusing the inheritance.

In the event of inheriting escheat property a refusal of the inheritance shall not be permitted.

2. An heir shall have the right to refuse an inheritance within the period established for acceptance of the inheritance (Article 1154), including when he already has accepted the inheritance.

If an heir has committed actions testifying to the actual acceptance of the inheritance (Article 1153[2]), a court may upon the application of this heir deem him to have refused the inheritance also upon the expiry of the established period if it finds the reasons for the lapse of such period to be justified.

3. A refusal of an inheritance may not be subsequently changed or taken back.

4. A refusal of an inheritance when the heir is a minor or is a citizen who does not have dispositive legal capacity or has limited dispositive legal capacity shall be permitted with the prior authorization of a trusteeship and guardianship agency.

Article 1158. Refusal of Inheritance to Benefit of Other Persons and Refusal of Part of Inheritance

1. An heir shall have the right to refuse an inheritance to the benefit of other persons from among the heirs by will or heirs by operation of law of any priority irrespective of being called to inherit, who are not deprived of inheritance (Article 1119[1]), and also to the benefit of those who have been called to inherit by right of representation (Article 1146) or by way of inheritance transmission (Article 1156) [as amended by Federal Law No. 22-ФЗ, 15 February 2016. СЗ РФ (2016), no. 7, item 910].

Refusal to the benefit of any of the said persons shall not be permitted:

from property inheritable by will, if all the property of the decedent was bequeathed to the heirs designated by him;

from an obligatory participatory share in the inheritance (Article 1149);

if the heir has subdesignated an heir (Article 1121).

2. A refusal of inheritance to the benefit of persons not specified in point 1 of the present Article shall not be permitted.

A refusal of an inheritance with reservations or on condition also shall not be permitted.

3. A refusal of part of an inheritance due to an heir shall not be permitted. However, if an heir is called to inherit simultaneously on several grounds (by will and by operation of law, or by way of inheritance transmission and as a result of the opening of an inheritance, and so on), he shall have the right to refuse the inheritance due to him under one of these grounds, several of their, or all the grounds.

Article 1159. Means of Refusal of Inheritance

1. Refusal of an inheritance shall be performed by filing at the place of opening the inheritance with the notary or official empowered in accordance with a law to issue a certificate on the right to inherit a statement of the heir concerning the refusal of the inheritance.

2. When a statement concerning refusal of an inheritance is filed with the notary not by the heir himself, but by another person or is sent by post, the signature of the heir on such statement must be certified by a notary, official empowered to perform notarial actions (Article 1125(7)), or by a person empowered to certify wills in accordance with Article 1127(1) of the present Code [as amended by Federal Law of 3 April 2023, No. 101-ФЗ. СЗ РФ (2023), no. 14, item 2378].

3. Refusal of an inheritance through a representative shall be possible if the power for such refusal has been specially provided for in the power of attorney. A power of attorney

shall not be required for a legal representative to refuse an inheritance.

Article 1160. Right to Refuse Receipt of Testamentary Legacy

1. The recipient of a legacy shall have the right to refuse receipt of a testamentary legacy (Article 1137). In so doing the refusal to the benefit of another person, refusal with reservations, or on condition shall not be permitted.

2. If the recipient of a legacy is simultaneously an heir, his right provided for by the present Article shall not depend upon his right to accept or to refuse the inheritance.

Article 1161. Increment of Inheritance Participatory Shares

1. If an heir does not accept an inheritance, refuses an inheritance without having specified in so doing that he is refusing to the benefit of another heir (Article 1158), has no right to inherit, or will be eliminated from inheriting on the grounds established by Article 1117 of the present Code, or as a consequence of the invalidity of a will, the part of the inheritance which would have been due to such heir who has fallen away shall pass to the heirs by operation of law called to inherit in proportion to their inheritance participatory shares.

However, when the decedent has bequeathed all property to heirs designated by him, the part of the inheritance due to an heir who has refused the inheritance or who has fallen away for the other specified grounds shall pass to the remaining heirs by will in proportion to their inheritance participatory shares unless the distribution of this part of the inheritance has been provided otherwise by the will.

2. The rules contained in point 1 of the present Article shall not apply if the heir who has refused the inheritance or fallen away on other grounds has subdesignated an heir (Article 1121[2]).

Article 1162. Certificate on Right to Inheritance

1. A certificate on the right to an inheritance shall be issued at the place of opening the inheritance by a notary or official empowered in accordance with a law to perform such notarial action.

The certificate shall be issued upon the application of an heir. At the wish of heirs the certificate may be issued to all heirs together or to each heir individually for all the inheritance property as a whole or for individual parts thereof.

A certificate shall be issued in the same procedure also in the event of the transfer of escheat property in accordance with Article 1151 of the present Code to the Russian Federation, subject of the Russian Federation, or municipal formation [as amended by Federal Law of 29 November 2007, No. 281-ФЗ. СЗ РФ (2007), no. 49, item 6042].

2. In the event inheritance property is elicited after the issuance of a certificate on the right to an inheritance for which such certificate was not issued, an additional certificate on the right to an inheritance shall be issued.

Article 1163. Periods for Issue of Certificate on Right to Inheritance

1. A certificate on the right to an inheritance shall be issued to heirs at any time upon the expiry of six months from the day of opening an inheritance, except for instances provided for by the present Code.

2. When inheriting either by operation of law or by will a certificate on the right to inheritance may be issued before the expiry of six months from the day of opening the inheritance if there is reliable data that, besides the persons who have had recourse for the issuance of the certificate, there are no other heirs having the right to an inheritance of respective part thereof.

3. The issuance of a certificate on the right to an inheritance shall be suspended by decision of a court, and also when there is a conceived but as yet unborn heir.

Article 1164. Common Ownership of Heirs

When inheriting by operation of law, if the inheritance property passes to two or several heirs, and when inheriting by will, if it was bequeathed to two or several heirs without specifying the specific property to be inherited by each of them, the inheritance property shall ensue from the day of opening the inheritance to the common participatory share ownership of the heirs.

The provisions of Chapter 16 of the present Code on common participatory share ownership, taking into account the rules of Articles 1165-1170 of the present Code, shall apply to the common ownership of heirs in the inheritance property. However, in the event of the division of inheritance property the rules of Articles 1168-1170 of the present Code shall apply for three years from the day of opening of the inheritance.

Article 1165. Division of Inheritance by Agreement Between Heirs

1. Inheritance property which is in common participatory share ownership of two or several heirs may be divided by agreement between them.

The rules of the present Code concerning the form of transactions and the form of contracts shall apply to an agreement concerning the division of an inheritance.

2. An agreement concerning the division of an inheritance in the composition of which there is immoveable property, including an agreement concerning the apportionment from the inheritance of the participatory share of one or several heirs, may be concluded by the heirs after the issuance to them of the certificate on the right to an inheritance.

State registration of the rights of heirs to immoveable property with respect to which an agreement has been concluded concerning the division of an inheritance shall be effectuated on the basis of an agreement concerning the division of an inheritance and previously issued certificate concerning the right to an inheritance, and in the event State registration of the rights of heirs to immoveable property was effectuated before the conclusion by them of an agreement concerning the division of an inheritance, on the basis of an agreement concerning the division of the inheritance.

3. The failure of the division of an inheritance effectuated by heirs in an agreement concluded by them to conform to the participatory shares due to the heirs specified in the certificate on the right to an inheritance may not entail a refusal of State registration of their rights to immoveable property received as a result of the division of the inheritance.

Article 1166. Protection of Interests of Child When Dividing Inheritance

When there is a conceived but as yet unborn heir, the division of an inheritance may be effectuated only after the birth of that heir.

Article 1167. Protection of Legal Interests of Minors, Citizens Lacking Dispositive Legal Capacity and Limited in Dispositive Legal Capacity When Dividing Inheritance

When there are among the heirs minors and citizens lacking dispositive legal capacity or having limited dispositive legal capacity, the division of an inheritance shall be effectuated in compliance with the rules of Article 37 of the present Code.

For the purposes of protection of the legal interests of the said heirs, the trusteeship and guardianship agency must be notified about drawing up an agreement concerning division of the inheritance (Article 1165) and consideration in a court of a case concerning division of the inheritance.

Article 1168. Preferential Right to Indivisible Thing When Dividing Inheritance

1. An heir who possessed jointly with the decedent the right of common ownership to an indivisible thing (Article 133), the participatory share in the right to which is within the composition of the inheritance, shall have when dividing the property a preferential right to receive at the expense of his inheritance participatory share the thing in common ownership

before heirs who previously were not participants of common ownership irrespective of whether they used this thing or not.

2. An heir who constantly used an indivisible thing (Article 133) within the composition of the inheritance shall have when dividing the property a preferential right to receive at the expense of his inheritance participatory share this thing before heirs who have not used this thing and were not previously participants of common ownership therein.

3. If within the composition of an inheritance there is a dwelling premise (dwelling house, apartment, and the like), the division of which in kind is impossible, when dividing the inheritance the heirs who resided in this dwelling premise on the day of opening the inheritance and who do not have another dwelling premise shall have a preferential right before other heirs who are not owners of the dwelling premise within the composition of the inheritance to receive this dwelling premise at the expense of their inheritance participatory shares.

Article 1169. Preferential Right to Ordinary Household Articles When Dividing Inheritance

An heir who lived on the day of opening the inheritance jointly with the decedent shall have when dividing the inheritance a preferential right to receive at the expense of his inheritance participatory share the ordinary domestic household articles.

Article 1170. Contributory Compensation for Incommensurateness of Inheritance Property from Inheritance Participatory Shares

1. The incommensurateness of inheritance property, the preferential right to receive which is declared by an heir on the basis of Article 1168 or 1169 of the present Code, the inheritance participatory share of this heir, shall be eliminated by the transfer of this heir to the remaining heirs of other property from the composition of the inheritance or granting of other contributory compensation, including payment of a respective monetary amount.

2. Unless established otherwise by agreement between all the heirs, the effectuation by any of them of a preferential right shall be possible after the provision of respective contributory compensation to the other heirs.

Article 1171. Protection and Management of Inheritance

1. In order to defend the rights of heirs, recipients of legacies, and other interested persons, measures specified in Articles 1172 and 1173 of the present Code, and other necessary measures with regard to the protection and management of the inheritance, by the executor of the will or notary at the place of opening the inheritance.

2. A notary shall take measures with regard to the protection and management of an inheritance upon the application of one or several heirs, executor of the will, agencies of local self-government, trusteeship and guardianship agency, or other persons acting in the interests of preserving inheritance property. When the executor of a will has been appointed (Article 1134), the notary shall take measures with regard to protection and management of the inheritance by agreement with the executor of the will.

The executor of a will shall take measures with regard to the protection and management of an inheritance autonomously or at the request of one or several heirs.

3. For the purposes of eliciting the composition of an inheritance and protection thereof, banks, other credit organizations, and other juridical persons shall be obliged at the request of the notary to notify him about information available with these persons concerning property belonging to the decedent. The notary may communicate information received only to the executor of the will and heirs.

4. A notary shall effectuate measures with regard to the protection and management of an inheritance during the period determined by the notary, taking into account the character and valuables of the inheritance, and also the time necessary for heirs to enter into possession of the inheritance [as amended

by Federal Law of 29 July 2017, No. 259-ФЗ. СЗ РФ (2017), no. 31(I), item 4808].

The executor of a will shall effectuate measures with regard to protection and management of the inheritance during the period necessary for performance of the will.

5. When inheritance property is situated in various places, the notary at the place of opening the inheritance shall send through territorial agencies of the federal agency of executive power effectuating law enforcement functions and functions with regard to control and supervision in the sphere of the notariat to the notary at the location of the respective part of the inheritance property a commission binding for execution concerning the protection and management of this property. If it is known by the notary at the place of opening the inheritance by whom measures with regard to protection of the property should be taken, such commission shall be sent to the respective notary or official [as amended by Federal Law of 29 December 2006, No. 258-ФЗ. СЗ РФ (2007), no. 1(I), item 21].

6. The procedure for the protection and management of inheritance property, including the procedure for the inventory of the inheritance, shall be determined by legislation on the notariat. The maximum amounts of remuneration under a contract of keeping of inheritance property and contract of trust management of inheritance property shall be established by the Government of the Russian Federation.

7. When the right to perform notarial actions has been granted by a law to officials of agencies of local self-government and consular officials of the Russian Federation, necessary measures for the protection of an inheritance and management thereof may be taken by the respective official [as amended by Federal Law of 28 February 2023, No. 46-ФЗ. СЗ РФ (2023), no. 10, item 1569].

Article 1172. Measures With Regard to Protection of Inheritance

1. In order to protect an inheritance, a notary shall make an inventory of inheritance property in the presence of two witnesses who meet the requirements established by Article 1124(2) of the present Code.

The executor of the will, heirs, and in respective instances, representatives of trusteeship and guardianship agencies, may be present when the inventory of property is made.

Upon the application of persons specified in paragraph two of the present point a valuation of the inheritance property must be made by agreement between the heirs. In the absence of agreement, the valuation of the inheritance property or that part thereof with respect to which agreement is not reached shall be made by an independent valuer at the expense of the person requiring valuation of the inheritance property, with subsequent distribution of these expenses between the heirs in proportion to the value of inheritance received by each of them.

2. Cash money within the composition of the inheritance shall be placed on deposit with the notary, and hard currency valuables, precious metals and stones, manufactures thereof, and securities not requiring management shall be transferred to a bank for keeping under a contract in accordance with Article 921 of the present Code.

3. If it has become known to a notary that a weapon is within the composition of the inheritance, he shall inform the federal agency of executive power empowered in the sphere of the turnover of a weapon or the territorial agency thereof [as amended by Federal Law No. 227-ФЗ, 3 July 2016. СЗ РФ (2016), no. 27(I), item 4160].

4. Property within the composition of an inheritance and not specified in points 2 and 3 of the present Article, unless it required management, shall be transferred by the notary under a contract for keeping to someone of the heirs, and, when it

is impossible to transfer it to heirs – to another person at the discretion of the notary.

When an inheritance is effectuated by a will in which the executor of the will is designated, the keeping of the said property shall be ensured by the executor of the will autonomously or by means of the conclusion of a contract with any of the heirs or other person at the discretion of the executor of the will.

Article 1173. Trust Management of Inheritance Property

1. If within the composition of an inheritance there is property requiring not only protection, but also management (enterprise, participatory share in charter (or contributed) capital of a corporate juridical person, share, securities, exclusive rights, and the like), a notary shall in accordance with Article 126 of the present Code as the founder of trust management conclude a contract of trust management for this property [as amended by Federal Law of 29 July 2017, No. 259-ФЗ. СЗ РФ (2017), no. 31(I), item 4808].

Before the conclusion of a contract of trust management of inheritance property, an evaluation must be conducted by an independent valuer of that part of the property which is transferred on trust management. The expenses for conducting the valuation shall be relegated to expenses for the protection and management of the inheritance (Article 1174) [paragraph added by Federal Law of 29 July 2017, No. 259-ФЗ. СЗ РФ (2017), no. 31(I), item 4808].

2. When inheriting is effectuated by will in which an executor of the will has been designated, the executor of the will shall be considered a trustee manager of the inheritance property from the moment of the expression by him of consent to be the executor of the will (Article 1134) [as amended by Federal Law of 29 July 2017, No. 259-ФЗ. СЗ РФ (2017), no. 31(I), item 4808].

3. The trust management of inheritance property shall be effectuated for the purposes of the preservation of this property and increasing the value thereof.

The beneficiary under a contract of trust management of inheritance property shall not be designated, except for an instance when a testamentary legacy is performed assuming the performance thereof to the benefit of a determined person for the period of the performance of actions relating to the protection and management of inheritance property. In such event the recipient of the legacy shall be designated as the beneficiary.

A trustee manager of inheritance property shall not have the right to perform obligations of the decedent at the expense of the property transferred to him on trust management until the issuance to one of the heirs of a certificate concerning the right to inherit, except for instances if the contract of trust management or will provides for the duty of the trustee manager to compensate expenses at the expense of property transferred on trust management indicated in Article 1174 of the present Code [point 3 added by Federal Law of 29 July 2017, No. 259-ФЗ. СЗ РФ (2017), no. 31(I), item 4808].

4. When performing actions relating to the protection and management of inheritance property in instances when the will of the decedent contains his instructions with regard to the management of the inheritance, the trustee manager and executor shall be obliged to act in accordance with such instructions of the decedent, including shall be obliged to vote in the higher organs of a corporation as was indicated in the will [added by Federal Law of 29 July 2017, No. 259-ФЗ. СЗ РФ (2017), no. 31(I), item 4808].

5. The notary effectuating the powers of founder of trust management under a contract of trust management shall be obliged to control the performance by the trustee manager of his duties no less than once every two months. In the event of the discovery of a violation by the trustee manager of his duties, the notary shall have the right unilaterally to dissolve the contract of trust management, demand the submission of a report from the trustee manager, and appoint a new trustee manager [added by Federal Law of 29 July 2017, No. 259-ФЗ. СЗ РФ (2017), no. 31(I), item 4808].

6. A person may be appointed a trustee manager under a contract who meets the requirements specified in Article 1015 of the present Code, including the assumed heir, who may be appointed with the consent of other heirs identified at the moment of appointment of the trustee manager, and in the event of objections thereof – on the basis of the decision of a court [added by Federal Law of 29 July 2017, No. 259-ФЗ. СЗ РФ (2017), no. 31(I), item 4808].

7. In the event of the transfer of inherited property to several trustee managers, each of them shall possess powers with regard to management of the inheritance property unless provided otherwise by the contract of trust management or the will that the trustee managers shall effectuate their powers jointly. In the event disagreements arise between the trustee managers with regard to the rights and duties effectuated by them, a notary shall be obliged to dissolve the contract of trust management concluded with such managers for the inheritance property, demand from the trustee managers the submission of reports by them, and appoint a new trustee manager or trustee managers [added by Federal Law of 29 July 2017, No. 259-ФЗ. СЗ РФ (2017), no. 31(I), item 4808].

8. A contract of trust management of inheritance property may be concluded for a period not exceeding five years. In any event at the moment of issuance of a certificate concerning the right to inherit to even one of the heirs, if in such certificate property is specified which is the subject-matter of trust management, or if such certificate was issued with respect to all the property of the decedent, however it was expressed and wherever it was located, to such heir (or such heirs) shall pass the rights and duties of the founder of trust management. The notary who founded the trust management shall be relieved from the effectuation of duties of the founder. The heir who has received the certificate concerning the right to inherit shall have the right to terminate the trust management and demand from the trustee manager the transfer of property in trust management, the right to which passed to this heir and the submission of a report concerning the trust management.

In the event of the failure of heirs to demand the transfer to them of property in trust management, the contract of trust management shall be considered to be prolonged for a period of five years, and the trust management may be terminated on the grounds provided by Article 1024 of the present Code [added by Federal Law of 29 July 2017, No. 259-ФЗ. СЗ РФ (2017), no. 31(I), item 4808].

Article 1174. Compensation of Expenses Caused by Death of Decedent and Expenses for Protection and Management of Inheritance

1. Necessary expenses caused by the fatal illness of the decedent, expenses for his dignified burial, including necessary expenses for payment of the site of interment of the decedent, expenses for the protection and management of the inheritance, and also expenses connected with execution of the will, shall be compensated at the expense of the inheritance within the limits of the value thereof.

2. Demands concerning compensation of expenses specified in point 1 of the present Article may be presented to heirs who have accepted the inheritance, and until acceptance of the inheritance – to the executor of the will or against the inheritance property.

Such expenses shall be compensated before payment of debts to creditors of the decedent and within the limits of the value of the inheritance property which passed to each of the heirs. In so doing expenses shall be compensated in first priority caused by the illness and burial of the decedent, in second – expenses for the protection and management of the inheritance, and in third – expenses connected with execution of the will.

3. In order to effectuate expenses for a dignified burial of the decedent any monetary means belonging to him may be used, including on deposit or in accounts in banks.

Banks in whose deposits or accounts monetary means of the decedent are situated, and also the Bank of Russia when there are digital rubles to be taken into account in a digital ruble account of the decedent, shall be obliged upon decree of a notary to provide them to the person specified in the decree of the notary for payment of the said expenses [as amended by Federal Law of 24 July 2023, No. 339-ФЗ. СЗ РФ (2023), no. 31(III), item 5765].

An heir to whom monetary means have been bequeathed (or placed on deposit or in any other accounts of the decedent in banks, and also digital rubles to be taken into account in in a digital ruble account of the decedent), including when they have been bequeathed by means of testamentary disposition (Article 1128), shall have the right at any time before the expiry of six months from the day of opening the inheritance to receive from the deposit or from the account, including the digital ruble account, of the decedent monetary means necessary for his burial [as amended by Federal Law of 24 July 2023, No. 339-ФЗ. СЗ РФ (2023), no. 31(III), item 5765].

The amount of means to be issued on the basis of the present point by a bank for burial to an heir or person specified in the decree of a notary may not exceed one hundred thousand rubles [as amended by Federal Laws of 2 December 2004, No. 156-ФЗ, 30 June 2008, No. 105-ФЗ, and 9 March 2016, No. 60-ФЗ. СЗ РФ (2004), no. 49, item 4855; (2008), no. 27, item 3123; (2016), no. 11, item 1487].

The rules of the present point respectively shall apply to other credit institutions which have been granted the right to attract monetary means of citizens in deposits or other accounts.

Article 1175. Responsibility of Heirs for Debts of Decedent

1. Heirs who have accepted an inheritance shall be liable for debts of the decedent jointly and severally (Article 323).

Each of the heirs shall be liable for debts of the decedent within the limits of the value of inherited property which has passed to him.

2. An heir who has accepted an inheritance by way of inheritance transmission (Article 1156) shall be liable within the limits of the value of this inherited property for debts of

the decedent to whom this property belonged and shall not be liable with this property for debts of the heir from whom the right to accept the inheritance passed to him.

3. Creditors of the decedent shall have the right to present their demands to heirs who accepted the inheritance within the limits of the periods of limitation established for respective demands. Until acceptance of the inheritance demands of creditors may be presented against the inheritance property for the purposes of the preservation of which the executor of the will or notary shall be enlisted to participate in the case. In the last event the court shall suspend consideration of the case until acceptance of the inheritance by heirs or transfer of escheat property in accordance with Article 1151 of the present Code to the Russian Federation, subject of the Russian Federation, or municipal formation [as amended by Federal Law of 29 November 2007, No. 281-ФЗ, and of 29 July 2017, No. 259-ФЗ. СЗ РФ (2007), no. 49, item 6042; (2017), no. 31(I), item 4808].

When demands are presented by creditors of the decedent the period of limitations established for the respective demands shall not be subject to interruption, suspension, or restoration.

Chapter 65. Inheriting of Individual Types of Property

Article 1176. Inheriting of Rights Connected with Participation in Economic Partnerships and Societies and Production Cooperatives

1. Within the composition of an inheritance of a participant of a full partnership or full partner in a limited partnership, participant of a society with limited or additional responsibility, and member of a production cooperative shall be the participatory share (or share) of this participant (or member) in the contributed (or charter) capital (or property) of the respective partnership, society, or cooperative.

If in accordance with the present Code, other laws, or constitutive documents of an economic partnership or society or production cooperative the consent of the other members of the partnership or society or members of a cooperative is required for entry of an heir into the economic partnership or production cooperative or transfer of a participatory share to an heir in the charter capital of an economic society and such consent is refused to the heir, he shall have the right to receive from the economic partnership or society or production cooperative the actual value of the inherited participatory share (or share) or part of the property corresponding to it in the procedure provided for by the rules of the present Code applicable to the said instance, other laws, or constitutive documents of the respective juridical person.

2. Within the composition of an inheritance of a contributor to a limited partnership shall be his participatory share in the contributed capital of that partnership. The heir to whom this participatory share passed shall become a contributor of the limited partnership.

3. Within the composition of an inheritance of a participant of a joint-stock society shall be the stocks which belonged to him. The heirs to whom these stocks have passed shall become participants of the joint-stock society.

Article 1177. Inheriting of Rights Connected with Participation in Consumer Cooperative

1. Within the composition of an inheritance of a member of a consumer cooperative shall be his share.

The heir of a member of a housing, dacha, or other consumer cooperative shall have the right to be admitted to membership in the respective cooperative. Such heir may not be refused admission to membership of the cooperative.

2. Deciding the question of who of the heirs may be admitted to membership of a consumer cooperative when the share of the decedent has passed to several heirs, and also the procedure, means, and periods for payment to heirs who do not become members of the cooperative the amounts due to them or issuance instead of property in kind shall be determined by legislation

on consumer cooperatives and constitutive documents of the respective cooperative.

Article 1178. Inheriting of Enterprise

An heir who on the day of opening an inheritance is registered as an individual entrepreneur, or a commercial organization which is an heir by will, shall have when dividing the inheritance a preferential right to receive at the expense of his inheritance participatory share the enterprise (Article 132) within the composition of the inheritance in compliance with the rules of Article 1170 of the present Code.

When none of the heirs has the said preferential right or does not take advantage of it, the enterprise within the composition of the inheritance shall not be subject to division and shall ensue to the common participatory share ownership of the heirs in accordance with the inheritance participatory shares due to them, unless provided otherwise by agreement of the heirs who have accepted the inheritance within the composition of which the enterprise is.

Article 1179. Inheriting of Property of Member of Peasant (or Farmer) Economy

1. After the death of any member of a peasant (or farmer) economy, an inheritance shall be opened and inheriting shall be effectuated on the general grounds in compliance in so doing with the rules of Articles 253-255 and 257-259 of the present Code.

2. If an heir of the deceased member of a peasant (or farmer) economy himself is not a member of this economy, he shall have the right to receive contributory compensation commensurate to the participatory share inherited by him in the property in the common joint ownership of members of the economy. The period for payment of contributory compensation shall be determined by agreement of the heir with members of the economy, and in the absence of agreement, by a court, but may not exceed one year from the day of opening the inheritance. In the absence of agreement between the members of the economy

and the said heir about otherwise, the participatory share of the decedent in this property shall be considered to be equal to the participatory shares of the other members of the economy. In the event of the admission of the heir to membership in the economy, the said contributory compensation shall not be paid to him.

3. When after the death of a member of a peasant (or farmer) economy this economy is terminated (Article 258[1]), including in connection with the fact that the decedent was the sole member of the economy and among his heirs there are no persons wishing that the effectuation of a peasant (or farmer) economy continued its activity, the property of the peasant (or farmer) economy shall be subject to division between the heirs according to the rules of Article 258 and 1182 of the present Code [as amended by Federal Law of 28 December 2013, No. 446-ФЗ. СЗ РФ (2013), no. 52(I), item 7011].

Article 1180. Inheriting of Things Limited in Circulability

1. A weapon, virulent and poisonous substances, narcotic and psychotropic means, and other things limited in circulability (Article 129(2), paragraph two) which belonged to the decedent shall be within the composition of the inheritance and shall be inherited on the general grounds established by the present Code. A special authorization shall not be required to accept an inheritance within those composition there are such things.

2. Measures with regard to the protection of things of limited circulability within the composition of an inheritance until an heir receives the special authorization for these things shall be effectuated in compliance with the procedure established by a law for the respective property.

In the event of a refusal to issue the said authorization to an heir, his right of ownership to such property shall be subject to termination in accordance with Article 238 of the present Code, and the amounts received from the realization of the property transferred to the heir, deducting expenses for the realization thereof.

Article 1181. Inheriting of Land Plots

A land plot belonging to the decedent by right of ownership or right of inheritable possession of the land plot for life shall be within the composition of the inheritance and shall be inherited on the general grounds established by the present Code. Special authorization shall not be required for acceptance of an inheritance within whose composition the said property is.

In the event of inheriting a land plot or right of inheritable possession of a land plot for life, the surface (earth) layer, water objects, and flora situated thereon un less established otherwise by a law within the boundaries of this land plot also shall pass by inheritance [as amended by Federal Law of 3 June 2006, No. 73-ФЗ. СЗ РФ (2006), no. 23, item 2380].

Article 1182. Peculiarities of Division of Land Plot

1. The division of a land plot belonging to heirs by right of common ownership shall be effectuated by taking into account the minimum size of a land plot established for plots of the respective special-purpose designation.

2. In the event it is impossible to divide a land plot in the procedure established by point 1 of the present Article, the land plot shall pass to the heir having a preferential to receive this land plot at the expense of his inheritance participatory share. Contributory compensation to the remaining heirs shall be granted in the procedure established by Article 1170 of the present Code.

In the event when no one of the heirs has a preferential right to receive the land plot or does not take advantage of this right, the possession, use, and disposition of the land plot shall be effectuated by the heirs on the conditions of common participatory share ownership.

Article 1183. Inheriting of Unpaid Amounts Granted to Citizen as Means for Existence

1. The right to receive amounts of earnings and payments equated thereto, pensions, stipends, benefits for social insurance, compensation of harm caused to life or health, alimony, and

other monetary amounts granted to a citizen as means for existence which are subject to payment to the decedent but not received by him while alive for any reason whatsoever shall belong to members of his family who resided jointly with the deceased, and also to his dependents without labor capacity irrespective of whether they resided or did not reside jointly with the deceased.

2. Demands concerning the payment of amounts on the basis of point 1 of the present Article must be presented to obliged persons within four months from the day of opening the inheritance.

3. In the absence of persons having the right on the basis of point 1 of the present Article to receive amounts not paid to the decedent, or in the event of the failure of these persons to present demands concerning payment of the said amounts within the established period, the respective amounts shall be included in the composition of the inheritance and shall be inherited on the general grounds established by the present Code.

Article 1184. Inheriting of Property Granted to Decedent by State or Municipal Formation on Privileged Conditions

Means of transport and other property granted by the State or municipal formation on privileged conditions to the decedent in connection with his disability or other similar circumstances shall be within the composition of the inheritance and shall be inherited on the general grounds established by the present Code.

Article 1185. Inheriting of State Awards, Marks of Honor, and Commemorative Marks

1. State awards which have been conferred on the decedent and to which legislation on State awards of the Russian Federation extends shall not be within the composition of an inheritance. The transfer of the said awards after the death of the awardee to other persons shall be effectuated in the procedure established by legislation on State awards of the Russian Federation.

2. State awards belonging to a decedent to which legislation on State awards of the Russian Federation does not extend, honorary, commemorative, and other marks, including awards and marks within collections, shall be within the composition of an inheritance and shall be inherited on the general grounds established by the present Code.

...

SECTION VII. INTERNATIONAL PRIVATE LAW

Chapter 67. Law Subject to Application When Determining Legal Status of Persons

...

Article 1202. Personal Law of Juridical Person

...

5. The application of foreign law to relations with the participation of the personal foundation, founder of this foundation, beneficiary of this foundation, and also persons who are members of organs of this foundation, if these are relations with the participation of foreign citizens or foreign juridical persons or relations complicated by another foreign element, may be provided by the charter of a personal foundation created under Russian law [point 5 added by Federal Law of 8 August 2024, No. 237-ФЗ. СЗ РФ (2024), no. 33(I), item 4393].

...

Chapter 68. Law Subject to Application to Property and Personal Nonproperty Relations

...

Article 1224. Law Subject to Application to Relations With Regard to Inheriting

1. Relations with regard to inheriting shall be determined according to the law of the country where the decedent had his last place of residence, unless provided otherwise by the present Article.

The inheriting of immoveable property shall be determined according to the law of the country where this property is situated, and the inheriting of immoveable property which has been entered in a State register in the Russian Federation, – according to Russian law.

2. The capacity of a person to draw up and revoke a will, including with respect to immoveable property, and also the form of such will or act of revocation thereof, shall be determined according to the law of the country where the testator had a place of residence at the moment of drawing up such will or act. However, the will or revocation thereof may not be deemed invalid as a consequence of the failure to comply with the form if it satisfies the requirements of the place of drawing up the will or act of revocation thereof or the requirements of Russian law.

FAMILY CODE OF THE RUSSIAN FEDERATION

[Excerpts]

...

SECTION III. RIGHTS AND DUTIES OF SPOUSES

...

Chapter 7. Legal Regime of Property of Spouses

Article 33. Concept of Legal Regime of Property of Spouses

1. The legal regime of the property of spouses shall be the regime of their joint ownership.

The legal regime of the property of spouses shall operate unless established otherwise by a marriage contract.

2. The rights of spouses to possess, use, and dispose of property which is the joint ownership of members of a peasant (or farmer's) economy shall be determined by Articles 257 and 258 of the Civil Code of the Russian Federation.

Article 34. Joint Ownership of Spouses

1. The property acquired by spouses during marriage shall be their joint ownership.

2. To property acquired by spouses during marriage (common property of spouses) shall be relegated the revenues of each of the spouses from labor activity, entrepreneurial activity and the results of intellectual activity, pensions and benefits received by them, and also other monetary payments not having a special special-purpose designation (amounts of material assistance, amounts paid in compensation of damage in connection with the loss of labor capacity as a consequence of mutilation or other impairment of health, and others). Moveable and immoveable things, securities, shares, contributions,

participatory shares in capital deposited in credit institutions, or in other commercial organizations also acquired at the expense of common revenues of the spouses, and any other property acquired by spouses in the period of the marriage, irrespective of in the name of which spouse it is acquired or in the name of which of the spouses monetary means have been deposited, also shall be the common property of spouses.

3. The right to common property of spouses shall also belong to the spouse who in the period of the marriage who effectuated the conducting of the household, care for children, or for other justifiable reasons had no autonomous revenue.

Article 35. Possession, Use, and Disposition of Common Property of Spouses

1. The possession, use, and disposition of common property of spouses shall be effectuated by the joint consent of the spouses.

2. When one of the spouses concludes a transaction with regard to the disposition of common property of the spouses it shall be presupposed that he operates with the consent of the other spouse.

A transaction concluded by one of the spouses with regard to the disposition of common property of the spouses may be deemed by a court to be invalid for reasons of the absence of consent of the other spouse only upon the demand thereof and only in instances if it is proved that the other party in the transaction knew or knowingly should have known about the lack of consent of the other spouse to conclude the particular transaction.

3. For one of the spouses to conclude a transaction with regard to the disposition of property, the rights to which are subject to State registration, a transaction for which the obligatory notarial form has been established by a law, or a transaction subject to obligatory State registration, it shall be necessary to receive the notarially certified consent of the other

spouse [as amended by Federal Law of 29 December 2015, No. 391-ФЗ].

A spouse whose notarially certified consent to the conclusion of the said transaction was not received shall have the right to demand the transaction be deemed to be invalid in a judicial proceeding within a year from the day when he knew or should have known about the conclusion of the particular transaction according to the rules of Article 173[1] of the Civil Code of the Russian Federation [as amended by Federal Law of 14 July 2022, No. 310-ФЗ].

Article 36. Property of Each of Spouses [as amended by Federal Law of 18 December 2006]

1. The property which belongs to each of the spouses before entry into marriage, and also the property received by one of the spouses during the marriage as a gift, by way of inheritance, or under other transactions with compensation (the property of each of the spouses) shall be the ownership thereof.

2. Things of individual use (clothing, footwear, and others), except for jewellery and other articles of adornment, although acquired in the period of the marriage at the expense of common assets of the spouses, shall be deemed to be the ownership of that spouse who used them.

3. The exclusive right to a result of intellectual activity created by one of the spouses shall belong to the author of such result [added by Federal Law of 18 December 2006].

Article 37. Deeming of Property of Each of Spouses to be Their Joint Ownership

The property of each of the spouses may be deemed by a court to be their joint ownership if it is established that in the period of the marriage investments were made at the expense of common property of the spouses or the property of each of the spouses or the labor of one of the spouses which significantly increased the value of this property (capital repair, reconstruction, re-equipping, and others) [as amended by Federal Law of 30 December 2015, No. 457-ФЗ].

Article 38. Division of Common Property of Spouses

1. The common property of spouses may be divided both in the period of the marriage and after the dissolution thereof at the demand of either of the spouses, and also in the event of the statement by creditors of a demand concerning the division of the common property of spouses in order to levy execution against the participatory share of one of the spouses in the common property of the spouses.

2. The common property of spouses may be divided between the spouses by their agreement. An agreement concerning the division of common property acquired by spouses during the period of marriage must be notarially certified [as amended by Federal Law of 29 December 2015, No. 391-ФЗ].

3. In the event of a dispute, the common property of spouses shall be divided, and also the participatory share of the spouses in this property shall be determined, in a judicial proceeding.

In the event of the division of the common property of spouses, the court at the demand of the spouses shall determine which property is subject to transfer to each of the spouses. If property is transferred to one of the spouses, the value of which exceeds the participatory share due to him, the other spouse may be awarded corresponding monetary or other contributory compensation.

4. The court may deem property acquired by each of the spouses in the period of their separate living when terminating family relations to be the ownership of each of them.

5. Things acquired exclusively in order to satisfy the requirements of minor children (clothing, footwear, school and sport appurtenances, musical instruments, children's library, and others) shall not be subject to division and shall be transferred without contributory compensation to that spouse with whom the children reside.

Contributions made by spouses at the expense of the common property of spouses in the name of their common minor children shall be considered to belong to these children and shall not be taken into account when dividing the common property of spouses.

6. In the event of the division of common property of spouses in the period of the marriage that part of the common property of spouses which was not divided, and also the property acquired by the spouses in the period of the marriage thereafter, shall comprise their joint ownership.

7. A three-year period of limitations shall apply to the demands of spouses concerning the division of the common property of spouses whose marriage is dissolved.

Article 39. Determination of Participatory Shares When Dividing Common Property of Spouses

1. When dividing the common property of spouses and determining the participatory shares in this property, the participatory shares of the spouses shall be deemed to be equal unless provided otherwise by the contract between the spouses.

2. The court shall have the right to depart from the principle of equality of participatory shares of the spouses in their common property by proceeding from the interests of the minor children and/or by proceeding from an interest deserving attention of one of the spouses, in particular in instances when the other spouse did not receive revenues for unjustifiable reasons or committed actions not in good faith which led to the diminution of the common property of the spouses, including such transactions concluded without the consent of the other spouse necessary by virtue of Article 35(3) of the present Code on unfavorable conditions with regard to the alienation of the common property of spouses to which the consequences of their invalidity were not applied by a court upon the demand of the other spouse [as amended by Federal Law of 14 July 2022, No. 310-ФЗ].

3. The common debts of spouses when dividing common property of the spouses shall be distributed between the spouses in proportion to the participatory shares awarded to them.

Chapter 8. Contractual Regime of Property of Spouses

Article 40. Marriage Contract

An agreement of the persons entering into a marriage, or the agreement of spouses determining the property rights and duties of spouses in the marriage and/or in the event of its dissolution, shall be deemed to be a marriage contract.

Article 41. Conclusion of Marriage Contract

1. A marriage contract may be concluded either before the State registration of the conclusion of the marriage or at any time in the period of the marriage.

A marriage contract concluded before the State registration of the conclusion of the marriage shall enter into force from the day of State registration of the conclusion of the marriage.

2. A marriage contract shall be concluded in written form and shall be subject to notarial certification.

Article 42. Content of Marriage Contract

1. The spouses shall have the right to change by a marriage contract regime of joint ownership (Article 34 of the present Code) established by a law and to establish a regime of joint, participatory share, or separate ownership to all the property of the spouses, to individual parts thereof, or to the property of each of the spouses.

A marriage contract may be concluded either with respect to existing and also in respect to the future property of the spouses.

The spouses shall have the right to determine their rights and duties in a marriage contract with regard to mutual maintenance, means of participation in the revenues of one another, the procedure for each of them to bear family expenses, to determine the property which will be transferred to each of the spouses in the event of dissolution of marriage, and also to include in the marriage contract any other provisions affecting the property relations of the spouses.

2. The rights and duties provided for by the marriage contract may be limited by determined periods or made dependent upon the ensuing or non-ensuing of determined conditions.

3. The marriage contract may not limit the legal capacity or dispositive legal capacity of spouses, their right to have resource to a court for the defense of their rights; to regulate personal nonproperty relations between the spouses, and the rights and duties of the spouses with respect to children; to provide provisions limiting the right of a needy spouse lacking labor capacity to receive maintenance; to contain other provisions which place one of the spouses in an extremely unfavorable position or contrary to the basic principles of family legislation.

Article 43. Change and Dissolution of Marriage Contract

1. The marriage contract may be changed or dissolved at any time by agreement of the spouses. An agreement concerning the change of or dissolution of the marriage contract shall be concluded in the same form as the marriage contract itself.

Unilateral repudiation of the performance of a marriage contract shall not be permitted.

2. At the demand of one of the spouses, the marriage contract may be changed or dissolved by decision of a court on the grounds and in the procedure which was established by the Civil Code of the Russian Federation for the change of and dissolution of a contract.

3. The operation of a marriage contract shall terminate from the moment of termination of the marriage (Article 25 of the present Code), except for those circumstances which have been provided for by the marriage contract for the period after termination of the marriage.

Article 44. Deeming of Marriage Contract to be Invalid

1. A marriage contract may be deemed by a court to be invalid in whole or in part on the grounds provided for by the Civil Code of the Russian Federation for the invalidity of transactions.

2. A court may also deem a marriage contract to be invalid in whole or in part at the demand of one of the spouses if the conditions of the contract place this spouse in an extremely unfavorable position. The conditions of a marriage contract violating other requirements of Article 42(3) of the present Code shall be void.

Chapter 9. Responsibility of Spouses for Obligations

Article 45. Levy of Execution Against Property of Spouses

1. Execution may be levied with regard to obligations of one of the spouses only against the property of this spouse. In the event of the insufficiency of this property the creditor shall have the right to demand the partition of the participatory share of the debtor-spouse which would be due to the debtor-spouse in the event of the division of the common property of the spouses in order to levy execution against it.

2. Execution shall be levied against the common property of spouses with regard to common obligations of the spouses, and also with regard to obligations of one of the spouses, if it is established by a court that everything received with regard to the obligations by one of the spouses was used for the needs of the family. In the event this property is insufficient, the spouses shall bear joint and several responsibility with regard to the said obligations by the property of each of them.

If it is established by judgment of a court that the common property of spouses was acquired or increased at the expense of means received by one of the spouses by criminal means, execution may be levied respectively against the common property of the spouses or against part thereof.

3. The responsibility of the spouses for harm caused by their minor children shall be determined by civil legislation. Levy of execution against the property of spouses in the event of compensation by them of harm caused by their minor children shall be made in accordance with point 2 of the present Article.

Article 46. Guarantees of Rights of Creditors When Concluding, Changing, and Dissolving Marriage Contract

1. A spouse shall be obliged to inform his creditor(s) about the conclusion, change, or dissolution of the marriage contract. In the event of the failure to fulfill this duty, the spouse shall be liable for his obligations irrespective of the content of the marriage contract.

2. The creditor(s) of a debtor-spouse shall have the right to demand the change of conditions or the dissolution of a contract concluded between them in connection with materially changed circumstances in the procedure established by Articles 451-453 of the Civil Code of Russian Federation.

...

SECTION VII. APPLICATION OF FAMILY LEGISLATION TO FAMILY RELATIONS WITH PARTICIPATION OF FOREIGN CITIZENS AND STATELESS PERSONS

...

Article 161. Personal Nonproperty and Property Rights and Duties of Spouses

1. Personal nonproperty and property rights and duties of spouses shall be determined by legislation of the State on whose territory they have a joint place of residence, and in the absence of a joint place of residence, by legislation of the State on whose territory they had the last joint place of residence. Personal nonproperty and property rights and duties of the spouses who did not have a joint place of residence shall be determined on the territory of the Russian Federation by legislation of the Russian Federation.

2. When concluding a marriage contract or agreement concerning the payment of alimony to one another, spouses not having a common citizenship or joint place of residence may choose the legislation subject to application in order to determine their rights and duties under the marriage contract

or agreement concerning the payment of alimony. If the spouses have not chosen the legislation subject to application to the marriage contract or to their agreement concerning the payment of alimony, the provisions of point 1 of the present Article shall apply.

...

SECTION VIII. CONCLUDING PROVISIONS

...

Article 169. Application of Norms of Present Code

...

5. The conditions and procedure for the conclusion of marriage contracts and agreements concerning the payment of alimony established according to Chapters 8 and 16 of the present Code shall apply to marriage contracts and agreements concerning the payment of alimony which are concluded after 1 March 1996. Marriage contracts and agreements concluded before 1 March 1996 concerning the payment of alimony shall operate in the part which is not contrary to the provisions of the present Code.

6. The provisions concerning joint ownership of spouses and the provisions concerning the ownership of each spouse established by Articles 34-37 of the present Code shall apply to property acquired by the spouses (or one of them) before 1 March 1996.

...

Bibliography

The following are a selected list of the principal monographs and treatises devoted solely or primarily to the law of inheritance in Russia. All general works on Russian civil law, of course, contain chapters or sections devoted to inheritance.

Abashin, E. A., Завещание [Will]. M., Zakonodatel'stvo, 2002.

Abova, T. E., Boguslavskii, M. M., Svetlanov, A. G. (eds.), Комментарий к Гражданского кодекса Российской Федерации, части третьи [Commentary to Civil Code of the Russian Federation] M., Iurait, 2004. 486 p.

Abramenkov, M. S., Коллизионно-правовое регулирование наследственных отношений в современном международном частном праве [Conflicts-Law Regulation of Inheritance Relations in Contemporary Private International Law]. Ul'ianovsk, UlGU, 2007.

Abramenkov, M. S., Chugunov,, P. V., Наследственное право [Inheritance Law]. M., izd-vo Iurait, 2013. 423 p.

Amfiteatrov, G. N., Solodilov, A. P., Право наследования в СССР [Law of Inheritance in the USSR]. M., 1946.

Amirov, M. S., Наследование имущества [Inheritance of Property]. Makhachkala, Iupiter, 2002.

Antimonov, B. S., Gerzon, S., Slifer, B., Наследование и нотариат [Inheritance and the Notariat]. M., Iuridicheskoe izd-vo, 1946. 76 p.

Antimonov, B. S., Grave, K. A., Советское наследственное право [Soviet Inheritance Law]. M., Iuridicheskaia literatura, 1955. 264 p.

Anufrieva, L. P. (ed.), Комментарий к Гражданскому кодексу Росссийской Федерации. Часть третья (постатейный) [Commentary to the Civil Code of the Russian Federation. Part Three (Article-by-Article)]. M., WoltersKluwer, 2004.

Aparova, T. V., Наследование в авторском и изобретательском праве [Inheritance in Author's and Inventor's Law]. M., 1963.

Barshchevskii, M. Iu., Если открылось наследство ... [If an Inheritance Opened …]. M., Iuridicheskaia literature, 1989. 192 p.

Barshchevskii, M. Iu., Наследственное право [Inheritance Law]. M., Belye al'vy, 2005.

Baryshev, A. I., Приобретение наследства и его юридические последствия [Acquisition of Inheritance and Legal Consequences Thereof]. M., Gosudarstvennoe izd-vo iuridicheskoi literatury, 1960. 94 p.

Batrova, T. A., Наследование бизнес-активов. Учебное пособие [Inheritance of Business-Assets. Instructional Manual]. M., Prospekt, 2023. 120 p.

Belov, V. A., Гражданское право [Civil Law] (2d ed.; M., Iurait, 2012. 3 vols.

Belov, V. A. (ed.), Практика применения Гражданского кодекса Российской Федерации [Practice of the Application of the Civil Code of the Russian Federation]. M., Iurait, 2009. 2 vols.

Bespalov, Iu. F., Bespalova, A. Iu., Дела о наследовании [Cases concerning Inheriting]. M., Prospekt, 2013. 104 p.

Bespalov, Iu. F., Kasatkina, A. Iu., Kameneva, Z. V., Наследование: спорный вопросы правоприменения [Inheritance: Disputed Questions of Law-Application]. 2d ed.; M., Prospekt, 2023. 240 p.

Bondarev, N. I., Eidinova, E. B., Право на наследство и его оформление [Right to Inheritance and Formalization Thereof]. M., Iuridicheskaia literature, 1971. 87 p.

Bondarev, N. I., Eidinova, E. B., Завещания, приравниваемые к нотариальным и их исполнение [Wills Equated to Notarial and the Execution Thereof]. M., Iuridicheskaia literatura, 1975. 59 p.

Bondarev, N. I., Il'ina, T. N., Shimalevich, S. Ia., Удостоверение и исполнение завещений [Attestation and Execution of Wills]. M., Iuridicheskaia literature, 1965. 131 p.

Bratus, S. N., Sadikov, O. N. (eds.), Комментарий к Гражданскому кодексу РСФСР [Commentary on the Civil Code of the RSFSR]. 3d ed.; M., Iuridicheskaia literatura, 1982. 675 p.

Budovnits, V., Исполнитель завещания. Домашний адвокат [Executor of Will. Home Advokat]. M., Norma; Infra-M, 2005.

Bugaevskii, A. A., Советское наследственное право [Soviet Inheritance Law]. Odessa, n.p., 1926. 122 p.

Butler, W. E., *Civil Code of the Russian Federation*. Clark, New Jersey, Talbot Publishing, 2021. 2 vols.

Butler, W. E., *Russian Foreign Relations and Investment Law*. Oxford, Oxford University Press, 2006. li, 580 p.

Butler, W. E., *Russian Inheritance Law*. London, Wildy, Simmonds, and Hill, 2014. x, 194 p.

Danilov, E. P., Наследование. Справочник адвоката [Inheritance. Manual of Advokat]. M., Pravo i zakon, 2001.

Demchenko, V., Существо наследства и призвание к наследованию по русскому право [Inheritance by Operation of Law and Call to Inherit under Russian Law]. Kiev, n.p., 1877. 112 p. (Vol. 1 only).

Demichev, A. A., Dukhan, A. B., Институт наследования в российском праве в XX – начале XXI в. в контексте соотношения интересов государства и личности [Institute of Inheritance in Russian Law in the XX and Early XXI Centuries in the Context of the Correlation of the Interests of the State and the Individual]. M., izd-vo Iurlitinform, 2014. 280 p. 1000 ptd.

Dronikov, V. K., Наследование по завещанию в советском праве [Inheritance by Will in Soviet Law]. Kiev, izd-vo Kievskogo gos. Universiteta, 1957. 134 p.

Dronikov, V. K., Наследственное право Украинской ССР [Inheritance Law of the Ukrainian SSR]. Kiev, Vishcha shkola, 1974. 159 p.

Druzhne, A. A., Наследование по праву представления [Inheritance by Right of Representation]. M., Iuridicheskaia literature, 2002.

Egorova, O. A., Bespalov, Iu. F., Настольная книга судьи по делам о наследовании [Manual of Judge for Cases on Inheriting]. M., Prospekt, 2013. 208 p.

Eidinova, E. B., Наследование по закону и завещанию [Inheritance by Operation of Law and by Will]. M., Iuridicheskaia literatura, 1984. 109 p.

Erdelevskii A. M. (ed.), Постатейный научно-практический комментарий части третьей Гражданского кодекса Российской Федерации [Article-by-Article Scientific-Practical Commentary to Part Three of Civil Code of Russian Federation]. M., 2001.

Goikhbarg, A. G., Буржуазные реформы наследственного права [Bourgeois Reforms of Inheritance Law]. M., izd-vo Narkomiusta RSFSR, 1925. 19 p.

Goikhbarg, A. G., Закон о расширении прав наследования по закону лиц женского пола и права завещания родовых имений [Law on Expansion of Rights of Inheritance by Operation of Law of Persons of Female Sex and Right to Bequeath Ancestral Estates] (Spb., Iuridicheskii knizhnyi sklad "Pravo", 1914). 128 p.

Goncharov, Iu. M., Брачно-семейное право Российской империи XIX-начала XX в. [Marriage-Family Law of the Russian Federation XIX-Beginning of XX Century]. Baranul, Azbuka, 2019. 148 p.

Gordon, M. V., Наследование по закону и по завещанию [Inheritance by Operation of Law and by Will]. M., Iuridicheskaia literature, 1967. 117 p.

Grave, K. A., Вопросы наследсевенного права в практике Верховного Суда СССР [Questions of Inheritance Law in the Practice of the USSR Supreme Court]. M., 1949.

Grishaev, S. P., Наследственное право [Inheritance Law]. M., Iurist, 2003.

Grishaev, S. P., Наследственное право: учебно-практическое пособие [Inheritance Law: Instructional-Practical Manual] M., Prospekt, 2011.

Grishaev, S. P., Наследственное право: учебно-практическое пособие [Inheritance Law: Instructional-Practical Manual] M., Prospekt, 2014. 184 p.

Grudtsyna, L. Iu., Наследование в вопросах и ответах [Inheritance in Questions and Answers]. M., Berator-Press, 2009.

Guev, A. N., Постатейный комментарий к части третьей Гражданского кодекса Российской Федерации M., Infra-M, 2010.

Gusakov, A. G., Курс семейного и наследственного права [Course of Family and Inheritance Law]. Spb., Kassa vzaimopomoshchi studentov Spb. Politekhnicheskogo instituta, 1911. 208 p.

Gushchin, V. V., Наследственное право: учебное пособие [Inheritance Law. Instructional Manual]. M., Dashkov i K., 2003.

Gushchin, V. V., Dmitriev, Iu. A., Наследственное право и процесс [Inheritance Law and Procedure]. M., Eksmo, 2004.

Iakovlev, V. N., Древнеримское и современное российское наследственное право. Рецепция права [Ancient Roman and

Contemporary Russian Inheritance Law. Reception of Law]. M., 2005.

Iaroshenko, K. B. (ed.), Наследственное право [Inheritance Law]. M., WoltersKluwer, 2005.

Intsas, V. L., Наследование как особый вид правопреемства в советском гражданском праве [Inheritance as Special Type of Succession in Soviet Civil Law]. Leningrad, 1975.

Khalfina, R. O., Право наследования в СССР [Law of Inheritance in the USSR]. 2d ed.; M., 1952.

Khodyreva, E. A., Предприятие как объект наследственного правопреемства [The Enterprise as Object of Inheritance Succession] M., izd-vo Norma, 2013. 192 p.

Khramtsov, K. V., Правовое регулирование наследования в Российской Федерации [Legal Regulation of Inheritance in the Russian Federation]. Omsk, Ministerstvo vnutrennykh del RF, 2002. 86 p.

Khvorenkov, A. A., Институт наследования по завещанию: история и современность [Institute of Inheritance by Will: History and Modern Times]. Izhevsk, 2003.

Kirillova, E. A., Основания наследования в гражданском праве Российской Федерации [Grounds of Inheriting in Civil Law of the Russian Federation]. M., Infra-M, 2012. 132 p.

Kirillovykh, A. A., Завещательное распоряжение в современном гражданском праве [Testamentary Disposition in Contemporary Civil Law]. M., 2011.

Komarov, B. K., Законодательство о наследовании [Legislation on Inheritance]. M., Gos. Izd-vo iuridicheskoi literatury, 1963. 25 p.

Krasheninninkov, P. V., Наследственное право [Inheritance Law] (M., Statut, 2016). 207 p.

Levshin, E. M., Правосудие по брачно-семейным спорам: историко-правовое исследование и анализ современного законодательства [Justice in Marriage and Family Disputes: Historical Legal Study and Analysis of Contemporary Legislation]. Nizhnii Novgorod, Nizhegorodskaia pravovaia akademiia, 2014. 124 p.

Limanskii, G. S., Наследование по закону: вопросы теории и практики [Inheritance by Operation of Law: Questions of Theory and Practice]. Samara, 2003.

Limanskii, G. S., Право наследования: теоретико-методологические и практические проблемы [Law of Inheritance: Theoretical and Methodological and Practical Problems]. Riazan, 2004.

Lukash, Iu. A., Права и обязанности участников отношений по наследованию [Rights and Duties of Participants of Relations Relating to Inheritance]. M., izd-vo Flinta, 2007. 496 p.

Makovskii, A. L., Sukhanov, E. A. (eds.), Комментарий к части третьей Гражданского кодекса Российской Федерации [Commentary to Part Three of the Civil Code of the Russian Federation]. M., Iurist, 2003.

Marrese, M. L., *A Woman's Kingdom. Noblewomen and the Control of Property in Russia, 1700-1861*. Ithaca and London, Cornell University Press, 2002. xvi, 276 p.

Marysheva, N. I., and Iaroshenko, K. B. (eds.), Комментарий к Гражданскому кодексу Российской Федерации, части третьи (постатейный) [Commentary to the Civil Code of the Russian Federation, Part Three (Article-by-Article)]. 3d ed.; M., Norma, 2011. 645 p.

Matison, A. V. (comp.), Духовные завещения, брачные договоры, документы о родственном разделе имущества (частноправовые акты Твери первой четверти XVIII века) [Wills, Marriage Contracts, and Documents on the Kinship Division of Property (Private Law Acts of Tver of the First

Quarter of the XVIII Century). M., Staraia Basmannaia, 2022. 248 p.

Medvedev, I. G., Комментарий к конвенциям в области имущественных отношений супругов и наследования [Commentary to Conventions in the Domain of Property Relations of Spouses and Inheritance]. M., WoltersKluwer, 2007.

Movchanovskii, B. F., Наследственное право по ГК РСФСР: практический комментарий [Inheritance Law under the Civil Code of the RSFSR: Practical Commentary]. M., 1923.

Mozolin, V. P. (ed.), Комментарий к Гражданскому кодексу Российской Федерации, части третьи [Commentary to the Civil Code of the Russian Federation, Part Three]. M., Norma, 2002.

Mun, V. A., Государственно-правовая охрана материнства и детства в России в середине XIX – начале XX в. [State-Law Protection of Maternity and Childhood in Russia in the Mid-Nineteenth – Early Twentieth Centuries]. M., Prospekt, 2023. 200 p,

Muromtsev, S. A., Гражданское право Древнего Рима [Civil Law of Ancient Rome]. M., Statut, 2003.

Nemkov, A. M., Очерки истории наследственного права [Survey of the History of Inheritance Law]. Voronezh, 1979.

Nikitiuk, P. S., Наследственное право и наследственный процесс: проблемы теории и практики [Inheritance Law and Inheritance Procedure: Problems of Theory and Practice]. Kishinev, Shtiintsa, 1973. 258 p.

Nikol'skii, V., О началах наследования по древнему русскому праву [On the Principles of Inheritance under Russian Law]. M., n.p., 1859. 375, 31 p.

Novitskaia, T. E., Правовое регулирование имущественных отношений в России во второй половине XVIII век [Legal

Regulation of Property Relations in Russia in the Second Half of the Eighteenth Century]. M., izd-vo Zertsalo, 2005. 568 p.

Novitskii, I. B., Pereterskii, I. S. (eds.), Римское частное право: учебник [Roman Private Law: Textbook]. M., Iurist', 1997.

Omarova, U. A., Наследственное право и социальная справедливость [Inheritance Law and Social Justice]. Makhachkala, 1999.

Orlovskii, P. E., Практика Верховного Суда СССР по гражданским наследственным делам [Practice of the USSR Supreme Court regarding Civil Inheritance Cases]. M., 1947.

Ospennikov, Iu. V., Брачно-семейные отношения в праве Северо-Западной Руси XII-XV вв. [Marriage-Family Relations in the Law of Northwestern Rus XII-XV Centuries]. Samara, izd-vo Samarskogo nauchnogo tsentra RAN, 2004. 258 p.

Petrov, E. Iu. (ed.), Наследственное право: Постатейный комментарий к статьям 1110-1185, 1224 Гражданского кодекса Российской Федерации [Inheritance Law: Article-by-Article Commentary to Articles 1110-1185, 1224 of the Civil Code of the Russian Federation]. M., Statut, 2018. 506 p.

Plekhanova, V. V., Исполнение завещания душеприказчиком [Execution of Will by Executor]. M., Norma, 2009.

Pobedonostsev, K. P., Курс гражданского права. Часть вторая: Права семейственные, наследственные и завещательные [Cours of Civil Law: Part Two: Family, Inheritance, and Testamentary Laws]. M., Statut, 2004.

Pokrovskii, I. A., Основные проблемы гражданского права [Basic Problems of Civil Law] M., Statut, 2003.

Pronina, M. G., Наследование по закону и завещанию [Inheritance by Operation of Law and by Will]. Minsk, 1978.

Pronina, M. G., Право наследования [Right of Inheritance]. Minsk, 1989.

Raevich, S. I., Rubinshtein, B. M., Наследственное право [Inheritance Law]. M., Iuridicheskoe izd-vo NKIu RSFSR, 1929. 62 p.

Riasentsev, V. A., Наследование по закону и по завещанию в СССР [Inheritance by Operation of Law and by Will in the USSR]. M., Znanie, 1972.

Rubanov, A. A., Наследование в международном частном праве (отношения СССР с капиталистическими странами [Inheritance in International Private Law (Relations of the USSR with Capitalist Countries]. M., Nauka, 1966. 235 p.

Rubanov, A. A., Наследование в международном частном праве (отношения между социалистическими странами [Inheritance in International Private Law (Relations with Socialist Countries]. M., Nauka, 1972. 284 p.

Rubanov, A. A., Право наследования [Inheritance Law]. M., 1978.

Rubanov, A. A., Заграничные наследства. Отношения между социалистическими и капиталистическими странами [Foreign Inheritances. Relations between Socialist and Capitalist Countries]. M., Nauka, 1975. 276 p.

Rubanov, A. A., [Law on Inheritance]. M., Znanie, 1984.

Rudnev, L. I., О духовных завещаниях по русскому праву [On Wills under Russian Law]. Kiev, n.p., 1894. vi, 182 p.

Ryndziunskii, G., Наследование по советским законам [Inheritance under Soviet Laws]. M., Iuridicheskoe izd-vo NKIu RSFSR, 1925. 46, 4, 8 p.

Sannikova, L. V., Институты частного права в Русской Правды [Institutes of Private Law in the Russkaia Pravda]. M., Statut, 2014. 80 p.

Serebrovskii, V. I., Избранные труды по наследственному и страховому праву [Selected Works on Inheritance and Insurance Law]. 2d ed.; M., Statut, 2003. 567 p.

Serebrovskii, V. I., Наследственное право [Inheritance Law]. M., 1948.

Serebrovskii, V. I., Наследственное право: Комментарий к ст. ст. 416-435 Гражданского кодекса Р.С.Ф.С.Р. [Inheritance Law: Commentary to Articles 416 to 435 of the RSFSR Civil Code]. M., Pravo i zhizn, 1925. 99 p.

Serebrovskii, V. I., Очерки советского наследственного права [Outline of Soviet Inheritance Law]. M., izd-vo Akademii nauk SSSR, 1953. 237 p.

Sergeev, A. P., Tolstoi, Iu. K., Eliseev, I. V., Комментарий к Гражданскому кодексу Российской Федерации (постатейный) [Commentary to the Civil Code of the Russian Federation (Article-by-Article). Part Three]. M., Prospekt, 2002.

Shilokhvost, O. Iu., Наследование по закону в российском гражданском праве [Inheritance by Operation of Law in Russian Civil Law]. M., Norma, 2012. 272 p.

Shirokova, I. B., Наследственное право [Inheritance Law]. M., Prior, 2001.

Shishmareva, T. P., Наследование земельных участков. Применение гражданского законодательства в нотариальной практике [Inheritance of Land Plots. Application of Civil Legislation in Notarial Practice]. Krasnoiarsk, 1997.

Shushkevich, B. A., Наследственное право Российской Федерации [Inheritance Law of the Russian Federation]. Tiumen, 1998.

Teliukina, M. V., Наследственное право: Комментарий Гражданского кодекса Российской Федерации Inheritance Law: Commentary to the Civil Code of the Russian Federation]. M., Pravo i zakon, 2002.

Tikhomirova, L. V., Наследство: приобретение и защита прав, вопросы налогообложения [Inheritance: Acquisition and Defense of Rights, Questions of Taxation]. M., 2012.

Tolstoi, M. K., Наследственное право [Inheritance Law]. M., Prospekt, 1999.

Vavilin, E. V., Gur'eva, E. V., Новый порядок наследования и дарения [New Procedure of Inheriting and Gift]. M., 2006.

Vinaver, M. M., Из области цивилистики. Дарение и завещание [From the Realm of Civilistics: Gift and Will]. Spb., tip. A. G. Rozen, 1908. 337 p.

Vlasov, Iu. N., Наследственное право Российской Федерации: общие положения, правовые основы, образцы типовых документов [Inheritance Law of the Russian Federation: General Provisions, Legal Foundations, Samples of Standard Documents]. 4th ed.; M., Iurait, 2000. 320 p.

Vlasov, Iu. N., Kalinin, V. V., Наследование по закону и по завещанию [Inheritance by Operation of Law and by Will]. M., Iurait, 1999; 2d ed., 2001. 246 p.

Wagner, William G., *Marriage, Property and Law in Late Imperial Russia*. Oxford, Clarendon Press, 1994. xiv, 413 p.

Zaitseva, T. I., Нотариальная практика: ответы на вопросы [Notarial Practice: Replies to Questions]. M.,, WoltersKluwer, 2007. 488 p.

Zaitseva, T. I., Судебная практика по наследственным делам [Judicial Practice in Inheritance Cases] M., WoltersKluwer, 2007.

Zaitseva, T. I., Krasheninnikov, P. V., Наследственное право в нотариальной практике [Inheritance Law in Notarial Practice]. 5th ed.; M., WoltersKluwer, 2005. xxxii, 765 p.

Zaitseva, T. I., Krasheninnikov, P. V., Наследственное право: Комментарий законодательства и практика его применения

[Inheritance Law: Commentary to Legislation and Practice of Application Thereof]. 6th ed.; M., Statut, 2009.

Zakirov, R. Iu., Grishina, Ia. S., Makhmutova, M. M., Наследственное право: учебное пособие [Inheritance Law: Instructional Manual]. M., 2009.

Index of Names

www.ingramcontent.com/pod-product-compliance
Lightning Source LLC
LaVergne TN
LVHW091523200926
848483LV00002B/292